Modern British Statesmen
1867–1945

MANCHESTER
UNIVERSITY PRESS

Modern British Statesmen 1867–1945

edited by
Richard Kelly
and John Cantrell

Manchester University Press
Manchester and New York
Distributed exclusively in the USA by St. Martin's Press

Copyright © Manchester University Press 1997

While copyright in the volume as a whole is vested in Manchester University Press, copyright in individual chapters belongs to their respective authors, and no chapter may be reproduced wholly or in part without the express permission in writing of both author and publisher.

Published by Manchester University Press
Oxford Road, Manchester M13 9NR, UK
and Room 400, 175 Fifth Avenue, New York, NY 10010, USA

Distributed exclusively in the USA by
St. Martin's Press, Inc.,
175 Fifth Avenue, New York, NY 10010, USA

Distributed exclusively in Canada by
UBC Press, University of British Columbia, 6344 Memorial Road,
Vancouver, BC, Canada V6T 1Z2

British Library Cataloguing-in-Publication Data
A catalogue record for this book is available from the British Library

Library of Congress Cataloging-in-Publication Data
Modern British statesmen, 1867–1945 / edited by Richard Kelly and
    John Cantrell.
        p.   cm.
      ISBN 0-7190-5079-0. — ISBN 0-7190-5080-4 (pbk.)
        1. Great Britain—Politics and government—1837–1901. 2. Great
Britain—Politics and government 1901–1936. 3. Great Britain—Politics and
government—1936–1945. 4. Statesmen—Great Britain—Biography. I.
Kelly, Richard N. II. Cantrell, John.
DA560.M58   1998
941.08—dc21   97–14152

ISBN 0 7190 5079 0 *hardback*
ISBN 0 7190 5080 4 *paperback*

First published in 1997

01 00 99 98 97   10 9 8 7 6 5 4 3 2 1

Typeset in Great Britain
by Action Typesetting, Gloucester

Printed in Great Britain
by Redwood Books, Trowbridge

Contents

List of illustrations		vi
Preface and acknowledgements		vii
Contributors		ix
Introduction: the road to social democracy *Richard Kelly and John Cantrell*		1
1	Benjamin Disraeli *Michael Lynch*	16
2	William Ewart Gladstone *Michael Lynch*	31
3	Charles Stewart Parnell *Michael Cunningham*	46
4	Robert, 3rd Marquess of Salisbury *Hugh Cecil*	64
5	Joseph Chamberlain *Jeremy Smith*	80
6	Arthur James Balfour *Jane Ridley*	97
7	Herbert Asquith *Harry Bennett*	113
8	David Lloyd George *Robin Barlow*	127
9	James Ramsay MacDonald *Robert Garner*	144
10	Stanley Baldwin *Stuart Ball*	161
11	Neville Chamberlain *Nick Smart*	179
12	Winston Churchill *Owen Hartley*	193
Appendix 1	Governments and major office holders, 1866–1945	205
Appendix 2	Leaders of principal political parties, 1867–1945	207
Appendix 3	Government revenue and income tax, 1867–1945	210
Appendix 4	General election results, 1867–1945	213
Appendix 5	Biographical summaries, 1867–1945	217
Index		224

List of illustrations

Benjamin Disraeli (1874) 16
© The Illustrated London News

William Ewart Gladstone (1898) 31
© The Illustrated London News

Charles Stewart Parnell 46
© By courtesy of the National Library of Ireland

Robert Gascoyne-Cecil, 3rd Marquess of Salisbury (1882) 64
by George Frederic Watts
By courtesy of the National Portrait Gallery, London

Joseph Chamberlain (1886) 80
by Frank Holl
By courtesy of the National Portrait Gallery, London

Arthur James Balfour, 1st Earl of Balfour (1891) 97
by Sir Lawrence Alma-Tadema
By courtesy of the National Portrait Gallery, London

Herbert Henry Asquith, 1st Earl of Oxford and Asquith (1919) 113
by Andre Cluysenaar
By courtesy of the National Portrait Gallery, London

David Lloyd George (1929) 127
© The Illustrated London News

James Ramsay MacDonald (1924) 144
© The Illustrated London News

Stanley Baldwin (c. 1923) 161
© The Illustrated London News

Neville Chamberlain (1940) 179
by Andrew MacLaren
By courtesy of the National Portrait Gallery, London

Winston Churchill (c. 1940) 193
© The Illustrated London News

Preface and acknowledgements

The period from 1867 to 1945 is one that is widely studied by those taking History at Advanced Level and beyond. It is also one that is rich in outstanding political personalities – politicians who, at various stages and in various ways, shaped the course of Britain's political history.

This has been recognised, of course, by those responsible for the setting and marking of Modern History examinations, which often require some assessment and comparison of the period's key figures. Although most of these figures have been the subject of weighty biographies, or more superficial treatment in wider-ranging textbooks, there has to date been no study which examines them in specific, compact chapters and in a manner accessible to sixth formers and first year undergraduates. With the help of eleven specialist historians, we have aimed to meet this particular need.

Following an Introduction which identifies what we believe to be the period's central theme – namely the growth of state intervention and a 'social democratic' political culture – the book consists of twelve chapters, each inspecting the career of a particularly influential politician. To enhance the book's user-friendliness, and to allow swift and effective comparison, each chapter will be divided into four sections.

The *Background* section will inspect the subject's early life and influences, charting the emergence of his central political beliefs. The *Apprenticeship* section will then recall his entry into public life and parliament, looking at the decisive moments – and tracing his progress – during the less conspicuous stages of his political career. The *Limelight* section, which accounts for the bulk of each chapter, will assess the subject's presence or clear influence upon the parliamentary front benches, offering (where applicable) an audit of his premiership. The *Legacy* section will record a verdict upon the achievements or failures of the particular career, as well as assessing its influence upon subsequent events and later politicians.

In keeping with the varied careers of the twelve politicians covered, we thought it inappropriate to impose upon authors precise word limits for each of the four sections. It will always be the case that, for some politicians, 'background' and 'apprenticeship' have a more lasting importance than for others, while the 'legacy' of certain figures is often more substantial than the zenith of their actual career. As such, the amount of attention devoted to each of the four sections does tend to vary from chapter to chapter.

We are also aware that the term 'statesman' is not unambiguous and some readers may wonder why certain politicians from the period have been excluded from this volume: why, for example, include two men who never attained the premiership – Parnell and Joseph Chamberlain – while excluding Derby, Rosebery, Campbell-Bannerman and Bonar Law? This would have been a valid criticism had we set out to produce a longer (and more expensive) volume, aimed more exclusively at the university market. We decided, however, to give the book a more utilitarian flavour, covering the twelve careers which we think had most effect upon the character of the British state, while providing essays which we think will be of most immediate use to our target audience of sixth formers and first year undergraduates. We should add at this point that most of the key politicians not included in this volume are the subject of potted biographies in Appendix 5, with the other appendices also providing easy-to-read information of the sort regularly required by our likely readers; indeed, we hope that our appendices will be as valued by those readers as the twelve core chapters.

Although our contributors were chosen on account of familiarity with their subject's primary material, this book does not involve much fresh assault upon such sources; we concede that it is unlikely to reveal many surprises to the graduate historian. The book's real strength, we believe, comes from a somewhat unusual marriage of professional scholarship and professional knowledge of classroom requirements. With contributors offering a sure, scholarly feel for both the period and the statesmen, it has been the editors' job – as schoolteachers – to insist this was done in a way the typical student finds useful. As a result, we hope that the book represents an authoritative summary of existing literature while providing the sort of crisp, concise commentary demanded by teachers and students alike. For those who wish to explore the subject in greater detail, there is a guide to further reading at the end of each chapter.

In compiling this volume, we would like to record our thanks to all eleven contributors for the speed and efficiency at which their chapters were produced. We would also like to thank our colleagues in the History and Politics Departments at the Manchester Grammar School for various forms of advice and encouragement. In this respect we are particularly grateful to W. J. Hardiman (Head of the History Department) for ideas concerning style and syntax, R. I. A. Martin (Head of Politics) for advice about chapter structure, and J. T. Bever for his scrutiny of the book's Introduction. Despite this assistance, responsibility for the book's content and presentation rests solely with the editors. The book is dedicated to Karen Hannah, whose support ensured its prompt completion.

R. N. Kelly and J. A. Cantrell

Contributors

Stuart Ball is Reader in History at the University of Leicester. He is author of *Baldwin and the Conservative Party: The Crisis of 1929–1931* (Yale University Press, 1988) and *The Conservative Party and British Politics 1902–1951* (Longman, 1995); editor of *Parliament and Politics in the Age of Baldwin and MacDonald: The Headlam Diaries 1923–1935* (Historians' Press, 1992) and co-editor of *Conservative Century: The Conservative Party since 1900* (Oxford University Press, 1994) and *The Heath Government 1970–1974: A Reappraisal* (Longman, 1996).

Robin Barlow is a former teacher of Politics and Modern History at Rugby School, and now Head Master of Spratton Hall School, whose doctoral thesis concerns Wales and the Great War. He has published three schools-based textbooks and several articles on the 1914–18 period.

Harry Bennett is Lecturer in History at the University of Plymouth and author of *British Foreign Policy During the Curzon Period* (Macmillan, 1995).

John Cantrell teaches History at the Manchester Grammar School and has been a Modern History examiner for the NEAB. He is author of *James Nasmyth and the Bridgewater Foundry* (Manchester University Press, 1985) and co-author of *The Normans in Britain* (Macmillan, 1987).

Hugh Cecil is Senior Lecturer in History at the University of Leeds. He is author of *The Flower of Battle: How Britain Wrote the Great War* (Steerforth, 1996) and co-editor of *Salisbury, the Man and His Policies* (MacMillan, 1987) and *Facing Armageddon: The First World War Experienced* (Pen & Sword, 1996).

Michael Cunningham is Lecturer in Politics at the University of Wolverhampton and author of *British Government Policy in Northern Ireland* (Manchester University Press, 1991).

Robert Garner is Lecturer in Politics at the University of Leicester, whose doctoral thesis concerns 'Ideology and Electoral Politics in Labour's Rise to Major Power Status 1918–1931'. His subsequent publications include *Animal Politics and Morality* (Manchester University Press, 1993), *British Political Parties Today* (Manchester University Press, 1993), *Animals Rights: The Changing Debate* (Macmillan, 1996) and *Environmental Politics* (Prentice Hall, 1996).

Owen Hartley is Senior Teaching Fellow at the University of Leeds' Institute for International Studies. He has written numerous published articles on local, British and international history.

Richard Kelly teaches Politics at the Manchester Grammar School and the University of Manchester. He is author of *Conservative Party Conferences* (Manchester University Press, 1989), co-author of *British Political Parties Today* (Manchester University Press, 2nd edn, 1998) and editor of *Changing Party Policy in Britain* (Blackwell, forthcoming).

Michael Lynch teaches History at the University of Leicester. His publications include *Gladstone and Disraeli* (Hodder and Stoughton, 1991), *Lloyd George and the Liberal Dilemma* (Holder and Stoughton, 1993) and *Ireland and England* (Hodder and Stoughton, 1995).

Jane Ridley is Senior Lecturer in History at the University of Buckingham. She is co-editor of *The Letters of Arthur Balfour and Lady Elcho* (Hamish Hamilton, 1992) and author of *Fox Hunting* (Collins, 1991) and *The Young Disraeli* (Sinclair Stevenson, 1995).

Nick Smart is Lecturer in History at the University of Plymouth. He edited the *Diaries and Letters of Robert Bernays* (Edwin Mellen, 1995) and is currently researching a book on the National Government of 1931–40.

Jeremy Smith is Head of History at Radley College, having previously lectured at the University of Wales, Lampeter. His publications include *The Taming of Democracy: A History of the Conservative Party, 1880 to 1924* (University of Wales Press, 1997) and *Home Rule and the Irish Question, 1879–1922* (Longman, forthcoming).

Introduction: the road to social democracy

Richard Kelly and John Cantrell

It is widely recognised that the 1945 general election is a crucial landmark in modern British history, comparable to (and arguably more important than) the Liberal landslide victory of 1906, the election of the first Thatcher government in 1979 and, of course, the Second Reform Act of 1867 – the starting point for both this edition and numerous history courses.

The reasons for this are well established. The 1945 election was the first to give Labour an overall parliamentary majority, underlining in spectacular form the electoral progress the party had made since 1918 and its position as the main anti-Conservative force in British politics. Labour's majority of 146 was not surpassed until the general election of 1997, and it remains the second largest majority obtained by any single party this century – an achievement rendered even more remarkable by Labour's dismal showing in most subsequent general elections: little wonder that 1945 is still regarded as the *annus mirabilis* of Labour politicians.

Of greater significance, however, was the fact that the 1945 election was the first to take account of the Second World War and its huge impact upon millions of British people – an impact which, as discussed below, largely explains Labour's success. For many historians, the endorsement given to Labour's programme by nearly 12 million voters (and 48 per cent of the electorate) marked the glorious emergence of British social democracy and the consummation of a new political order – one which easily survived the Labour government's fall six years later.[1]

As a political ideology, social democracy is not easily defined. During the late nineteenth and early twentieth centuries, it had strong associations with revolutionary politics. The German Social Democratic Party (SPD) was formed in the mid 1860s by followers of Marx, while Lenin's entry into politics came via the Russian Social Democratic Party formed at the end of the nineteenth century. In Britain, the Social Democratic Federation, founded by H. M. Hyndman in 1881, likewise advanced an essentially Marxist analysis of history and economics, and represented the first Marxist party to be formed in Britain. Indeed, prior to 1945, social democracy and Marxism were still widely seen as synonymous.[2]

The situation is complicated further by the fact that 'social democracy' was a term not generally used by mainstream politicians in Britain until an official Social Democratic Party (SDP) was formed in 1981. The sort of Labour politicians attracted to the new SDP (Shirley Williams, David Owen, William Rodgers *et al.*) had hitherto preferred to describe themselves as democratic socialists rather than social democrats, with the new party's supporters, 'more easily identified socially than described ideologically'.[3]

The SDP did serve, however, as a vivid illustration of how social democracy's connotations had changed in the course of the present century: from being a gospel of revolution, it had developed into a euphemism for consensus, moderation and incremental reform. Like social democracy itself, the reasons for this are not clear-cut, but important clues are provided by two particular developments within the German (and then West German) SPD – the first in the 1890s, the second in the 1950s.

Edward Bernstein, editor of the SPD's newspaper and often hailed as the father of modern social democracy, told his party in 1899 that its aims did not after all require insurrection and could in fact be accommodated within the existing parliamentary system – a view founded upon Bernstein's observation that capitalism was not as 'contradictory' as Marx had prescribed and could generate constant, material improvements for the bulk of society. Although Bernstein's analysis was rejected by the SPD in 1899, it was vindicated half a century later at the party's Bad Godesburg conference of 1958, when one of Europe's most influential left-wing parties finally rejected the revolutionary, non-parliamentary approach to politics. But the implications of Bad Godesburg went beyond the policies of the SPD: thereafter the reputation and perception of European social democracy were fundamentally altered.

Britain's own 'social democrats', in the mid to late twentieth century, were therefore unsurprising in their commitment to representative, parliamentary democracy. As such, the movement in Britain after 1867 towards universal adult suffrage, the elimination of electoral corruption, the brake on hereditary power and so on could be seen as important to the development of a modern, social democratic state. Yet a belief in parliamentary democracy has never been exclusive to the social democratic agenda and it would be wrong to declare that all those who instigated parliamentary reform after 1867 were proto-social democrats.

Like Conservatives and Liberals, modern social democrats have regarded parliamentary democracy as a means to a more important end. In social democracy's case, this involved greater social justice and economic equality, brought about by judicious state intervention and government expenditure (ultimately sanctioned by a parliamentary majority). With this in mind, it is clear why Labour's general election victory of 1945 is seen as social democracy's key moment, with Attlee's government paving the way for a new 'social democratic' consensus – a consensus which arguably existed in Britain until the late 1970s, and which even today (with government spending at 43 per cent of Gross National Product) has strong echoes in public administration.

It is undeniable that, between 1945 and 1951, the Labour government pushed the British state strongly in the direction of collective provision and government control, the strategic aim being the alleviation of inequality and socio-economic hardship. In that relatively short period an astonishing legislative programme was enacted, amounting to a phenomenal record of reform: the National Insurance Act and establishment of the National Health Service in 1946, the rent control Acts of 1946 and 1949, and the nationalisation of coal, civil aviation and the Bank of England (1946), railways and gas (1948) and iron and steel (1949) being the best known examples.

Yet this bold drive towards social democracy did not mark a complete break from government policy before 1945. Attlee's reforms were distinguished not by their inherent, statist character but by the quickfire manner in which they were implemented and the overt egalitarian principles upon which they were based. But again this rather brave approach would have been much less feasible without a series of uneven developments between 1867 and 1945 – developments which had gradually shifted the ideological and administrative culture of British politics.

It is possible to group these developments into four categories, all of which are touched upon by our contributors: Tory paternalism, New Liberalism, World War and Labourism.

Tory paternalism

At the start of 1867, Britain was far removed from the social democratic ideal. Owing to strict property qualifications, only one in five male adults could vote, while women were excluded altogether. This restricted franchise was accompanied by a distinctively *laissez-faire* approach to government, with a meagre number of state departments spending a mere 8 per cent of Gross National Product. Parliament met less frequently (hardly at all from August to Christmas), with its Members – drawn almost exclusively from the ranks of society's 'haves' – attaching little importance to the passage of new legislation. For the parliamentarians of 1867, the most pressing functions were to check the activities of ministers and to restrain taxation – and *ergo* public spending and governmental action. This belief in limited politics seemed justified by Britain's pre-eminence half-way through the nineteenth century – responsible for over 40 per cent of Europe's manufactured exports and arguably a third of the world's manufactured goods.

Yet Britain's relatively advanced condition also bred a certain degree of political instability. With the growth of the press and improvements in communication, political agitation from groups such as the National Reform Union (founded in 1864) and the Reform League (founded in 1865) became more widespread and effective. Pressure from such quarters prompted Britain's governing class to reappraise the limited franchise, which eventually produced the Reform Act of August 1867. The Act's 'democratic' impact was limited, with women and two-thirds of adult males still excluded from the franchise. Nevertheless, it still enfranchised over a million new voters – including perhaps half the adult males living in the towns – many of whom were without any strong vested interest in the *status quo*.

As Michael Lynch explains in Chapter 1, this new situation presented a particular challenge for the Tory Party, even though it had been a Tory government (led by Derby and Disraeli) which completed and steered through the final Reform Bill. As a party whose support seemed rooted in agriculture and the established Church, it had a pressing need to widen its appeal to the new and more diverse electorate. Part of its response was organisational, with the setting up of a new National Union of Conservative and Constitutional Associations, designed to help Tory MPs campaign more effectively amid the enlarged electorate. But there was also a subtle, philosophical shift, designed to show that the established order could meet the more urgent socio-economic demands of a less privileged electorate.

Between 1874 and 1880, Disraeli's ministry passed eleven major, and assorted minor, pieces of legislation which have given it a reputation (albeit a disputed one) for social reform and state intervention. Such reforms – illustrated by the Factory Act of 1874 and the Artisans Dwellings and Public Health Acts of 1875 – are often held up as examples of Disraeli's brand of Tory paternalism, founded upon a belief that in an unequal society the fortunate (as embodied by the state) should attend to the condition of the less fortunate. This idea, though perpetuating hierarchical power structures and justifying the uneven spread of wealth and power, is not wholly unrelated to the practice of social democracy, which places great faith in the governing class to remedy social injustice and thereby avert revolutionary upheaval. Indeed, following the Tories' defeat in 1945 and their rush to adopt much of Labour's own agenda, 'Disraelian Toryism' was often cited by Conservatives anxious to dispel the notion that they were being opportunistic and untrue to 'Tory principles'.[4]

As Lynch points out, the effect of Disraeli's social reforms is easily exaggerated; the Public Health Act, for example, merely built upon two earlier pieces of legislation, while much of the reformist legislation sprang from the reports of Royal Commissions set up by the earlier ministry of William Gladstone. Yet even if much of this legislating approach to social reform was cosmetic, satisfying Disraeli's theatrical instincts, it still inaugurated a new brand of Tory politics which was to have residual appeal once the party's 'natural' voters were heavily outnumbered.

Hugh Cecil (Chapter 4) confirms that Lord Salisbury's achievements as Tory Prime Minister between 1886 and 1892 and from 1895 to 1902 were mainly in the field of foreign policy. Indeed, certain authors recall Salisbury's ministries for 'legislative paralysis' and 'producing little in the way of constructive legislation' – a fitting reminder that the drift to social democracy was far from remorseless after 1874.[5] Yet even these conservative administrations produced 'a steady stream of remedial legislation and increased spending', placing upon local authorities additional responsiblity for roads, bridges and asylums (Local Government Act 1888), education (Technical Instruction Act 1889) and housing (Housing of the Working Classes Act 1890).[6]

The Tories' paternalist elements were bolstered by their capacity to absorb those reared in other political traditions – notably the Liberal Unionists following the great Liberal rupture of the 1880s. As Jeremy Smith indicates in Chapter 5, the defection to the Tories of Joseph Chamberlain strengthened the forces of intervention inside the party at the turn of the century, although here again the course of statism did not run true – his Workmen's Compensation Act was plagued by opposition from Conservatives in both Houses, while his plans for an old-age pension scheme were blocked by Michael Hicks Beach at the Exchequer. Yet his crusade for tariff reform and imperial preference, which had gripped the bulk of the extra-parliamentary party by 1903, was linked to the financing of further social reform without recourse to punitive taxation. An inspection of local party records prior to the Tory conferences of 1903–11 shows that this double example of statist thinking (tariffs plus state benefits) had particular appeal to party activists increasingly worried by the threat from Labour and the Liberals;[7] as Jane Ridley shows in Chapter 6, this strain of Edwardian Toryism effectively ended Balfour's premiership and leadership of the party.

For most of the twentieth century, in fact, there has been within Tory thinking an acceptance that state intervention – the modern, bureaucratic equivalent of *noblesse oblige* – is the price to pay for the maintenance of an inegalitarian society.[8] Recent surveys of older Tory activists bear this out, showing a sceptical view of *laissez-faire* and many echoes of the 'One Nation' (*qua* statist) Toryism associated with Disraeli and Chamberlain.[9]

These paternalistic (and electorally sensitive) tendencies again allowed statist solutions during the predominantly Conservative coalition of 1918–22 – albeit encouraged by the presence of lingering Liberals such as Lloyd George and Addison. The 1919 Housing Act obliged local authorities to build homes subsidised by the Exchequer, while the Maternity and Child Welfare Act imposed similar obligations in respect of clinics and pre-natal provision. Once again, however, such examples have to be balanced by instances of the state being rolled backward as well as forward: the Geddes economies of 1921–22 proposed £76 million worth of cuts in public spending, while the coal mines were returned to private ownership in 1921. There was certainly no sense within the Tory Party that the growth of state provision was inexorable and that *dirigisme* on an epic scale was inevitable.[10] The party's approach was essentially *ad hoc*, governed by pragmatism rather than any grand philosophical design. Even so, this approach still served subtly to condition both the electorate and the governing class to the more serious forays into state provision after 1945.[11]

As Stuart Ball reveals (Chapter 10), the second government of Stanley

Baldwin (1924–29) offered no coherent strategy of intervention in industry and the economy. Instead, Baldwin's government offered a number of half-baked responses to mounting unemployment in the old industrial regions – such as the Mining Industry Act 1926 (encouraging amalgamation of struggling pits) and a scheme launched in 1928 to help miners find work in the more prosperous regions.

There was, however, some consolidation of the state's welfare responsibilities. As Owen Hartley reminds us in Chapter 12, Winston Churchill's period as Chancellor is overshadowed by the return to the Gold Standard; yet his budget of 1925 was also significant in that it introduced a contributory pension for widows and orphans, while reducing the pensionable age from seventy to sixty-five. Nick Smart (Chapter 11) also points out that Neville Chamberlain's concurrent spell as Minister of Health is remembered largely for its twenty-one Acts involving collective provision – housing, health and leisure being among the beneficiaries. The 1924–29 government also unveiled the concept of public corporations (creating the BBC and Central Electricity Board in 1926) which were later to prove central to the Attlee government's nationalisation programme. Of even more importance to the nascent, social democratic state was perhaps the Equal Franchise Act of 1928, which at last 'equalised' voting rights by enfranchising all women over twenty-one – in effect, a tidying-up measure from the Representation of the People Act ten years earlier (which removed the property qualification and made age, rather than means, the main criterion of voting). When one recalls that, prior to 1918, only about a quarter of adults were voters, a case can be made that parliamentary democracy finally arrived in Britain only during Conservative or mainly Conservative ministries.

The Tory-dominated National Government of the 1930s is chiefly remembered for its savage cuts in public spending following the crisis of 1931. Yet the slump which occasioned those cuts, and the social problems it created, only highlighted the shortcomings of *laissez-faire* to a country that no longer enjoyed economic pre-eminence. Furthermore, it would be wrong to assume that the Tory ministers of the 1930s resisted any further invasions by the state into social and economic policy. The Housing, Public Health and Factory Acts (1935–37), the Wheat Act (1932) and the Agricultural Marketing Acts (1931 and 1933) all gave the state more regulatory powers, while the Special Areas Act (1934) saw governments venture tentatively into the field of economic planning. In comparison with what followed after 1945, the terms of these Acts may seem tame and unimaginative. However, they did set important, statist precedents which again allowed the Conservatives to feel easier about their appeasement of social democracy in the late 1940s.[12]

New Liberalism

The social democratic consensus is often described as a Liberal consensus, and those who assaulted it from the late 1970s onwards often used the term 'Liberalism' as one of abuse and derision. There is a historical irony here, because much of what Thatcherism emphasised (e.g. self-reliance) had a clear Liberal pedigree, while much of what social democracy stood for (e.g. collectivism) was a repudiation of traditional Liberalism.

This implies that, between 1867 and 1945, there was an enormous change in the character of British Liberalism: from being a creed which championed minimal government it became one which saw state intervention as a force for good. The one consistency was its emphasis upon human perfectibility and individual freedom; the change which took place involved the state no longer being an enemy of these ideals but a valuable ally.[13]

For Liberal Party leader William Gladstone, the essential Liberal state was already in place by the end of 1867 – one characterised by minimal state interference and therefore minimal taxation, relative freedom of speech, publication and religion, and non-autocratic, constitutional government. At that time, Liberalism's radical fringe seemed more interested in issues such as temperance and secular education than any serious extension of the government's responsibilities. (As Michael Cunningham explains in Chapter 3, Gladstone's own preoccupation was Ireland rather than far-reaching domestic reform.) Even W. E. Forster's much heralded Education Reform Act of 1870 had the limited objective of 'filling up gaps at the least costs of public money'.[14] 'Old' Liberalism's main contribution to the future social democratic state arguably came in the form of further constitutional reform (the Ballot Act 1872, Judicature Act 1873, Franchise and Distribution Acts 1885), pushing Britain slowly towards proper, representative democracy.

If the ethos of *laissez-faire* sprang largely from Britain's economic ascendancy, its demise sprang largely from economic decline (from being responsible for perhaps a third of the world's manufacturing, Britain's share would fall to 13.6 per cent in 1914 and a mere 10 per cent by 1939). Even by the 1880s, it was becoming clear that Britain's economy was being eclipsed by those of Germany and the USA – hence the growing demands, from farmers in particular, for protection from foreign competition. Complacency was also undermined by abject poverty in the industrial areas (highlighted by the creation of a Sanitary Commission in 1869) and a resulting acceptance that personal economic misfortune was not always due to personal error or wickedness.[15] Although certain Liberals, such as Herbert Spencer, continued to preach the doctrine of self-help and limited government, by 1879 the Oxford philosopher T. H. Green had already planted the seeds of an alternative Liberalism, one which required a more active state to remove the new socio-economic obstacles to individual liberty and fulfilment.[16]

Gladstone's ministries offered little tangible evidence of Green's New Liberalism; government spending as a percentage of Gross National Product actually reached an all-time low under his premiership in the 1880s. Yet Gladstone did give both the Liberal Party and British politics generally a *rhetorical* legacy which was evident in future administrations. As Michael Lynch points out in Chapter 2, this partly involved a 'moral' view of government, one which held that the state was obliged by its conduct to set an example to its subjects and foster an improved code of behaviour (hence Gladstone's loathing of Turkey at a time when this made little geopolitical sense). The sort of moralistic language beloved of Gladstone was to be adopted expediently by more than a few of his successors in British government, seeking to 'put a sanctimonious gloss on their own meddlesome instincts'.[17] Yet Gladstone also bequeathed a distaste for passivity and fatalism – a distaste which became the hallmark of politicians after 1945. For Gladstone the 'vital principle' of the Liberal Party was 'action, and that nothing but action will ever make it worthy of the name of a party'.[18] Even modern Tory politicians, with an ideological affinity for *laissez-faire*, have often found this hyperactive legacy impossible to resist – Margaret Thatcher being the prime example.[19]

At the start of the twentieth century, however, there were few signs that New Liberalism had detained most of the Liberal leadership. Campbell-Bannerman showed little interest in legislative reform, while Asquith told an audience in 1904 that the party's 'first duty' in government would be to reduce public spending.[20] Yet pressure for more remedial action by governments was already becoming more intense. Seebohm Rowntree's survey of 1899 had estimated that nearly a third of Britons were paupers, the effects of which were shown shortly afterwards by the poor physical quality of Boer War recruits. The Liberal MP, L. C. Money also noted in 1905 that, although there was more of it, Britain's wealth was so unevenly shared as to make class conflict a worrying possibility – a possibility both reflected and heightened by the emergence of the Labour Party and its clear pitch for traditional Liberal supporters.[21]

As Harry Bennett and Robin Barlow observe (Chapters 7 and 8), these forces conspired to make the last Liberal governments (1906–15) among the most significant landmarks in the evolution of Britain's 'welfare state'. Also encouraged by the dynamic German Empire, which suggested that bold intervention and economic success were compatible, the reforms carried out by these governments led to a doubling of social service spending between 1906 and 1914 by which time (for example) over 30,000 children were receiving free lunches courtesy of the School Meals Act. The government also reworked the state's relationship with industry and the workforce. In addition to enhancing the status of trade unions under the 1906 Trades Disputes Act, the Trade Boards Act of 1909 applied the criteria of a national minimum wage to occupations such as chain- and box-making, while the coal strike of 1912 prompted the expanding Board of Trade to set up District Boards to oversee wage negotiations – a clear forerunner of the incomes policies practised by successive social democratic governments from 1962 to 1979.

Yet it is the 'People's Budget' of 1909, and the later National Insurance

Act of 1911, for which the Asquith/Lloyd George ministries are mainly remembered, representing in many ways the apogee of 'new' Liberalism and the prototype for social democratic governments later in the century. After 1945, Liberal supporters claimed – with some justification – that the welfare reforms of the Attlee government were a mere extension of their party's own measures between 1909 and 1911.[22] Certainly the central idea behind the reforms of the late 1940s – redistributive taxation helping to finance state welfare schemes to which the likely recipients made clear contributions – had its roots in the Asquith/Lloyd George measures, but without being anything like as controversial as it had been forty years earlier.

Although the last purely Liberal government ended in 1915, New Liberalism's contribution to British social democracy did not end with it. If the 'welfare state' represents one pillar of the post-war social democratic consensus, then the other is represented by an approach to economics usually described as 'Keynesian' – again involving a more interventionist state and a clear moral dimension (*vide* the prevention of mass unemployment). As a post-war Tory Chancellor said of his Labour predecessor: 'We both spoke the language of Keynes but with different accents.'[23] Yet Keynes, a young Treasury official, was recruited to the Liberal Party in the late 1920s in order to devise an alternative approach to the mounting economic crisis. Subsequent policy documents – the Green, Yellow and Orange Books – carried interventionist remedies which, though rejected by the cautious electorates of 1929 and 1931, were accepted by the two major parties after 1945.

In fact it is considered a paradox of post-war politics that the Liberal Party almost disappeared at a time when Liberalism seemed to be flourishing in British government (the party won only 2.5 per cent of votes cast at the 1951 general election). This paradox is further highlighted by the fact that the principle architect of post-war welfare policy, William Beveridge, also had strong Liberal connections. On the other hand, it may be argued that the Liberal Party's 'near-death experience' after 1945 was entirely predictable: with the main, class-based parties having accepted the 'new' Liberal (or quasi-social democratic) agenda, at a time of strong voter–class alignment, there seemed little incentive to support a party still confused about its own social and ideological identity.

The inter-war period has bred many myths about the nature of government and society. It was clearly not a period in which market forces and *laissez-faire* were still unchallenged; neither was it a period of unremitting misery for the mass of ordinary people. The admirably meticulous studies of both Fraser (1973) and Addison (1977) confirm that the 1930s, far from representing the 'last fling' of minimal government, actually saw Britain's governing class make innumerable contributions to the country's gestating welfare state.[24] Furthermore, Rowntree's later surveys showed that, by 1936, 'the economic condition of the workers' had improved by 30 per cent since 1899, with housing, health and education all 'immeasurably better' than thirty years earlier.[25]

The revisionist case, however, is easily overstated. Rowntree's 1936 report also asserted that 30 per cent of workers in urban areas were suffering 'absolute' deprivation, with almost half the children of working-class parents destined to spend the first five years of their lives in poverty. Neither should the various statist responses of inter-war governments be confused with the more systematic (and comprehensive) reforms of the post-war Labour government. The interventionist social policies of the 1920s and 1930s, though paving the way for more radical reform after 1945, were still 'a totally *ad hoc*, unplanned response to events ... a process of devising expedients as the need arose'.[26] It is too easy, when tracing the origins of social democracy in Britain, to overlook the huge difference the Attlee governments were to make in the space of just six years. The fact remains that, in the 1930s, no free medical treatment was universally available; there was no free secondary education for the vast majority, no family allowances, no free school milk for all children, few council houses and no comprehensive system of old-age pensions.[27] In fact the movement towards a statist political culture during the inter-war era was cautious and equivocal compared with the half-decades which both preceded and followed it.

World War

Britain's involvement in the century's two World Wars was obviously different in a number of vital respects – the sheer scale of casualties, during two relatively short periods, being an obvious and staggering illustration (750,000 between 1914 and 1918; 325,000 between 1939 and 1945). Yet the unprecedented pressures imposed upon the country by both World Wars forced British governments to adopt new powers and enact new measures of intervention undreamt of before war broke out. As Fraser noted, 'a sort of inexorable logic forced the state forward, every step necessary as an effective enforcement of the previous one'.[28]

During the First World War, the advance of state power stemmed mainly from the Defence of the Realm Act 1914 – a response to the need for national mobilisation which enabled the government to regulate a wide range of social and economic activities. Following various amendments, this duly allowed conscription into both the armed forces and heavy industry, and eventually led to food rationing in 1918. The Ministry of Munitions, after 1915, acquired vast powers of regulation in industry, aided by strict controls over profits, prices and wages (a Rent Restriction Act was also passed to abet a more mobile workforce). Likewise, County Agricultural Committees – strengthened by the Corn Production Act 1917 – were set up to direct farmers towards achieving centrally determined quotas of production. At the Exchequer, Reginald McKenna briskly disregarded the principles of *laissez-*

faire by raising income tax to almost 10 per cent, with a 50 per cent excess profits tax in 1915. Free trade was also sacrificed to a 33 per cent tariff on all luxury imports. Yet the key point of all these developments was that they were generally considered effective, strengthening the confidence of those, such as the Fabians and their New Liberal allies, who claimed that social progress and limited government were incompatible.

As with the Boer War, the First World War highlighted the mean condition of a population subjected to largely unfettered market forces; surveys revealed that only one in three conscripts satisfied the original medical criteria for active service.[29] Such findings fuelled the creation of a Ministry of Reconstruction in 1917, which was designed to investigate how state action could tackle health, education, housing and employment problems once the war was over. The ideals invested in the Ministry by Lloyd George were scarcely justified by subsequent governments, even though the Housing Act 1919 (already mentioned) and the Education Act 1918 (raising the school leaving age and abolishing fees in elementary schools) represented significant advances. Yet the failure (or inability) of inter-war governments to realise fully the 'land fit for heroes' idea and build upon the potential for state action revealed in the Great War, did not dent the confidence of contemporary social democrats. It merely strengthened their determination to consolidate state power more effectively once it burgeoned again – and even more dramatically – between 1939 and 1945.

The encroachments made by central government during the First World War were to pale in comparison with those which took place during the Second. An estimated 22 million Britons (roughly half the population) were called into service by the state for both military and non-military purposes, while the Emergency Powers Act 1940 gave the Coalition Government unlimited powers over British citizens and their property. As one diarist recorded, the Second World War witnessed 'the stiffest dose of totalitarian principles a democracy has ever had to swallow', with Michael Foot later claiming that the war was 'the nearest thing I have seen in my lifetime to the operation of a democratic socialist state'.[30] Virtually no aspect of civilian society – employment, prices, incomes, leisure activities, diet, fuel consumption, transport, child care, health care, domicility – was exempt from bureaucratic regulation.

The apparent effectiveness of these measures naturally strengthened social democracy's cause after 1945; having been deployed to beat an external enemy, it was easy to argue that widespread state direction could now be used to defeat the perennial 'enemies within', such as unemployment, poverty and ill-health. Indeed there were signs during the war that the state was already addressing itself to this task. The Beveridge Report of December 1942 recommended a comprehensive system of social insurance and the creation of a national health service; the Education Act 1944 (fashioned by the Conservative minister, R. A. Butler) established the principle of free secondary education for all; and the Employment White Paper of 1944 – heavily influenced by Keynesian thinking – acknowledged a more interventionist role for governments in a capitalist economy, giving priority to 'a high and stable level of employment after the War'.

Yet of equal importance was the effect the Second World War had upon millions of voters – the same voters who would later give Attlee's Labour Party its mandate for change. As Hennessy observed:

> Almost six years of total war had left no citizen untouched by the rigours of state control, whether in the form of a siege economy on the home front or by military service abroad. The population was used to strict regulation which helped create an atmosphere in which carefully conceived and centrally directed schemes of national improvement became a norm and not a pipedream.[31]

Yet the public mood was not just a case of bureaucratic conditioning. Even more than during the First World War, the 1939–45 conflict bolstered the public's belief that such tribulations merited an altogether 'better' (*qua* equal) society once peace was resumed. This belief was endemic even among the middle classes, which (on account of conscription and evacuation, for example) had experienced first hand and for the first time the grim condition of people living in the same society as themselves.[32] The classless *esprit de corps* fostered in both military and non-military spheres of activity, allied to the perceived efficiency of state regulation, translated easily into a general conviction that governments could and should engineer limitless social improvement. The public's reaction to the Beveridge Report, for example, was so enthusiastic that it 'established a national consensus ... to believe in Beveridge was to believe in a successful outcome to the War'.[33]

Labourism

The points just raised have encouraged among certain scholars a 'deterministic' view of the Labour governments' record between 1945 and 1951, one which claims that much of what they carried out was almost preordained given the public mood and state of the nation.[34] This view is rather unfair given the formidable opposition encountered by many of Attlee's reforming ministers – particularly Aneurin Bevan at the Ministry of Health.[35] It is also a view which ignores Labour's own contribution to the mood which swept it to power, and the impact of 'Labourism' between 1900 and 1945.

After 1900 the very existence of the Labour Party (and its progenitor, the Labour Representation Committee) served to push British politics in a collectivist direction, with the influence of 'Labourism' extending beyond the labour movement. 'Labourism' represents an essentially short-term and pragmatic brand of left-wing politics – committed to the doctrine of equality, yet adamant that nothing should eclipse the immediate needs of the labouring classes. Labourism holds that these needs are best met through steady, incremental reform, effected through the industrial action of trade unions and the complementary legislative action of their 'labour' allies in parliament.[36]

Labourism has not been the only ideological strand within the Labour Party – Marxism, Fabianism and Christian socialism have all played an important role in the development of Labour's political thought – yet it has normally been the guiding strategy.[37] And although it is easily portrayed as a half-hearted doctrine (particularly by revolutionary socialists, who decry the Labour Party's influence), the impact it made at the start of the century was significant.

It needs to be emphasised that, despite the claims of Tory paternalism and New Liberalism, the enactment of new laws was but a small part of parliamentary life in the early 1900s; in 1911 (a relatively heavy year for legislation) there were only 450 pages of new statutory orders, compared with over 3,000 in 1975.[38] The Labour Party represented a phenomenon in British politics in that it was committed, as a matter of fundamental principle, to large quantities of new legislation – first, as a way of alluring the new breed of working-class voter, and second, as a method of transforming society in the manner prescribed by those leading the Labour movement.

Much has been made of how Labour in the 1920s was 'absorbed' into the political establishment, an 'achievement' for which Baldwin has received much credit (see Stuart Ball, Chapter 10). Yet it is often overlooked that Labour's *a priori* commitment to social reform, via extensive legislation, was also absorbed by the Establishment's existing parties, particularly after the franchise extension of 1918 (which flooded the electorate with working-class voters) and Labour's arrival as principal Opposition and party of government between 1922 and 1923. Although the frontiers of state control did recede between 1918 and 1922, Labour's advance thereafter was to impede any whole-hearted return to *laissez-faire* by other parties.

When tracing the roots of social democracy, it is also easy to disparage the record of Ramsay Macdonald's two Labour governments (1924 and 1929–31). As Robert Garner shows in Chapter 9, the legislative record of these governments is far from impressive, even though Wheatley's Housing Act of 1924 led to an important expansion of council housing. Yet, as Garner points out, Macdonald's real achievement lay in admitting voters to the idea of Labour in power, and Labour politicians to the constraints and realities of governing – a strategy which arguably bore fruit in the election victory of 1945.

Labour's performance after the débâcle of 1931, when Macdonald's government collapsed and a vital section of the party seceded, can also be misread. Despite the party's huge loss of seats in the 1931 general election, its share of votes remained respectable, while its share in 1935 was higher than when it took office in the 1920s (see Appendix 4). Moreover, Labour's electoral progress after 1931 was not achieved through any dilution of its historic, statist ideals. In *Labour's Immediate Programme* of 1937, Dalton outlined plans for a generous state benefits and pensions scheme, while endorsing Keynesian-style full employment – policies which were restated in *Labour's War Aims* of 1939.[39]

Labour's status by 1940 was such that Churchill could not exclude its senior figures from his wartime Coalition. Attlee, Dalton, Greenwood, Cripps and Morrison were not only given positions that were critical, but positions which allowed them to hone and test labourist ideas. As Deputy Prime Minister, Attlee was given almost unhindered responsibility for domestic policy, orchestrating with gusto many of the interventionist schemes permitted by the Emergency Powers Act (see above). Greenwood meanwhile, assumed responsibility for Reconstruction after 1941, enabling him to develop several of the ideas instigated by Labour in the 1930s. When Labour's conference of 1944 reaffirmed its support for public ownership, it was able to cite existing practice – rather than abstract theory – as proof of its utility.

Labour's inclusion in government between 1940 and 1945 therefore stoked that government's statist tendencies, which in turn made Labour's post-war proposals seem like a logical, administrative extension rather than a cerebral, ideological crusade. Furthermore, the wartime Coalition strengthened Labour's credibility at the 1945 election, equipping it to extol policies which sounded not just resonant but practicable.

This introduction has tried to show that the 1867–1945 period left behind vital foundations for the social democratic accord which later emerged. What the period could not foresee, however, were the problems which eventually beset a heavily bureaucratised state and politicians faced with exponentially large responsibilities – problems which, by the 1970s, sparked a 'crisis of governability' in British politics. This was to be the troubled inheritance of those who governed (or sought to govern) Britain after 1945 – and we hope to examine their record more closely in a second volume of essays.

Notes

1. R. Eatwell, *The 1945–1951 Labour Governments* (London, Batsford, 1979).
2. See D. Howell, *British Social Democracy* (London, Croom Helm, 1976).
3. *The Spectator*, editorial, 13 February 1981.
4. Q. Hogg, *The Case For Conservatism* (Harmondsworth, Penguin, 1948).
5. M. Pearce and G. Stewart, *British Political History 1867–1990* (London, Routledge, 1992), p. 94.
6. Pearce and Stewart, *British Political History*, p. 93.
7. R. Kelly, 'The party conference', in A. Seldon and S. Ball (eds), *Conservative Century* (Oxford, Oxford University Press, 1994), pp. 232–4.
8. P. Buck (ed.) *'How Conservatives Think* (Harmondsworth, Penguin, 1975), pp. 121–78.
9. P. Whiteley, P. Seyd and J. Richardson, *True Blues* (Oxford, Oxford University Press, 1994), pp. 54–9.
10. J. Barnes, 'Ideology and factions', in Seldon and Ball *Conservative Century*.

11 M. Pugh, *The Making of Modern British Politics 1867–1939* (Oxford, Blackwell, 1982), pp. 207–13.
12 Pugh, *Modern British Politics*, pp. 273–83.
13 P. Clarke, 'Liberals and social democrats in historical perspective', in V. Bogdanor (ed.), *Liberal Party Politics* (Oxford, Clarendon Press, 1983).
14 Quoted in Pearce and Stewart, *British Political History*, p. 36.
15 D Fraser, *The Evolution of the British Welfare State* (London, Macmillan, 1973), pp. 115–35.
16 See M. Freeden, *The New Liberalism* (Oxford, Oxford University Press, 1978).
17 M. Beloff, *The Tide of Collectivism: Can It Be Turned?* (London, Conservative Political Centre, 1978), p. 9.
18 M. Bentley, *The Climax of Liberal Politics 1868–1918* (London, Arnold, 1978), p. 110.
19 J. Ranelagh, *Thatcher's People* (London, Fontana, 1992), pp. 15–38.
20 T. Wilson, *The Downfall of the Liberal Party* (London, Collins, 1966), p. 84.
21 Pearce and Stewart, *British Political History*, p. 187.
22 J. Grimond, *The Liberal Challenge* (London, Hollis and Carter, 1963), p. 74.
23 Lord Butler, *The Art of the Possible* (London, Hamish Hamilton, 1971), p. 160.
24 Fraser, *Welfare State*, Ch. 8; P. Addison, *The Road To 1945* (London, Cape, 1977), Chs 1 and 2.
25 Fraser, *Welfare State*, p. 190.
26 Fraser, *Welfare State*, p. 171.
27 P. Clarke, *A Question of Leadership* (London, Hamish Hamilton, 1991), pp. 193–211.
28 Fraser, *Welfare State*, p. 164.
29 Fraser, *Welfare State*, p. 166.
30 Quoted in Pearce and Stewart, *British Political History*, p. 433.
31 P. Hennessy and A. Seldon (eds), *Ruling Performance* (Oxford, Blackwell, 1987), pp. 32–3.
32 See S. Briggs, *Keep Smiling Through: The Home Front 1939–1945* (Cambridge, Cambridge University Press, 1986).
33 A. Sked and C. Cook, *Post-War Britain* (London, Penguin, 1993), p. 19.
34 D. Coates, *The Labour Party and the Struggle for Socialism* (Cambridge, Cambridge University Press, 1975), p. 47.
35 See K. O. Morgan, *Labour People* (Oxford, Oxford University Press, 1991), pp. 135–48, 204–19.
36 G. Elliott, *Labourism and the English Genius* (London, Verso, 1993), pp. 22–66.
37 G. Foote, *The Labour Party's Political Thought* (London, Croom Helm, 1985), pp. 1–6.
38 D. Butler and G. Butler, *British Political Facts 1900–1994* (London, Macmillan, 1994), p. 205.
39 Addison, *Road to 1945*, p. 51.

Benjamin Disraeli

Michael Lynch

Background

In February 1868 Queen Victoria wrote to one of her daughters: 'Mr Disraeli is Prime minister, A proud thing for a man "risen from the people" to have obtained'.[1] Her description was a touch misleading. It is true that he and the Duke of Wellington were the only Prime Ministers in the nineteenth century not to have attended public school and Oxbridge, but Benjamin Disraeli's background can hardly be described as humble. He came from a comfortable, middle-class Jewish family which had formally converted to Anglicanism when Benjamin was aged thirteen in order to avoid the social and political barriers that confronted practising members of the Jewish faith.

Disraeli cannot be said to have had a proper job until he was appointed Chancellor of the Exchequer in 1852. By then he was forty-eight years old. He had survived by borrowing heavily and by writing. Initially his literary efforts brought in only a meagre income, but in the 1840s he gained success with a trilogy of political novels, which have come to be accepted as his most accomplished works. What continues to make them interesting to later generations is that they represent an insider's view of early Victorian politics.

Disraeli made four unsuccessful attempts, the first as a radical, to win a parliamentary seat before eventually being elected in 1837 as a Conservative MP under the patronage of Lord Lyndhurst, a leading Tory. As a young politician, Disraeli exploited his distinctive Jewish appearance and adopted a deliberately outrageous style of dress in order to make himself known. He calculated that effective self-publicity would help offset the disadvantage of not belonging to the social class from which politicians were traditionally drawn. His tactics sometimes invited ridicule, but there was no doubting he was a person of exceptional ability. A local paper described him on the hustings in Dorset in 1835:

> He commenced in a lisping, lackadaisical tone of voice ... He minced his phrases in apparently the most affected manner ... he would lean affectedly on the table, supporting himself with his right hand; anon he would push aside the curls from his forehead ... But as he proceeded all traces of the dandyism and affectation were lost ... His voice at first so finical, gradually became full, musical and sonorous ... The dandy was transformed into a practised orator and finished elocutionist.[2]

In his early years in politics, in the 1830s and 1840s, Disraeli expressed a deep distrust of the times in which he lived, an attitude he happened to share with Gladstone, the man destined to be his great political rival. Gladstone was disturbed by what he saw as the godlessness of the age; Disraeli by the prevailing spirit of utilitarianism which he considered was changing so much of British society for the worse. In response he became a leading member of Young England, a movement which looked to a romantic, golden English past which was to be restored under the leadership of the aristocracy.

Apprenticeship

Although the British aristocracy remained a matter of life-long fascination for Disraeli, it is unlikely that he took the ideas of Young England very seriously for very long. The movement was a means of promoting himself and it provided a platform from which to attack Robert Peel, the leader who had transformed the Tories into the Conservative Party. In 1846 Disraeli denounced Peel for betraying his party by introducing the repeal of the Corn Laws, the symbol of the protectionist interests of the landed classes, who were the chief supporters of traditional Toryism. Yet in helping to bring down Peel in 1846, Disraeli was in part responsible for the split in the Conservative Party that was to deny it majority government for nearly thirty years.

Robert Blake, his outstanding modern biographer, remarks that Disraeli's only certain feature in his early years was an 'unrelenting determination to get to the top'.[3] Everything Disraeli did in public life was dedicated to that end. What is fascinating is that judged by this standard he had relatively limited success. Of his thirty-one years in politics before 1868, arguably the time when he was at his best, he had been a minister for only four, and then only occasionally and briefly in minority governments. Furthermore, until 1868 he was under the shadow of the Earl of Derby, who, although a peer and therefore not a member of the Commons, dominated the Conservative Party.

Disraeli's success and importance as a politician were concentrated into the last quarter of his forty-four year career. In 1868, having 'climbed to the top of the greasy pole' and become Prime Minister for the first time, he confided that power had come to him too late.[4] He regarded the middle years of his life between 1846 and 1867 as having been a time of lost opportunity. But perhaps he was too harsh in his self-assessment. By 1868 he had certainly made a major impact on British politics. His political gifts, evinced by his work as Chancellor of the Exchequer, in 1852, 1858–59 and 1867, had made him a key figure in the Conservative Party. As early as 1853, the *Edinburgh Review* had said that Disraeli 'glittered in the political horizon as a star of the first magnitude'.[5]

Despite having advanced his early career by attacking Peel, Disraeli – once he had risen to the top of the Conservative Party by the late 1860s – adopted policies that were essentially Peelite. He followed Peel in acknowledging that the economic and social changes that Britain was experiencing in the wake of industrialisation made it necessary for government and parliament to introduce reforms and for the Conservative Party to modify its policies in the light of these. He calculated that it would be far less disruptive if reforms that could not be resisted were to be initiated by the traditional ruling classes. In this way they would remain in control of the political situation. This was the essence of Disraeli's concept of 'Tory democracy'. The Conservatives would not resist the extension of the vote to a widening range of the population but their aim would be to continue to direct affairs so as to prevent democracy from going too far. This could best be achieved not by weakening Britain's institutions, but by building on them. Disraeli's approach can be illustrated by examining his role in the major issues in which he was involved after he had risen to the leadership of his party: the reform of parliament, the reshaping of the Conservative Party, Imperialism and the Eastern Question.

Limelight

Disraeli and the Second Reform Bill, 1867
By the late 1860s it was broadly accepted that the 1832 Reform Act had not gone far enough to accommodate the social shifts occurring in Britain and that a further measure of electoral reform was unavoidable. The question was which of the parties would be responsible for introducing it – the Liberals or the Conservatives? Disraeli did not believe in sweeping change, but he was a realist. He judged that if the Conservative Party was to survive as a dominant force in politics it had to win the support of the growing middle classes. It was they, the commercial and business interests of Britain, who were the most vociferous in demanding that the franchise be modified so as to represent them more fully. Disraeli resolved that the Conservatives must seize the initiative over franchise reform, thereby putting themselves in a position to limit its scale and effects. Accordingly, when Gladstone introduced a Reform Bill in 1866, Disraeli chose to attack it. Supported by the 'Adullamites', a group of anti-reform Liberal rebels, the Conservatives were able to defeat Gladstone's measure. This brought the Conservatives back into government, with Derby as Premier and Disraeli as Chancellor of the Exchequer.

Having 'dished' the Liberals, Disraeli then introduced his own Bill in 1867. Its main clauses extended the vote to rate-paying householders in the boroughs. Although Disraeli spoke of his Bill in terms of principle, as a measure in keeping with 'the manners, the customs, the laws, the traditions of the people',[6] his approach was essentially expedient. This was shown by the readiness with which he accepted the Hodgkinson Amendment, a radical proposal which widened the franchise to include some half-million 'compounders', the class of occupiers who shared costs with their landlords rather than paying full rates. The Amendment contradicted the basic principle which Disraeli had originally claimed underlay his Bill, that the franchise was a privilege not a right and should be granted only to direct ratepayers. The reason for his shift was that he saw electoral advantage for the Conservatives in a modified Bill. Although it considerably increased the number of middle- and working-class voters in the urban boroughs, the 1867 Act enhanced Conservative voting strength in the county constituencies. In the words of Maurice Cowling, a modern analyst, Disraeli 'was prepared to let Radicals have their way in the boroughs, so long as he had his in the counties'.[7]

Disraeli's adroitness greatly impressed many of his contemporaries; they attributed the passing of the 1867 Reform Bill to the power of his personality and his great skill as a parliamentary tactician. His opportunism had proved a double success: it had stolen the Liberals' thunder and it had consolidated his own standing in the Conservative Party.

However, it was precisely this second factor which offended those Conservatives who looked upon Disraeli as an upstart. The Marquess of Salisbury was prominent among a disaffected group who believed that Disraeli was simply intent on advancing his own position. According to Salisbury, Disraeli was a cavalier adventurer, 'without principles and honesty'.[8] Salisbury regretted the personal esteem that Disraeli had gained in the party and the government. His gravest complaint was that Disraeli's lack of breeding and lineage put him 'under a temptation to Radical measures to which no other Minister is subject'. Not being a natural Conservative, Disraeli was obliged to adopt a radical posture in order to sustain his position: 'He alone can silence and paralyse the forces of Conservatism ... in an age of singularly reckless statesmen he is I think beyond question the one who is least restrained by fear or scruple'.[9]

Salisbury's bitterness is an interesting example of the Conservative distrust that dogged Disraeli throughout his career. Traditionalists in the party never fully accepted him. They recognised his outstanding abilities and they knew the party could not dispense with him, but at the same time they regarded him as an affront to their Conservative values. He had become, in the words of Robert Blake, 'an indispensable liability' to the Conservative Party.[10] Yet it was this 'liability' who was to give new shape and purpose to Conservatism and to enable it to make the transition into the world of modern politics.

Disraeli's reshaping of Conservatism
By one of those ironies that frequently occur in British politics, Disraeli's achievement in piloting through the Second Reform Bill was followed not by success but by apparent failure. Having briefly become Prime Minister for the first time on Derby's retirement in February 1868, he found himself out of office by November when, in the first election after the 1867 Act, the Liberals were returned with a substantial majority. However, it was the subsequent six years of Conservative Opposition that were to prove the most politically productive period in Disrali's career. In retrospect it can be seen that Disraeli's great opportunity 'to educate' his party, as he put it,[11] came not so much with the 1867 Reform Act as with the years that immediately followed when Gladstone headed his first government, the great Liberal reforming administration of 1868–74. The reforms which were introduced during this 'high tide of Liberalism' left hardly any of the major state institutions untouched. The propertied, the commercial and the industrial classes began to fear that their interests were under deliberate and systematic threat. Disraeli deftly played upon their fears, representing the Liberal government as being intent on nothing less than the destruction of the British way of life: '[The] tone and tendency of Liberalism cannot be long concealed. It is to attack the institutions of the country under the name of Reform, and to make war on the manners and customs of the people of the country under the pretext of Progress'.[12]

He personalised the threat by portraying Gladstone as an irrational demagogue who was imperilling the nation. But Disraeli did not limit himself to attacking the Liberals and their leader. His complementary aim was to convince the electorate of the positive virtues of Conservatism. What Disraeli did in the early 1870s was to undertake a major campaign, aimed at projecting an image of himself and the Conservative Party as bastions of reason and committed guardians of the national interest. In a series of major speeches in parliament and in the country, he set out to show that the Conservative Party truly understood the nation's needs and had a programme for realising the aspirations of the people. He identified three major objectives in Conservative policy: the defence of the nation's traditional institutions; the preservation and enlargement of the British Empire; and 'the elevation of the condition of the people', Disraeli's term for social reform. These were calculated appeals to a wide cross-section of the nation: traditionalists, the middle classes and the newly enfranchised working-class voter. Disraeli was concerned to prove that the Conservatives were 'the National Party'.[13]

The reward for his efforts came in 1874 with a substantial victory over the Liberals at the general election. Diraeli became Prime Minister at the head of a government with a comfortable parliamentary majority, something the Conservatives had not enjoyed since 1846. He now had the opportunity to give practical effect to the policies he had been advocating so vigorously. For the next six years, Disraeli, gout-ridden and asthmatic and in his late seventies, led a ministry which was no less significant than its predecessor in legislative achievement. Social reform figured prominently in the Conservative government's programme. Among the outstanding measures were: the Artisans Dwelling Act, providing for slum clearance and re-housing; two Factory Acts, protecting female workers and confirming the ten hour day; the Sale of Food and Drugs Acts, forbidding the adulteration of foodstuffs; a Public Health Act, codifying over one hundred regulatory statutes; Trade Union Acts, establishing the right to peaceful picketing and protecting union funds; an Education Act, making primary school attendance compulsory; and a Merchant Shipping Act, requiring ship owners to conform to statutory safety standards.

The measures make an impressive list. Yet to contemporaries they did not seem particularly remarkable and Disraeli himself showed little enthusiasm for the finer points of detail. He left his ministers to do the essential task of preparation. Richard Cross, Disraeli's Home Secretary, expressed disappointment at his leader's lack of initiative in this area: 'From all his speeches, I had quite expected that his mind was full of legislative schemes, but such did not prove to be the case; on the contrary, he had to rely on the various suggestions of his colleagues'.[14] But this is to judge Disraeli by the wrong measure. His personal interest in social reform is a question of secondary importance. The critical point is that he had grasped the political necessity of appearing to redeem his election pledges to elevate the condition of the people. It was the logical corollary of his conviction that a modern party had to be visibly responsive to the demands of a broadening electorate.

Disraeli's Imperialism
Disraeli had always shown an interest in Britain's Empire. Although as a younger politician he had spoken of the colonies as 'millstones round our necks', his reference at the time had been to a particular problem with regard to Canada. Historians now accept that too much has been made of that statement and that the extension of British possessions overseas had always appealed to Disraeli.[15] What is certain is that from the early 1870s he began to express a distinct commitment to the Empire as an essential aspect of Conservatism. He was encouraged in this by Gladstone's hostility to any form of foreign involvement. Disraeli judged that the idea of British greatness, exemplified by imperial expansion, would prove a vote-winner with the growing electorate. He publicised his party's attitude towards Empire in a series of powerful speeches in the early 1870s. It was part of his campaign to convince the voters that Gladstone's reforming Liberal government was engaged in destroying the nation's true character. Denouncing Liberal attempts over forty years to reduce Britain's status as an overseas and imperial power, Disraeli pledged his party to the restoration and enlargement of the Empire.

Disraeli's translation of the concept of Imperialism into practical policy is evident in four characteristic episodes which occurred during his 1874–80 administration. In 1875, when the bankrupt Khedive of Egypt was forced to sell off his holdings in the Suez canal project, currently being constructed under French direction, Disraeli used his influence with Rothschilds, the banking giants, to raise the necessary capital to purchase the shares for Britain. He wrote exultantly to the Queen: '... you have it, Madam; the French Government has been outgeneraled ... the entire interest of the Khedive is now yours'.[16] The following year Disraeli took equal satisfaction in introducing the Royal Titles Bill, which conferred on the Queen the title of 'Empress of India', thus making her the personification of the imperial idea. Victoria, beguiled and delighted by her Premier, sent him a Christmas card, signed 'Regina et Imperatrix'.[17]

Disraeli's determination to resist any challenge to Britain's position in India, 'the Jewel in the Crown', led directly to a crisis over Afghanistan, India's northwestern neighbour. Worried by Russia's expansion into southern Asia, which by the 1870s appeared to threaten India, Disraeli judged it necessary for Britain to take control of Afghanistan as a buffer state. When Sher Ali, the Afghan Amir, resisted Britain's demands that he reject Russian overtures and accept British authority, an army was despatched from India to compel him to comply. This occasioned the Second Afghan War of 1879–81, a British success militarily but one which offended Liberal opinion and led to renewed denunciations of Disraeli's disregard of morality in state affairs. Gladstone was subsequently to reverse Britain's aggressive policy in the region.

A similar set of incidents had occurred in Africa. In 1876 Disraeli sent a British army to the Transvaal in support of the Dutch Boers in their war with the native Zulus. His primary aim was not to assist the Boers but to assert British authority in Southern Africa. Things went badly at first – the Zulus inflicted a major defeat on the British forces at Isandhlwana in 1879 before being finally overcome later that same year at Ulundi.

Disraeli and the Eastern Question

It has been said of Disraeli that the only nationalism he was prepared to recognise was the English variety.[18] His overriding concern in foreign affairs was the protection of British interests. He never shared any of Gladstone's grand and airy concepts of the concert of nations. This was clear from his approach to the Turkish Question. Here Disraeli's basic aim was to prevent the Russians exploiting the terminal decline of the Ottoman Empire to their own advantage. His anxiety was that as Turkey's hold over its Balkan and Middle Eastern territories weakened Russia would move in, thus menacing the route to India in particular and Britain's strategic and commercial position more broadly.

Disraeli was pursuing traditional British policy. Britain's entry into the Crimean War in the 1850s had been a demonstration of its anti-Russian disposition. The Treaty of Paris which ended that war had forbidden Russian warships to enter the Black Sea. In 1871, however, Russia had ignored that prohibition. Disraeli had feared that this might be a prelude to a Russian advance into the Balkans and he had attacked Gladstone as Prime Minister for failing to respond to the Russian threat. In office himself after 1874, Disraeli continued his anti-Russian line, refusing to be pushed into action by the accounts of Turkish barbarities against Christians in the Balkans. When in 1876 Gladstone came out of retirement to publish his anti-Turkish tirade, *The Bulgarian Horrors and the Question of the East*, Disraeli countered it with mockery. He described Gladstone's pamphlet as 'vindictive and ill-written' and 'of all the Bulgarian horrors, perhaps the worst'.[19] He rejected Gladstone's charge that in refusing to denounce the Turks he was sacrificing morality to expediency by asserting that in any international question Britain's interests must be paramount. In 1877, in accordance with that principle, Disraeli adopted an openly aggressive stance towards Russia by ordering British land and sea forces to the Dardanelles.

But no fighting ensued. When it became known that the Russians had made considerable territorial gains under the Treaty of San Stefano, which they had forced upon the Turks in March 1878, Disraeli was able to persuade Germany and Austria to join Britain in imposing a new settlement to cancel out Russia's gains. The major European powers met formally at the Congress of Berlin to reconsider the Eastern Question. The gathering proved a major diplomatic success for Disraeli. Bismarck, the German Chancellor, acknowledged the British Prime Minister as the dominant influence in shaping the Treaty of Berlin, under which Russia returned the territories it had gained at San Stefano and Britain guaranteed to protect Turkey in return for the cession of Cyprus.

Despite Disraeli's success in bringing back 'peace with honour' from Berlin in 1878, a triumph met with huge popular acclaim, his days in office were numbered. The Conservatives had begun to lose their administrative edge, the situation in Ireland had grown increasingly threatening, Britain had undergone a serious agricultural depression and the economy overall had taken a down-turn. Moreover, in a reversal of roles, Gladstone performed the task in Opposition that Disraeli had achieved during the Liberal administration; in his famed Midlothian campaign undertaken in 1879, Gladstone had revivified the Liberals and undermined the credibility of the Conservatives. Disraeli, weary and weakened by severe bronchitis, could not stem the Liberal tide; the Liberals returned to office following their election victory of March 1880. Twelve months later Disraeli was dead.

Legacy

Throughout his life Disraeli professed an abiding admiration for the British aristocracy. He believed it gave order and stability to British society. The established Church, the House of Lords, the authority of the JPs in the counties and, above all, the Crown: these were the institutions which for him symbolised the nation's identity. Yet he was sufficiently a realist to know that times were changing and that political adjustments had to be made in keeping with them. Moreover, as John Vincent has pointed out, 'Disraeli's unrestrained delight in aristocracy was aesthetic, not political'.[20]

The striking point about Disraeli's career is that, in all major respects, he remained a Peelite. From the late 1860s, he pursued policies which were essentially developments of what Peel had earlier begun. The acceptance of free trade was one obvious example of this. But it went much further. Disraeli followed Peel in transforming the Conservative Party from an oligarchy of landed magnates into an alliance of moderate opinion capable of representing the interests of the commercial and industrial world. While he obviously had no wish to undermine aristocratic tradition, he understood that it was the middle classes that mattered. They were the possessors of the wealth created by industrialisation; now that they had the vote they were the most influential stratum in politics and society. No party could survive that did not adapt itself to this fundamental social shift.

Disraeli's remarkable coup in outmanoeuvring the Liberals and pushing through the Conservatives' own Reform Act in 1867 has often been cited as evidence of his genuine wish to extend democracy by enfranchising the working classes. Modern historians, however, tend to regard the Act as primarily a measure designed to safeguard the electoral interests of the Conservative Party rather than a genuine broadening of the representative character of parliament. Similarly they question Disraeli's claim that the Reform Act, which swelled the electorate by nearly a million, had both enlarged the rights of the British people and strengthened the institutions of the country. They interpret his role as one of political expediency rather than idealism. Ian Machin suggests that in all that Disraeli did, 'the furthering of his party and of his own political fortunes was paramount. He had a genuine wish to carry certain reforms but only if and when they assisted his political objectives'.[21]

But although doubts remain concerning Disraeli's motives in widening the franchise, there was one area where undoubtedly he did win over working-class support to the side of Conservatism. His judgement that Imperialism would have special appeal for a large part of the electorate proved remarkably percipient. For all the high-flown rhetoric that so often accompanied Imperialism, the reality was that colonial expansion was an affair of British armies on the ground in foreign lands. Since the rank and file came from the working classes, most ordinary families had a father, son or brother for a soldier; they were thus linked in a chain of personal interest in Britain's foreign ventures. It is arguable that, in the last quarter of the century, Imperialism – with its appeal to patriotism – proved as popular as social reform in persuading the bulk of the working class to give Disraeli's new brand of Conservatism a sympathetic hearing.

The past is always viewed through the lens of the present. In the early 1990s there were attempts to enlist Disraeli as the progenitor of 'one nation Conservatism'. Interpretations were produced based on the idea that because

Disraeli, particularly in his novels, had lamented the division of Britain into two nations, the rich and the poor, he had been essentially a social healer who wished to lead the Conservative Party in a policy of ending class antagonisms and economic inequality.[22] Recently Paul Johnson has powerfully restated that view: 'Democracy turned out to be the Conservatives' secret weapon, and since Britain became a democracy they have held power more than three-quarters of the time. Disraeli was the first to perceive this truth and make use of it'.[23]

But this is to invest Disraeli with values and ideas that belong to a different era. There are key features of modernity about Disraeli but it is important not to exaggerate them. He was not a believer in the welfare state. His model was *ad hoc* reform, introduced when the pressure for change was too great to resist without occasioning serious political risk. His approach was pragmatic not idealistic. The political fact was that both Liberal and Conservative Parties were now prepared to contemplate necessary reform. They might differ on detail and timing and seem to present sharp alternatives to each other, but that was necessary in order to appear to offer genuine choice to voters. Assessed in the light of their social reform measures when in office, there was little to separate them; they were both liberalising parties. Despite Disraeli's campaign against what he depicted as the excesses of Gladstone's 1868–74 government, the legislation introduced by the succeeding Conservative administration was not substantially different in character from that of the Liberals.

Yet, notwithstanding this evident continuity of policy, it remains the case that it was at this time that the two-party system, with its attendant pattern of alternating governments – the 'swing-of-the-pendulum' – consolidated itself as the basic process by which British politics operated. The explanation for this is that the great divide between Liberal and Conservative was not principally over domestic policies but over imperial and foreign affairs. Gladstone and Disraeli came to personify diametrically opposed attitudes towards the question of Britain's place in Europe and the world at large. Opinion in the country divided bitterly over the morality of the stances taken by the two leaders. They came to be seen as offering distinct moral alternatives. The Governor of the Isle of Man, writing in 1878 about Disraeli's Afghan and Turkish policies, described the intensity of the passions aroused among ordinary people in Britain by the two leaders: '... it is all *purely personal*, the divergence of opinion not being so much upon the merits of the questions which seldom seem understood, but upon the feelings that are entertained either towards Lord Beaconsfield or Mr Gladstone'.[24]

It is fascinating to reflect that, had the accidents and events of politics been even slightly different, it is quite possible that Gladstone might have remained a Conservative and that Disraeli's radicalism might have led him into the Liberal Party. That such speculations may be legitimately made indicates how close the major parties were in many areas. It is easy to be too impressed by the rigidity and formality of the modern two-party system and to forget how fluid the pattern had been before it hardened around Disraeli and Gladstone. The fragmenting of the Conservative Party after 1846 and the uncertain evolution of the Whig into the Liberal Party had led to political uncertainty. There was no immutable reason why the Conservatives and Liberals should have settled into distinct and opposed parties. The social and economic backgrounds of Members of Parliament were often indistinguishable; since they were unpaid, they were of necessity overwhelmingly drawn from the propertied or moneyed classes. Shifts and adjustments had been common and labels such as Conservative, Liberal and Radical did not always convey a precise description, which is why compound adjectives, such as Liberal-Tory and Conservative-Radical, were frequently used. The historical importance, therefore, of both Disraeli and Gladstone is that the more closely they became identified with their respective parties, the more politics polarised around them as individuals. In that sense it can be claimed that the two men were the first leaders of mass parties in British politics.

Here it is important to understand the character of party politics as they have operated in Britain since the age of Disraeli and Gladstone. The record shows that, in action, party government has been essentially a reactive exercise, a response to economic and social changes after they have taken place. Parties in office have seldom initiated change according to a particular philosophy. Indeed ideology has played little part in practical politics. Judged by what parties actually do when in power, there has been far greater convergence between them than the adversarial character of their political debate would suggest. Insofar as one can talk of political philosophy in Britain, it has been largely a set of justifications for what governments have done rather than a body of ideological precepts laying the base for future action.

Herbert Morrison, a prominent Labour Party spokesman of a later generation, once defined Socialism as 'what Labour governments do'. With the appropriate adjustment of the party label, the same might be said of Conservatism as practised under Disraeli. It is true that he devoted considerable time, particularly in the early 1870s, to redefining the objectives of Conservatism; but his greatest claim to modernity is not as a political thinker but as a practical politician who had a gift for presentation and a remarkable instinct for seizing the moment. The charge often made against him in his own time and since – that he was an opportunist – overlooks the essential consideration that opportunism was a necessary requirement for success. Not to have been opportunist would have been to condemn himself to political and administrative impotence. Interestingly, Gladstone also showed this same sense of right timing and of knowing how to respond to the public mood; he could be as much an opportunist as Disraeli. Ironically, it may be that it was their similarities as much as their differences that made them such bitter foes.

Disraeli often did things for effect. He could play the dilettante or he could play the statesman, but the essential thing was that he was playing. It was, of course, a serious game in which he engaged; he was an opportunist, ever willing to adjust to changed circumstances. It is difficult to know how deeply, if at all, he held to the principles which he advanced. It is quite legitimate to try, as this chapter does, to define the ideas that made up his Toryism or Conservatism, but it is not easy to tell how sincerely he believed in them.

Not surprisingly, his calculated levity damaged his reputation. It seemed that he was too entertaining to be trusted. In his own self-mocking analysis: 'The British People being subject to fogs and possessing a powerful Middle Class require grave statesman'.[25] A similar charge levelled against him was that he lacked consistent principles. Yet total consistency in politics is more likely to be a handicap than an asset and the fact remains that he contributed as much to Conservatism as any other leader in its modern history. Whatever the sincerity of his own beliefs, he identified his party with modernity and progress. Moreover, he brought to Conservatism a sense of romance and glamour. It was this, indeed, which led many of his Conservative contemporaries to distrust him. And yet a century later he is still the most consistently revered figure in Conservative Party folklore.[26]

It is also worth considering that contemporaries may have been misled by Disraeli's apparent insouciance and have failed to notice his industry and underlying seriousness of purpose. The image of him as a carefree adventurer does not always match the record. There are, for example, strong grounds for suggesting that there was something distinctly orthodox, even staid, about his financial policies. He was no irresponsible spendthrift. He described his approach to the management of the nation's finances as 'frugally but wisely to administer the public treasure'.[27] His Budgets as Chancellor of the Exchequer and his fiscal policies when Prime Minister were as much about retrenchment as Gladstone's ever were.[28]

We probably know as much about Disraeli now as we ever shall. All the many sources have been gathered. What changes are the interpretations of him. All historical figures are reassessed through the insights of succeeding generations. While Disraeli scholars might differ in their appraisals of his policies, they tend now to concur in accepting that what he did was less important than what he was. It was his personality that made him so distinctive. A representative voice is that of Paul Smith who, in his biography, suggests that 'Disraeli's art and legacy lay not in the manufacture of measures but in the management of impressions'.[29] Indeed, he comments:

> Disraeli lives on as a source of political inspiration less because of his contributions to Conservative strategy and discourse, or his sense of the profound forces shaping the flow of events, or his attributes of the seer, than because of the brilliance and excitement that he found in, and imparted, to life.[30]

One feature of this brilliance was the way he excelled in the company of women. He had a great capacity for winning their affection and loyalty. As his collected correspondence shows, he could be light-hearted without descending into mere chit-chat, or serious without becoming merely solemn. His art lay in appearing to treat women as equals. Princess Marie Louise, one of Queen Victoria's granddaughters, related: 'After sitting next to Mr. Gladstone I thought he was the cleverest man in England. But after sitting next to Mr. Disraeli I felt I was the cleverest woman in England'.[31] Disraeli's subletly was nowhere better illustrated than in his relations with the Queen. He knew how to charm her and to say what she wanted to hear. She loved his attention and flattery, and their audiences more often had the air of mild flirtation than of formal constitutional business.[32] Such mutual affection was of considerable political importance since there is little doubt that she sided with his Conservatism. The prospect of Disraeli as Prime Minister filled her with barely hidden delight as much as the thought of Gladstone in the same capacity filled her with scarcely concealed gloom. Disraeli was always careful to slip into their conversations frequent and reverential allusions to her beloved Albert, the Prince Consort, from whose death in 1861 she never fully recovered emotionally. There is a story that as Disraeli himself lay dying in 1881 he was asked whether he would welcome a visit from the Queen. 'No,' he replied, 'she would only ask me to take a message to Albert.'[33]

A particularly absorbing aspect of modern analyses of Disraeli is the stress that is laid on his Jewishness, which was not merely a background influence but a main determinant of his artistry and his striving to reach the top. But the influence of Judaism upon him was as a culture not as creed, for religion sat lightly on him. He found Gladstone's ecclesiastical fervour amusing, but he was aware of the importance of formal religion in public life and was careful not to offend unnecessarily those in his party who wished to make a stand against unwelcome developments in the Anglican Church. Disraeli was impressed by Christianity, to which his family had converted in his youth, but largely because he saw it as a logical extension of Judaism. For him, Christ's Jewishness was more important than His divinity.

Disraeli presents a marked contrast with the solemn Gladstone but, though his manner and style may have lacked gravity, his desire for success was entirely sincere. Disraeli wrote political novels whereas Gladstone wrote theological and classical works. But even novelists deserve to be taken seriously sometimes.

Chronology

1804	born in London into a genteel Jewish family
1817	his family convert to Christianity
1832	stands for parliament as a radical but is unsuccessful
1837	enters parliament at the fifth attempt as Conservative MP for Maidstone
1841–46	becomes a leading figure in the Young England movement
1844–47	his three major novels, *Coningsby*, *Sybil* and *Tancred*, are published
1845–46	leads a campaign against Peel over repeal of the Corn Laws

1852	becomes Chancellor of the Exchequer in Derby's government
1858–59	Chancellor of Exchequer in Derby's second government
1866–67	pushes through the Second Reform Bill
1868	becomes Prime Minister for the first time, but is defeated in the subsequent general election
1868–74	rejuvenates the Conservative Party in Opposition
1872	makes a series of key speeches redefining the role of the Conservative Party
1874	wins general election and becomes Prime Minister for the second time
1874–80	leads one of the major reforming ministries of the century
1876	becomes Lord Beaconsfield
1878	attends the Congress of Berlin
1880	Conservatives defeated in the general election
1881	dies

Notes

1 Robert Blake, *Disraeli* (London, Eyre and Spottiswoode, 1966), p. 487.
2 W. F. Monypenny and G. E. Buckle, *The Life of Benjamin Disraeli, Earl of Beaconsfield* (London, John Murray, 1910–20), Vol. I, pp. 284–5.
3 Blake, *Disraeli*, p. 757.
4 Blake, *Disraeli*, p. 487.
5 Michael Lynch, *Gladstone and Disraeli* (London, Hodder and Stoughton, 1991), p. 18.
6 Speech in Edinburgh, 1867, in Lynch, *Gladstone and Disraeli*, p. 26.
7 Maurice Cowling, *1867 Disraeli, Gladstone and Revolution* (Cambridge, Cambridge University Press, 1967), p. 233.
8 Salisbury to Mr Gaussen of the Hertfordshire Conservative Association, April 1868, in Lynch, *Gladstone and Disraeli*, p. 43.
9 Lynch, *Gladstone and Disraeli*, p. 43.
10 Blake, *Disraeli*, p. 758.
11 Speech in 1867, in Lynch, *Gladstone and Disraeli*, p. 26.
12 Speech at Crystal Palace, June 1872, in Lynch, *Gladstone and Disraeli*, p. 43.
13 Lynch, *Gladstone and Disraeli*, p. 43.
14 Paul Adelman, *Gladstone, Disraeli and Later Victorian Politics* (London, Longman, 1970), p. 89.
15 See for example, John K. Walton, *Disraeli* (London, Routledge, 1990), p. 37.
16 Blake, *Disraeli*, p. 584.
17 Disraeli to Lady Bradford, December 1876, in Marquis of Zetland, (ed.), *The Letters of Disraeli to Lady Bradford and Lady Chesterfield* (London, Ernest Benn, 1929), p. 96.
18 See Blake, *Disraeli*, p. 760.
19 Disraeli to Derby, September 1876, in Blake, *Disraeli*, p. 602.
20 John Vincent, *Disraeli* (Oxford, Oxford University Press, 1990), p. 119.
21 G. I. T. Machin, *Disraeli* (London, Longman, 1995), p. 169.
22 See the discussion in Walton, *Disraeli*, p. 66.
23 Paul Johnson in *The Spectator*, 18 May 1996, p. 16.
24 Henry Loch to Lord Lytton, November 1878, in Blake, *Disraeli*, p. 761.

25 Blake, *Disraeli*, p. 766.
26 See Paul Smith, *Disraeli: A Brief Life* (Cambridge, Cambridge University Press, 1996), p. 211.
27 Speech in 1862, in Lynch, *Gladstone and Disraeli*, p. 42.
28 See P. R. Ghosh, 'Disraelian Conservatism: a financial approach', *English Historical Review*, (April 1984), 268–96.
29 See Smith, *Disraeli*, p. 217.
30 Smith, *Disraeli*, p. 220.
31 *The Spectator*, 28 September 1996, p. 55, quoting from John G. Murray (ed.), *A Gentleman Publishers Commonplace Book* (London, John Murray, 1996).
32 See Robert Blake, *Gladstone, Disraeli, and the Queen* (Oxford, Clarendon Press, 1993).
33 Sarah Bradford, *Disraeli* (New York, Stein and Day, 1983), p. 388.

Further reading

The standard reference work and mine of information remains W. F. Monypenny and G. E. Buckle, *The Life of Benjamin Disraeli, Earl of Beaconsfield*, 6 vols (London, John Murray, 1910–20). The outstanding modern authority on Disraeli is Robert Blake; among his most accessible works are *Disraeli* (London, Eyre and Spottiswoode, 1966); *The Conservative Party from Peel to Thatcher* (London, Methuen, 1985); and *Gladstone, Disraeli and the Queen* (Oxford, Clarendon Press, 1993). Three informed and highly stimulating biographies, which contain provocative reappraisals of Disraeli's influence upon British politics are John Vincent, *Disraeli* (Oxford, Oxford University Press, 1990); G. I. T. Machin, *Disraeli* (London, Longman, 1995); and Paul Smith, *Disraeli* (Cambridge, Cambridge University Press, 1996). An interesting Jewish perspective is presented by Stanley Weintraub in his *Disraeli: A Biography* (London, Hamish Hamilton, 1993). Bruce Coleman's *Conservatism and the Conservative Party in Nineteenth-Century Britain* (London, Edward Arnold, 1988) places Disraeli in the context of Victorian party politics. Three outstanding studies of Disraeli's attitude towards democracy are: Maurice Cowling, *1867 Disraeli, Gladstone and Revolution* (Cambridge, Cambridge University Press, 1967); E. J. Feuchtwanger, *Disraeli, Democracy and the Tory Party* (Cambridge, Cambridge University Press, 1968); and Richard Shannon, *The Age of Disraeli 1868–1881: The Rise of Tory Democracy* (London, Longman, 1992). Interesting insights into Disraeli as a literary and social figure are offered by Sarah Bradford in her *Disraeli* (New York, Stein and Day, 1983). Useful documentary studies with accompanying commentaries are Paul Adelman, *Gladstone, Disraeli and Later Victorian Politics* (London, Longman, 1970) and Michael Lynch, *Gladstone and Disraeli* (London, Hodder and Stoughton, 1991).

William Ewart Gladstone

Michael Lynch

Background

'A comic genius' is how a former Labour Party leader recently referred admiringly to Disraeli.[1] The noun might be applied equally appropriately to Gladstone, but not the adjective. The great Liberal leader of the nineteenth century was never comic, at least never intentionally. He was a man of the highest seriousness in a highly serious age. His character was neatly captured by Disraeli when he remarked that Gladstone did not possess 'a single redeeming defect'.[2]

Born in 1809 into a prosperous merchant family of Scottish extraction, whose wealth had been originally derived from the slave trade, William Ewart Gladstone was from the first a deeply religious person with an abiding sense of his own unworthiness. For him every moment of life was a gift from God and had to be accounted for; hence the diaries that he wrote daily from the age of eleven until failing eyesight forced him to stop in his late eighties. His entries help to provide a fascinating picture of a man described by his latest biographer, Roy Jenkins, as 'the most remarkable specimen of humanity of all the fifty who ... have so far held the office of British Prime Minister'.[3]

Gladstone had a sustained mental and physical energy that few could equal. Contemporaries spoke in awe of his ability to do in one hour what it took everyone else two hours to accomplish and to maintain that output for eighteen hours a day. One example of this is that during his lifetime he read a total of 20,000 books, an average of five a week. All this could, of course, be extremely irritating to observers who were unable to match his industry. His wife, Catherine, once remarked: 'Oh William dear, if you weren't such a great man, you would be a terrible bore'.[4]

Gladstone's rescue work among prostitutes, which he engaged in throughout his career in fulfilment of a commitment made as a student at Oxford to perform a redeeming work of Christian charity, was an activity which the modern tabloid press would make impossible for a contemporary politician to attempt. Although from time to time doubts have been cast on Gladstone's motives,[5] there are still grounds for seeing his nightly vigils among fallen women as an expression of both his sense of morality and his innocence of spirit.

Apprenticeship

On leaving Oxford with a double first in 1831, Gladstone considered becoming an Anglican priest, and even though he subsequently chose instead to enter politics as a Tory MP he still regarded his public life as being primarily the service of God. As a young politician he believed the age in which he lived was uniquely sinful. He found the democracy of the Great Reform Act of 1832 unacceptable and denounced the Whig reforms of the 1830s, particularly those relating to the established Church, as godless. However, service in the 1830s and 1840s as a junior minister under Robert Peel, whom Gladstone regarded as his political mentor, tempered the severity of his earlier views.

He followed loyally as Peel moved from protection to free trade, an evolution which culminated in the repeal of the Corn Laws in 1846. His veneration for Peel convinced many contemporaries that Gladstone was his natural Conservative heir. But, with the fracturing of party alignments after 1846 and Peel's death in 1850, Gladstone was no longer sure that his future was as a Conservative. An important experience that helped direct him towards Liberalism as an ideal was his witnessing of the oppression of political dissidents in Naples in the early 1850s.

The vital stage in the turning of his burgeoning Liberal ideas into practical politics came with his work as Chancellor of the Exchequer, first in Lord Aberdeen's Coalition Government of 1852–55 and then in Palmerston's Whig-Liberal ministry of 1859–65. His budgets of those years overhauled the system of government finance and consolidated Britain's position as a free-trade nation. Gladstone's 1859 acceptance of office under Palmerston, a man whom he had previously distrusted as much as he had Disraeli, was a clear sign that he had moved from his previous Conservative moorings. From now on he could be counted a Liberal.

Such was Gladstone's stature in his new party that within a decade of joining it in 1859 he had risen to the leadership. In 1868 he became Prime Minister for the first time. By then he was already in his sixtieth year and yet his extraordinary political life was to run for another quarter of a century. It is appropriate to study his late career by reference to its three outstanding phases: his leadership of the great Liberal reforming government of

1868–74; his arousing of the moral outrage of at least half the nation against the Turkish atrocities and Beaconsfieldism; and his prolonged, though doomed, attempt to bring a peaceful resolution to the Anglo-Irish Question.

Limelight

Gladstone's first ministry, 1868–74
Gladstone later described the Cabinet he assembled during this ministry as, 'one of the best instruments for government that ever was constructed'.[6] Its legislative record certainly merits such a claim. Often described as 'the high tide of Liberalism', Gladstone's first ministry undertook a range of reforms that affected nearly all the major institutions of the state.

In 1870, W. E. Forster, Vice-President of the Committee for Education, tackled the contentious issue of education by introducing a Bill for the creation of a national system of elementary schooling. The problem he faced was a religious one. While there was broad acceptance of the need for a universal system, there were deep divisions regarding how it was to be achieved. On one side was the National Education Union, the voice of the established Church, which claimed that reform of education should include government financing of the existing Anglican 'voluntary' schools. On the other was the National Education League, the representative body of the Nonconformists, who fiercely objected to state funds being used, as they saw it, to subsidise the teaching of Anglican doctrines. Forster's scheme aimed at meeting both demands: it provided aid to Church schools and also grants for the founding of non-denominational 'Board schools'. The compromise satisfied neither side; each felt betrayed by the concession to the other. The most worrying aspect of this for Gladstone's government was the reaction of the Nonconformists, previously one of the strongest groups among Liberal supporters. Joseph Chamberlain, their spokesman and a radical-Liberal, declared that the government's decision, 'deliberately to defy us leaves us no alternative. The "Nonconformist Revolt" long threatened has begun'.[7]

The problems inherent in trying to reconcile opposing interests were evident in the response to each of the reforming measures of the 1868–74 ministry. On the labour relations front, the credit gained by the Liberals for the Trade Union Act of 1871, which gave the unions extended legal rights and protection of funds, was dissipated by the accompanying Criminal Law Amendment Act, which subjected picketing to the charge of conspiracy. Similar loss of government popularity followed from the University Test Act of 1871, which ended formal discrimination against Dissenters at Oxford and Cambridge, and the Civil Service reforms begun in 1870, which introduced open competitive examinations for entry to the Service and promotion within it.

Progressive though these reforms were, they offended the traditionalists, who saw their personal status and the character of their institutions being undermined. The Ballot Act of 1872 also had its critics. The obvious virtue of the measure lay in its ending of electoral corruption by the introduction of secret balloting. However, critics forecast – correctly as events were to show – that the effect in Ireland would be to enable the electorate to vote in defiance of their landlord's wishes by returning pro-Home Rule MPs.

The reform of the British Army, the work of Edward Cardwell at the War Office, was based (like the Civil Service measures) on the principle of promotion on merit and the abolition of the custom of auctioning commissions to the highest bidder. It was a necessary prerequisite for the formation of a modern armed service, but it, too, met the sternest opposition, this time from the officer class which resented the attack upon its privileges.

Posterity has applauded the reforms introduced during Gladstone's first ministry as marking a significant move towards the modernising of Britain. But, at the time, the hostility of the various vested interests brought the government growing opposition, often from within its own ranks. Measures which encountered notably fierce resistance included the 1872 licensing reforms. The attempt to lessen the destructive social effects of uncontrolled drinking – by imposing limitations on opening hours and the rights of admission to public houses – was condemned by the liquor trade as an assault on civil and commercial freedom. In the House of Lords, the Bishop of Peterborough declared that 'it would be better that England should be free than that England should be sober'.[8] After the Liberals' election defeat in 1874, Gladstone wrote characteristically that his government had been 'borne down in a torrent of gin and beer'.[9] He resigned as Prime Minister and party leader and announced that he was retiring from politics in order to read theology and prepare himself for death. However, two years later there began what might justifiably be described as his second career.

Gladstone, the Eastern Question and Beaconsfieldism
Gladstone's short-lived withdrawal from public life ended in 1876 when he learned of the Turkish massacres of the Christians in the Balkans. Despite being bed-ridden with lumbago, he dashed off an impassioned pamphlet, *The Bulgarian Horrors and the Question of the East*, denouncing the Turks in the most uncompromising terms for perpetrating:

> crimes and outrages so vast in scale as to exceed all modern example, and so utterly vile as well as fierce in character, that it passes the power of heart to conceive, and of tongue and pen adequately to describe them. These are the Bulgarian horrors ... An old servant of the Crown and State, I entreat my countrymen ... that our Government, which has been working in one direction, shall work in the other; and shall apply all its vigour to concur with the other States of Europe in obtaining the extinction of the Turkish executive power in Bulgaria.[10]

Gladstone's thunderings did not begin the anti-Turkish campaign in Britain; that was already underway. But his condemnation of Turkey for its atrocities, and his castigation of Disraeli's government for allowing 'the hobgoblin of

Russia' to scare it into a pro-Turkish stance, had the effect of polarising opinion in Britain. The nation divided in support between Gladstone, the protector of oppressed peoples, and Disraeli, the guardian of the nation's interests.

So ensued what Roy Jenkins describes as 'the greatest setpiece drama of Victorian politics'.[11] Jenkins also suggests that Gladstone had never truly intended to retire and that the Bulgarian horrors provided the perfect pretext for him to launch himself back into political life for a moral cause. It is certainly true that once Gladstone had returned to the fray he showed every sign of wanting to remain. He did not immediately retake the Liberal leadership from Lord Hartington, his successor in 1874, but his pre-eminence in the party made it only a matter of time before he did so.

Gladstone broadened his attack upon Disraeli into a bitter excoriation of the evils of Beaconsfieldism, the term that he coined to define the immorality of the Conservative leader's foreign and imperialist policies. This was not mere party-political rhetoric. Gladstone had a profound dislike of Disraeli. He believed that it was 'Dizzy's crypto-Judaism' that helped to explain his inability to sympathise with the ravaged peoples of the Balkans.[12] For his part, Disraeli regarded his rival as a madman; he spoke of 'that unprincipled maniac Gladstone – extraordinary mixture of envy, vindictiveness, hypocrisy, and superstition'.[13]

Gladstone refused to join in the general rejoicing at Disraeli's triumph in bringing back 'peace with honour' from the Congress of Berlin in 1878. He dismissed the treaty that Disraeli had negotiated as 'an insane convention' and considered that Britain had been unworthily represented by the Prime Minister and his Foreign Secretary, Lord Salisbury: 'I do affirm that it was their part to take the side of liberty; and I do also affirm that as a matter of fact they took the side of servitude'.[14]

The Liberal attack on Beaconsfieldism reached its climax in Gladstone's groundbreaking election campaign in the Midlothian constituency in Scotland in 1879. In one typical week of this campaign Gladstone made nine speeches, five of them major oratorical performances, at different venues to mass audiences ranging from 2,500 to 20,000. Midlothian may be fairly described as the first 'whistle-stop tour' in British politics. Remarkably, as John Morley, Gladstone's Liberal colleague and first major biographer, pointed out:

> he took care to address all these multitudes of weavers, farmers, villagers, artisans, just as he would have addressed the House of Commons, – with the same breadth and accuracy of knowledge, the same sincerity of interest, the same scruple in right reasoning, and the same appeal to the gravity of public life.[15]

Gladstone's audiences reciprocated, listening transported to speeches which seldom lasted less than an hour and were often twice as long. Angrily, the Conservative press accused him of playing the demagogue and subverting the Constitution. Historians see such a reaction as an unwitting tribute to what is now regarded as the first calculated and successful deployment of populism in modern British politics.

The immediate consequence of the Midlothian campaign was to make Gladstone once again the unchallenged leader of the Liberal Party. This was soon followed by his return to office as Prime Minister in 1880. His personal duel with Disraeli finally ended with the latter's death in 1881. The prospect of having to give the customary formal tribute in the Commons to the rival he had detested brought on a prolonged bout of diarrhoea. To avoid hypocrisy, Gladstone in his speech made no reference to Disraeli's principles; instead he praised him for his consistency of purpose and parliamentary courage.

Gladstone's personal commitment to parliamentary reform was evident in the major domestic measure of his 1880–85 administration. The 1884 Third Reform Act saw the extension of the franchise to county householders. But this second ministry did not achieve the legislative success of his first and it encountered particular difficulties over foreign affairs. In 1882 Gladstone felt it necessary to sanction the British occupation of Egypt, a decision that opponents and many within his own party challenged as a mockery of his previous censures of Conservative imperial expansion. Gladstone's prestige was further eroded by what was widely perceived to be his culpability in the death in the Sudan in 1885 of the British military hero, General Gordon. It appeared that out of pique Gladstone procrastinated over sending an army to the assistance of Gordon, who had been besieged by the followers of the Mahdi. When Gladstone did eventually authorise the despatch of a relief force it arrived too late; Gordon had already been killed. The Queen let it be known publicly that she regarded Gladstone as being heavily responsible for the tragedy. Embarrassing for the Liberal government though these crises were, it was the Irish problem that dominated Gladstone's 1880–85 government, as it would both his subsequent ministries.

Gladstone and Ireland

Gladstone's involvement with Ireland, which preoccupied him for the last twenty-five years of his career, is the stuff of Greek tragedy. His persistence in seeking a solution denied him the chance to attend fully to the pressing domestic issues of his day and finally broke the Liberal Party.

In 1868, when invited to form the first of his four governments, Gladstone had resolutely declared: 'My mission is to pacify Ireland'.[16] His initial reading of the Anglo-Irish Question did not suggest to him that the problem was essentially a political one. He judged that Ireland would achieve a condition of 'contentment' if three outstanding grievances were removed: religion, land and education. Accordingly, in 1869 he introduced a Bill to disestablish and disendow the Anglican Church in Ireland, the 'tall tree of noxious growth' whose privileges had been an affront to the overwhelmingly Catholic population.[17] In the following year came the first Land Act, intended to safeguard Irish tenants against eviction except for non-payment of rent. The Irish University Bill of 1873 was Gladstone's attempt to tackle the education issue; it sought to bring higher education within the reach of

Catholics by the establishment of a university for them in Dublin.

Of these three measures only Church disestablishment proved effective. The Land Act did not prevent landlords from forcing eviction by raising rents to unreasonable levels, while the University Bill proved unacceptable to Catholics since it forbade the new institution to teach theology. Far from improving matters, Gladstone's measures had served to increase Irish bitterness. By the start of his second ministry in 1880, the situation in Ireland had deteriorated further. Government coercion was being met with terrorism by the Fenians. Yet Gladstone still clung to the notion that legislation to redress grievances was the best means of ending Anglo-Irish hostility. His second Land Act, introduced in 1881, sought to provide protection for Irish tenants by establishing the 'three Fs': fair rents, fixity of tenure and free sale.

But the British government and parliament were now confronted by Charles Stewart Parnell, the astute leader of the Irish Land League and of the Irish Nationalist MPs in the Commons. Parnell, confident that Gladstone's series of attempted reforms was proof that further agitation would produce further concessions, directed his followers in a twin policy of agrarian disturbances in Ireland and obstruction at Westminster. In 1881 Parnell was charged with sedition and held in Kilmainham Gaol in Dublin. Still believing that conciliation offered a better way forward, Gladstone, through the offices of Joseph Chamberlain, negotiated the 'Kilmainham Treaty', an unofficial agreement with Parnell that in return for his release he would move to lessen the violence in Ireland.

In 1882 the Irish crisis struck Gladstone in a directly personal way when his nephew, Lord Frederick Cavendish, the new Irish Secretary, was stabbed to death in Phoenix Park in Dublin. Interestingly, the murder, rather than spurring Gladstone to retaliation, reinforced his developing line of reasoning. He was moving to the conclusion that ameliorative action could not of itself bring 'contentment'. Ireland, he now acknowledged, needed some form of self-government: 'A popular and responsible Irish body – competent to act for its own portion of the country'.[18] It followed that the Act of Union, which for eighty years had tied Ireland to England, would have to be modified, if not ended altogether.

Gladstone knew that to contemplate Home Rule for Ireland risked party unity: both wings of the Liberal Party – the Hartington Whigs on the Right and the Chamberlain Radicals on the Left – would oppose it. But he was convinced that the strength of the Irish Nationalist vote in the 1885 election, the first to be held under the newly extended franchise, was a mandate that made Home Rule a moral necessity. Gladstone was so resolved upon a solution that he was prepared to put it beyond party politics. He let it be known to the Conservatives that he was willing to consider a bi-partisan approach or even to support them if they were prepared to bring in their own measure for an Irish constitutional settlement.

His manoeuvres were nullified, however, by his son's inadvertent public disclosure that his father had been converted to Home Rule. The Conservatives under Salisbury considered that Gladstone's decision effectively removed any possibility of a two-party agreement. Gladstone would have to go on alone. What compounded Gladstone's difficulties at this critical juncture was the loss of the services of Charles Dilke, one of the leading radicals among the Liberals. Gladstone had hoped to rely on Dilke to swing radical opinion in the party behind Home Rule, thus offsetting the opposition of Chamberlain. But in 1885 Dilke's reputation was irreparably damaged by the revelation of his involvement in a salacious three-in-a-bed divorce scandal.

Nevertheless, Gladstone pressed on. But by now the greatest single obstacle to Home Rule was the attitude of Ulster. That region's largely Protestant population was passionately determined to remain part of the United Kingdom. It was to preserve the rights of Protestant Ulster that the Conservative Party and a significant number of Liberals now adopted an unyielding 'Unionist' stance. This was sufficient to defeat Gladstone's first Home Rule Bill in 1886. Despite giving what was perhaps his greatest parliamentary performance in introducing the Bill, he saw it rejected on its second reading, over ninety Liberals joining the Conservatives to vote against it.

Yet Gladstone was as determined as ever; he estimated that, since the Irish Nationalist MPs now held the balance between the Liberals and the Unionists in the Commons, their support made it possible still to achieve Home Rule. But fate again intervened. In 1890 news broke of Parnell's adulterous affair with the wife of one of his own Nationalist MPs. The majority of Parnell's followers felt he had forfeited their loyalty and the party split, so depriving Gladstone of a major block of support.

He remained undaunted. In 1893, during his fourth and last ministry, he introduced a second Home Rule Bill. It passed narrowly through the Commons, only to be thrown out by the Lords, a rejection that occasioned his last parliamentary speech, an angry denunciation of the unelected and undemocratic Upper House.

Legacy

Gladstone became a Victorian institution, as much a personification of the Victorian age as the Queen herself. In many of those things which are thought of as definitively Victorian – gravitas, religious devotion and scrupulous soul-searching – Gladstone was the epitome. He was more than simply a Prime Minister and party leader; he became a moral force in British public life, the keeper of the nation's conscience. Yet, outstanding though he undoubtedly was as a statesman and public figure, his record of political achievement as Liberal leader is much more open to question.

Historians recognise the significance of 'the High Tide of Liberalism', but see the legislation of his 1868–74 ministry as piecemeal rather than a systematic social and economic reform programme. Emphasis is now laid on the insoluble problems that weakened Gladstone's first government. The basic difficulty was that the Liberal Party was not yet a single movement with a fixed agenda, but merely a collection of interests; this tended to result in internal disputes. Indeed in modern British politics this has been the characteristic weakness of all left-of-centre parties. In a sense the Liberals in government were their own worst enemies. Gladstone wrote in 1874 that Liberalism 'has no present public *cause* upon which it is agreed'.[19] He complained that too many Liberals were simply using the party to advance their careers, which made them only too ready to oppose its leaders and policies. Powerful though Disraeli's onslaught on Gladstone's first ministry was, the defeat of the government in 1874 was due less to external Conservative pressure than to internal divisions. Colin Matthew, today's leading authority on Gladstone, remarks that between 1868 and 1874 Gladstone spent the greater part of his time in conflict with colleagues and groups on both the Left and Right of the party. Gladstone's first ministry 'followed the Liberal stereo-type: every Liberal government between 1830 and 1895 ended by the disintegration of its own support in the Commons'.[20]

Matthew discerns three dominant characteristics in Gladstone's Liberalism: first, a belief in the minimal state, which exists not to regulate conduct but to create the necessary civil stability that allows citizens the freedom to pursue their own legitimate interests; second, a recognition, as witnessed by his Irish policy, that the retention of the unitary character of the United Kingdom was not an absolute principle; and third, a conviction, manifest in his government's Parliamentary Reform Act of 1884, that ultimate political authority lay with the people.[21] The continuing centrality of these three concerns in British public life gives Gladstone a powerful claim to modernity.

A notable feature of that modernity was his development as a popular politician. The Midlothian campaign can now be seen as the beginning of a momentous stage both in Gladstone's Liberalism and in British party politics. Richard Shannon writes that Gladstone, building on his success in stimulating national anger over the Bulgarian horrors, made 'a holy drama' of Midlothian: 'He was appealing over the heads of the classes to the virtuous masses; and his demand was essentially that the classes voting in Midlothian should vote in this sense as moral proxies to a higher electorate'.[22]

By appealing directly to the people, Gladstone aimed to circumvent the customary barriers that preserved politics as an activity for an exclusive elite. He was seeking to establish an immediate relationship between himself and the nation. For the first time in British politics a leader was taking on the role of populist, claiming not just to understand but to represent the real aspirations of the people. Gladstone began a tradition which later leaders, such as Lloyd George and Margaret Thatcher, would seek to revive.

It was Gladstone's attempt to represent the feelings and hopes of the electorate in a personal sense that earned him the popular title of 'the people's

William'. He had developed a belief in the basic moral worth of the British people; his instinct, he said, was always 'to back the masses against the classes'. He reflected: 'In 1880, Midlothian leading the way, the nation nobly answered to the call of justice and broadly recognised the brotherhood of man. It was the nation, not the classes'.[23]

Yet not surprisingly, given the depth and complexity of his character, there are a number of paradoxes about Gladstone. He was one of those rare individuals who become more tolerant and understanding as they grow older, as manifested in his progressive approach to Ireland; but it was this same Gladstone who in 1874–75 worked himself into a lather over the Vatican Decrees. To the bewilderment of most of his colleagues, he devoted his prodigious energies to attacking the Papacy for daring to claim infallibility in matters of faith and doctrine. Rather than treat it as the purely theological question that it was, he reacted as if a great moral principle was involved, writing intemperately of the Roman Church – to which the great majority of the Irish and a large number of the British population belonged – as, 'an Asian monarchy: nothing but one giddy height of despotism and one dead level of religious subservience'.[24]

Other anomalies relate to Gladstone as a public figure. Despite his ability to arouse and represent public opinion, his own tastes and outlook remained essentially elitist. He once revealingly remarked: 'I am a firm believer in the aristocratic principle – the rule of the best. I am an out-and-out *inequalitarian*'.[25] His preoccupations often detached him from the ordinary concerns of politics and made him slow to adapt himself and the Liberal Party to the growing pressures of popular politics in what was becoming an increasingly democratic age. The outstanding example is the way he allowed his passionate commitment to the Eastern Question and Ireland to divert him and his party from the domestic issues that increasingly imposed themselves on late Victorian Britain.

Gladstone's ability to strike grand moral stances gave him the image of a prophet risen above ordinary politics. But this same loftiness of spirit often made it difficult for him to communicate at a personal level. This was well illustrated by his strained relations with the Queen. He never developed Disraeli's charm of manner, that sense of knowing how to speak to her as a woman as well as a queen. Victoria memorably remarked that Gladstone addressed her as though she were a public meeting, a jibe that Roy Jenkins counters by suggesting that had the Queen occasionally permitted Gladstone to sit down in her presence, as she did Disraeli, it might have softened the formality of their dealings.[26]

Gladstone managed to be both remarkably old-fashioned and strikingly modern. He believed in the concert of Europe and he actively espoused the principle of arbitration for resolving international disputes. Yet his own personal values belonged to an attitude of mind that was already passing away. His deep religious convictions in a man of his eminence were odd in an age which, although formally still committed to the trappings of organised religion, was increasingly erastian in politics and sceptical in matters of faith.

Gladstone acknowledged that from the 1870s his own personal beliefs had distanced him from his own party: 'I felt myself to be in some measure out of touch with some of the tendencies of the Liberal party especially in religious matters. I thought they leant to the dethronement of the private conscience and to a generalised religion'.[27] His estrangement from the Liberals in key areas was a crucial factor. It was at this time, the last quarter of the century, that the Liberal Party was faced with the problem of defining its role in a new age: what, in a progressively democratic Britain, did Liberalism represent? For the radicals, the answer was quite clear: their party should be grappling with the exigent social problems of an industrialising Britain – destitution, deprivation, squalor and disease. They viewed Gladstone's obsession with Ireland as an unnecessary distraction from these vital concerns.

Opinion continues to be divided over Gladstone and Ireland. His policy is sometimes described as courageous and noble. Through trial and error over a period of twenty-five years, he came to realise that Ireland was fundamentally a political question and therefore could be settled only by a political answer. He concluded that, no matter what the difficulties, a just settlement of the Irish Question was central to the polity of Britain; to leave the issue unresolved would be to betray the notion of the Liberal state. A contrary view is that his approach was essentially misguided in that it ignored the current political realities; by obdurately persisting for a quarter of a century with his efforts to reach a solution, he polarised attitudes and made an eventual solution even more difficult to achieve.

But that perhaps is to be wise after the event and to overlook how close he came to fulfilment. Sheer bad luck played a critical role, as it frequently does in political affairs. Had the news of his conversion to Home Rule not leaked out in 1885, had Dilke not been destroyed by sexual scandal in the same year, and had the news of Parnell's involvement in the O'Shea divorce case not broken when it did, it is conceivable that Home Rule would have been carried by either a Conservative or a Liberal government and certainly without the Liberals being torn asunder.

Whatever the judgements on his Irish policy, there is a strong case for saying that Gladstone stayed in politics too long for his party's good. His reluctance to withdraw frustrated the younger contenders for the Liberal leadership. Not only was this a bar on the aspirations of such hopefuls as Chamberlain; it meant that, as long as Gladstone remained leader, the Liberal Party was personally identified as *his* party. It could not become primarily a party of policies. When he did finally retire in 1894 it was too late; the party had already split. The Whig remnant had become Liberal-Unionists and had begun to gravitate towards full Conservatism. As for the radicals, many of them seriously doubted whether Liberalism was any longer politically relevant since it had failed to attract sufficient support from the growing ranks of organised labour. This seemed to fulfil Chamberlain's warning that, unless the Liberals modernised their stance on social issues, their natural supporters among the working class would desert them for a separate party directly representative of labour.

Yet though Gladstone may have made political misjudgments at critical moments, this was not the whole story. Differences of personality were as important as disagreements over principle in causing the fissures in the Liberal Party. If there had been more sympathetic personal relations between Gladstone, Chamberlain and Hartington, there need not have been an irrevocable division over policy.

In assessing Gladstone's place in the development of modern politics attention must be paid to his relations with Disraeli. Interestingly, their gladiatorial contest as party leaders covered a relatively short period of time – from 1868 to 1881. Moreover, for the last five of those years Disraeli was no longer in the House of Commons. However, it was not the duration of their animosity that was important but the intensity. Their disagreements did much to define the modern political agenda and consolidate the two-party system as the basic pattern of British politics.

Here a distinction needs to be made between high and low politics, between the politics that concerns itself with major moral issues and Britain's role as a nation in them, and the down-to-earth politics involved in the amelioration of social conditions and the improvement of the nation's infrastructure. Save perhaps in tone, there was little real difference between Gladstone and Disraeli over low politics. The Liberals and the Conservatives were both liberalising parties. Their social reform programmes were barely distinguishable from each other. The two great reforming ministries, the Liberal of 1868–74 and the Conservative of 1874–80, present a line of continuity not contradiction. It is this that gives the confrontation between Gladstone and Disraeli such a recognisably modern character. Although British politicians often talk in terms of principle, claiming moral propriety for themselves while denying it to their opponents, the truth is that it is very rarely that the parties really differ from each other over matters of principle. The rhetoric often obscures this point, but British parliamentary parties in the age of the two-party system have been essentially coalitions of moderate opinion.

The great clash between Gladstone and Disraeli came over high politics and had as much to do with style and presentation as policy. What their dominance of their time left was the notion that politics is as much about personality as it is about principles, as much about image as ideas, as much about presentation as policy. In this resides the most enduring legacy of both men.

Chronology

1809	born into a merchant family in Liverpool
1831	graduates from Oxford
1832	enters parliament as a Tory MP
1835	serves as junior minister in Peel's government
1843	President of the Board of Trade under Peel
1850–51	agitates against Neapolitan tyranny
1852	appointed Chancellor of the Exchequer under Aberdeen
1859	joins Palmerston's Whig-Liberal government as Chancellor of the Exchequer
1867	opposes Disraeli's Reform Bill
1868	becomes leader of the Liberal Party
1868–74	his first ministry
1874	resigns as Prime Minister; writes 'The Vatican Decrees in Their Bearing on Civil Allegiance'
1875	gives up his leadership of the Liberal Party and retires from politics
1876	writes *The Bulgarian Horrors and the Question of the East*
1879	undertakes the Midlothian campaign and resumes as Liberal leader
1880	becomes Prime Minister for the second time following a major electoral victory over 'Beaconsfieldism'
1880–85	his second ministry
1882	British troops occupy Egypt
1884	Third Parliamentary Reform Act
1885	Gladstone resigns as Prime Minister; his conversion Irish Home Rule revealed
1886	becomes Prime Minister for the third time; his first Irish Home Rule Bill splits his party and is lost in the Commons
1892–94	his fourth ministry
1893	second Home Rule Bill passes in the Commons but is defeated in the Lords
1894	resigns as Prime Minister and finally retires from politics
1898	dies

Notes

1 Michael Foot, quoted in Matthew Parris, *Scorn with Added Vitriol* (London, Hamish Hamilton, 1995), p. 125.
2 Disraeli quoted in Parris, *Scorn*, p. 125.
3 Roy Jenkins, *Gladstone* (London, Macmillan, 1995), p. xiv.
4 Jenkins, *Gladstone*, p. 55.
5 Roy Jenkins, for example, judges that the diary entries indicate that Gladstone did succumb to sexual temptation. See Jenkins, *Gladstone*, p. 106.
6 Jenkins, *Gladstone*, p. 293.
7 From a speech by Chamberlain in 1870, in Michael Lynch, *Gladstone and Disraeli* (London, Hodder and Stoughton, 1991), p. 34.
8 E. S. Turner, *Roads to Ruin: The Shocking History of Social Reform* (London, Michael Joseph, 1950), p. 191.

9 Gladstone to Robertson Gladstone, February 1874, in Philip Magnus, *Gladstone* (London, John Murray, 1954), p. 228.
10 Lynch, *Gladstone and Disraeli*, p. 95.
11 Jenkins, *Gladstone*, p. 401.
12 Gladstone to the Duke of Argyll, September 1876, in John Morley, *The Life of William Ewart Gladstone* (London, Macmillan, 1903), Vol. II, p. 552.
13 Disraeli to Lady Bradford, 1876, in Robert Blake, *Disraeli* (London, Eyre and Spottiswoode, 1966), p. 606.
14 Speech in the Commons, July 1878, in Morley, *Gladstone*, Vol. II, p. 577.
15 Morley, *Gladstone*, Vol. II, p. 589.
16 Recorded by Evelyn Ashley, in the *National Review*, June 1869, in Lynch, *Gladstone and Disraeli*, p. 18.
17 Speech in Wigan, October 1868, in Magnus, *Gladstone*, p. 193.
18 Gladstone to Lord Granville, January 1883, in Agatha Ramm (ed.) *The Political Correspondence of Mr Gladstone and Lord Granville 1876–86* (Oxford, Oxford University Press, 1962), Vol. II, p. 10.
19 Entry for 7 March 1874, in H. C. G. Matthew (ed.), *The Gladstone Diaries* (Oxford, Oxford University Press, 1982), Vol. VIII, p. 472.
20 H. C. G. Matthew, *Gladstone 1809–1874* (Oxford, Oxford University Press, 1988), p. 230.
21 H. C. G. Matthew, *Gladstone 1875–1898* (Oxford, Clarendon Press, 1995), p. 388.
22 Richard Shannon, *The Crisis of Imperialism 1865–1915* (London, Hart-Davis, 1974), pp. 139–40.
23 John Brooke and Mary Sorensen (eds), *The Prime Ministers' Papers: W. E. Gladstone 1: Autographica* (London, HMSO, 1971), p. 113.
24 Jenkins, *Gladstone*, p. 391.
25 John Ruskin, recounting a conversation with Gladstone in 1878, in Morley, *Gladstone*, Vol. II, p. 582.
26 Jenkins, *Gladstone*, p. 338.
27 Brooke and Sorensen, *W. E. Gladstone 1: Autographica*, p. 112.

Further reading

Of the many biographies, Roy Jenkins' *Gladstone* (London, Macmillan, 1995), has quickly established itself as one of the best informed and most readable, while the most authoritative are the two definitive studies by the outstanding Gladstone scholar, H. C. G. Matthew, the editor of Gladstone's diaries: *Gladstone 1809–1874* (Oxford, Oxford University Press, 1988) and *Gladstone 1875–1898* (Oxford, Clarendon Press, 1995). Other renowned biographies are Philip Magnus, *Gladstone*, (London, John Murray, 1954); E. J. Feuchtwanger, *Gladstone* (London, Allen Lane, 1975); Agatha Ramm, *William Ewart Gladstone* (Cardiff, University of Cardiff Press, 1989). Despite its age and over-respectful approach, John Morley's classic study, *The Life of William Ewart Gladstone* (London, Macmillan, 1903) is well worth dipping into. Robert Blake's published lecture, *Gladstone, Disraeli, and the Queen* (Oxford, Clarendon Press, 1993) is an entertaining analysis of the relations between the three dominant figures of the Victorian era. Eugenio F. Biagini, in his *Liberty, Retrenchment and Reform: Popular Libralism in the Age of Gladstone, 1860–1880* (Cambridge, Cambridge University Press, 1992), is concerned with Gladstone's emergence as a populist politician, while an important study of his later career is D. A. Hamer's, *Liberal Politics in the Age of Gladstone and Rosebery*, (Oxford, Oxford University Press, 1972). A brief but informed survey is M. Winstanley's, *Gladstone and the Liberal Party*, (London, Routledge, 1990). Though now somewhat dated, J. L. Hammond's *Gladstone and the Irish Nation* (with an Introduction by M. R. D. Foot) (London, Frank Cass, 1964) remains an absorbing account of Gladstone's Irish crusade. A more recent study of this theme is W. C. Lubenow, *Parliamentary Politics and the Home Rule Crisis* (Oxford, Clarendon Press, 1986). A seminal treatment of Gladstone's involvement in the Eastern Question is Richard Shannon, *Gladstone and the Bulgarian Agitation* (London, Nelson, 1975). Later researches in this area are covered in Ann Pottinger Saab, *Reluctant Icon: Gladstone, Bulgaria and the Working Classes 1856–78* (Cambridge Mass, Harvard University Press, 1991). Two key studies on overlapping themes are T. A. Jenkins, *Gladstone, Whiggery and the Liberal Party 1874–1886*, (Oxford, Clarendon Press, 1988) and J. P. Parry, *Democracy and Religion. Gladstone and the Liberal Party*, (Cambridge, Cambridge University Press, 1986). Helpful documentary studies are Paul Adelman, *Gladstone, Disraeli and Later Victorian Politics*, (London, Longman, 1970), and Michael Lynch, *Gladstone and Disraeli* (London, Hodder and Stoughton, 1991).

Charles Stewart Parnell

Michael Cunningham

Background

Parnell's inclusion in a book entitled *Modern British Statesmen* may appear anomalous and his reaction can only be guessed at; however, as will be discussed in more detail below, both his personal history as a member of the Anglo-Irish Ascendancy and his pivotal role in Anglo-Irish relations in the late nineteenth century argue strongly for his inclusion. It is not only perhaps Parnell's influence that has deemed him worthy of such extensive study (among a mass of literature, three of Ireland's most eminent historians have produced biographies), but also the personal characteristics of the man. The tragic nature of his fall contributed to his entry into the pantheon of Irish nationalist heroes which has, over time, led to more scholarly reassessments. Parnell has proved a fertile subject for such study, partly because of the political context in which he operated, partly because of his charismatic and often aloof personality, and partly because he left no detailed written accounts of his actions and ideas. This means that trying to locate and define the 'real' Parnell, if such a creature existed, has exercised many writers. This should be borne in mind by readers when the question of Parnell's political beliefs is discussed below.

One of the more obvious paradoxes of Parnell is how a Protestant member of the landlord and Anglo-Irish Ascendancy class should become the undisputed leader of a predominantly Catholic Irish nationalism. Two factors can be identified which help, at least partially, to resolve this.

First, although Parnell was to promote policies and ideas which would be unrepresentative of his class, earlier forms of Irish nationalism did not by any means imply a desire for a total separation with Britain or the establishment of a more 'Catholic' ethos within Ireland. The strands and forms of Irish nationalism are many and diverse; the basic point is that, being either Protestant or socially conservative – as Parnell was – did not necessarily mean that one was opposed to either social reform in Ireland or some form of renegotiation of the constitutional link with Britain. Second, Parnell's own family background was not typical of the class to which he belonged, but rather exhibited somewhat more 'progressive' tendencies. Parnell's great-grandfather, Sir John Parnell, had opposed the Act of Union of 1800 by which the Dublin parliament was dissolved. Although its independence *vis-à-vis* Westminster was limited, and it represented only an elite strand of Irishmen, it had a symbolic importance, and Parnell himself was often to invoke the traditions and precedent of Grattan's parliament. Parnell's paternal grandfather, William, had been an MP for Wicklow, the county in which the family estate was situated, and displayed liberal tendencies in relation both to tenants' rights and those of Catholics, while his father's outlook has been described as 'an essentially decent reformist liberalism'.[1]

If Parnell's paternal family was atypical of the landlord class, so too were his maternal links. His mother was American and the daughter of an admiral who had fought against the British in 1812. Although she is credited with vague republican sentiments, most recent writers on Parnell doubt the consistency of her anti-Britishness or her influence on her son's beliefs. The point to be made here is that, while Parnell's future role and political thought were far from preordained, they are not perhaps as anomalous as his privileged position would at first glance indicate.

There was little in Parnell's early life that indicated his later political engagement. It was not until his late twenties that he became involved in politics. Prior to this, he had had an undistinguished education, failing to return to graduate at Cambridge having been sent down after being fined for his part in a brawl, and had inherited his father's estate at Avondale in Wicklow. This provided him with scope to pursue his interests in engineering and to engage in the recreational pursuits of the landed gentry, including shooting-parties and, in Parnell's case, a keen and not particularly sporting approach to cricket.

Parnell's first attempt to stand as a parliamentary candidate came in 1874, but he was ineligible for nomination in Wicklow as he was High Sheriff for the county and, as such, would have been responsible for counting his own votes. The decision to attempt to enter parliamentary politics seems to have been a result of a combination of family tradition, the political conjuncture and personal circumstances. As outlined above, his family had been politically active and Parnell himself held local administrative posts as befitted his social status, while in later campaigns the ancestral tradition and his landlord status were frequently invoked by his campaigners. Roy Foster has argued that, despite his support for amnesty for Fenian insurrectionists, he was little influenced by their failed uprising in 1867 and that a developing movement promoting tenants' rights and the Ballot Act of 1872 were more important in honing Parnell's political interest.[2] In respect of personal circumstances, a degree of unfulfilment and the lack of more intimate commitments given the failure of a previous liaison provided the 'space' which political service was to fill.

Apprenticeship

The period considered as Parnell's 'apprenticeship' is difficult to define precisely, but may be roughly dated from his election to parliament as MP for Meath in 1875 to his becoming the first President of the Irish National Land League (INLL) in 1879. The brevity of this period is an indication of both Parnell's energy and aptitude and also the relative weakness of alternative strategies of Irish nationalism in this period – from the timid parliamentarianism of Butt's Home Rule Party to the failed insurrectionism of the Fenian tradition.

Prior to his election in 1875, Parnell had unsuccessfully contested a Dublin seat against the incumbent Tory the previous year. Although he was relatively inactive in the campaign, he expressed support for ideas that lay markers for his future development: these included support for tenants' rights (e.g. in relation to tenure), amnesty for Fenian prisoners, denominational education, restoration of a domestic parliament and a strategy of independence for the Irish Party in the House of Commons. He also emphasised the economic development that Home Rule would produce and the important role that the landlord class would play when its connection with Britain was broken; this was to be a constant in his political thought. The support for denominational education was significant in that clerical support was important in Parnell's victory in Meath in 1875, and support for the Fenian amnesty signalled to the more radical elements in Irish nationalism that Parnell was potentially a parliamentarian with whom they could effect some form of alliance.

More will be said later of Parnell's 'balancing' strategy, which, for Conor Cruise O'Brien, was his major contribution to nationalist politics. It may be briefly noted here that there were diverse and often antagonistic forces at work in Irish politics which Parnell had to appease, dominate or nullify to later mould a united movement. These included agrarian radicals, whom both the Church hierarchy and much of Isaac Butt's conservative and loose-knit Home Rule Party distrusted, and the Fenian tradition, which was particularly strong in America and an important source of finances. (It was also largely contemptuous of the constitutional tradition on the grounds that freedom would not be granted through such channels and that attendance at Westminster would only emasculate and corrupt.[3])

What, then, were the principal achievements and ideas of Parnell in this formative period? In parliament, he became associated with the policy of 'obstructionism', along with Biggar and O'Connor Power, by which the workings of the Commons were disrupted in protest at the British parties' refusal to introduce Home Rule. This was a response to the failure of the more accommodating approach of Butt to win concessions and also helped to secure support from more radical elements of Irish nationalism. However, in the latter case this was more than purely tactical; Parnell was acutely aware of the dangers of being seduced by the 'clubbability' of Westminster, and attendance was premised initially on disruption and later on parliamentary arithmetic providing the Home Rule Party with the leverage to 'push' for its ends. The party was riven by personal animosities and a lack of discipline, and Lyons has argued that at an acrimonious meeting concerning obstructionism in July 1877 the Home Rule Party as an entity '... may be said to have ceased to exist'.[4] This is significant, for Butt's declining health and influence marked the beginning of the end of an essentially conservative and exclusively parliamentary-focused strand of home rule politics that feared the implications of land agitation, while Parnell's high-profile tactics had marked him out as a future leader. It is ironic that with Butt probably went the chance of Irish nationalism retaining a significant Protestant and landlord influence, despite the fact that this was, of course, Parnell's heritage.

The closing years of the 1870s saw a strengthening of Parnell's position, principally because of his links with what have been termed 'neo-Fenians': those who distrusted constitutional politics but would co-operate with the more uncompromising elements within it. In 1877 Parnell became President of the Home Rule Confederation of Great Britain with Fenian support, and the following year the 'New Departure' was engineered. This was a policy of collaboration between advocates of physical force nationalism (in particular Devoy, a leading Fenian) and constitutional nationalism, with the former offering support subject to five conditions among which were support for peasant proprietorship, support for self-government (rather than the federal relationship which Butt favoured) and an aggressive approach in parliament including energetic resistance to all coercive legislation for Ireland. The tensions such a collaboration could provoke and the question of the relationship between the land and the national question will open the following section as an introduction to the years of Parnell's dominance.

Limelight

The land question and the party leadership
The relationship between the issue of some form of self-government and the land question is a complex one. As indicated above, some strands of nationalist thought were relatively unconcerned about the land question, while some believed that Home Rule would precurse an improvement of the situation of the tenant class since they believed a British government would never

challenge the position of landlords through reduction in rents or the establishment of peasant proprietorship. At the risk of over-simplifying, Parnell believed, unlike the Fenians, that there was the possibility of gaining concessions on land reform through constitutional action. Furthermore, the connection between the two issues was important because Parnell both hoped and believed that the landlord class could play a positive role in both a national government in Ireland and in its future social and economic development. However, this could not be achieved as long as the British government unreservedly backed their position since they had no incentive to achieve a rapprochement with other social forces in Ireland. These ideas about the role of the landed classes partly reflect Parnell's own social conservatism and partly a belief that more enlightened landlords might realise that an impoverished tenantry threatened both the financial security of landlords and violent agrarian protests.

Historians differ in their analyses of Parnell's order of priorities and of whether he held a consistent position. Yet Bew emphasises clearly the interrelationship he perceived: 'The way forward was to fight for progressive reforms, particularly land reforms, which removed the privileges of the Irish landlords and removed simultaneously the barrier to their association in the Home Rule movement.'[5]

The land question had come to the fore again with the agricultural depression of 1879 and Parnell became President of the newly formed INLL, the main policy of which was to campaign for rent reduction and a more formal commitment to peasant proprietorship. In theory these objectives were distinct and separable from nationalist ones, but, at that period, almost all would see them as connected. By the end of the 1870s, there were indications that Parnell was endorsing a radical position and it appeared thus to the British political Establishment. He had come to attention as a 'militant constitutionalist' advocating obstructionism, linking himself to both extra-parliamentary political and agrarian agitation through the New Departure and the INLL. In late 1879, he also moved away from the old Buttite position of federalism to a more 'open-ended' position on the possible future constitutional relationship between Britain and Ireland. This view was reinforced when Parnell toured North America in early 1880 to raise funds for the campaign of land agitation while engaging in a series of radical speeches. In retrospect, many commentators have seen this as a highpoint of Parnell's radicalism; yet even at this period there are indications of his caution and the strategy of 'balancing' as he endeavoured to avoid a too-close relationship with the Fenian wing of the New Departure.

In May 1880 Parnell defeated William Shaw by twenty-three votes to eighteen for the position of Sessional Chairman and *de facto* leader of the parliamentary party, which augured closer links between the parliamentary campaign and agrarian agitation. In an early attempt to improve the cohesion and discipline of the party it was decided in December 1880 that all home rule MPs should sit on the Opposition benches, and the following month twelve of the 'moderate' MPs seceded from the party.

The following two years were dominated by land agitation and governmental responses. The strategy of 'boycotting' and attempting to mobilise mass support in Britain for INLL action was supported by Parnell, and coercive legislation was employed in an attempt to deal with agrarian outrages and those who advocated the withholding of rents. However, it is perhaps indicative of Parnell's later trajectory that secession from parliament was rejected and, according to O'Brien, not seriously considered following parliamentary expulsion, impending coercive legislation and the arrest of Michael Davitt, a leading Land League activist. Indeed, O'Brien views Parnell in this period as making radical gestures while remaining fundamentally committed to a parliamentary role so as not to be outflanked by more militant groups in both Ireland and America.[6]

The government response was a mixture of coercion and conciliation, with Parnell seeking to maintain the unity of the nationalist and agrarian movement in the face of the potentially destabilising tendencies of such action. In 1881 a Land Act was introduced, the main provision of which was to allow for the control of agrarian rents for freehold tenants in an attempt to undermine the INLL. The Act was inadequate in at least two respects in that it offered no remedy for those – particularly in the impoverished west of Ireland – who could not afford to pay any rents, while the provisions did not cover leaseholders. It did, however, present serious tactical problems for Parnell in that it would be difficult to endorse an inadequate Act in the face of Left hostility, while rejection would risk losing what amelioration the government was offering along with the possibility of further reform through parliament which Parnell had believed possible. He abstained on both second and third readings (although many of the party supported the measure and managed to persuade the INLL to engage in 'test cases' by which the level of rents was challenged through the courts) and appeased the Left by making a series of speeches hostile to the Act. A newspaper, *United Ireland*, was also launched to act as a mouthpiece against coercion.

In October 1881, following an intemperate speech, Parnell was imprisoned for inciting others to prevent people from seeking redress through the land courts under the 1881 Act. It is fair to say that imprisonment did no harm to Parnell's reputation in Ireland and neither did papal denunciation of INLL activities. He was released in May 1882 after negotiating the 'Kilmainham Treaty' with the Liberal government (Kilmainham was the Dublin prison in which he was held). The treaty was an informal agreement by which the provisions of the Land Act would be extended to leaseholders, while those tenants in arrears – originally outside the terms of the original Act – would now be included and coercive measures would also be scaled down. In return, the Home Rule Party would support the Liberals in parliament. The Arrears Bill was passed and proved successful in that while it did not solve the land question, it removed many of the more pressing grievances and reduced the level of land agitation and agrarian violence.

The Irish National League and the growth of party discipline
The period following Parnell's release from prison is frequently seen as characterised by a move to the Right, in that it involved a renewed focus on parliamentary strategy, an attempt to downplay agrarian agitation and, relatedly, an effort to assert his dominance in the movement over figures such as Davitt and Dillon. The position of Davitt – one of the Land League activists – was weakened by his adoption of land nationalisation, which Parnell foresaw would not be favoured by the mass of the Irish peasantry. Two important indicators of Parnell's growing dominance are the establishment and form of the Irish National League in 1882, and the increasing discipline and unity of the parliamentary party.

In October 1882, a conference in Dublin was convened to establish the League. The five major objectives contained in its constitution were the establishment of national self-government, reformed local government, land reform, extension of the parliamentary and municipal franchise and the encouragement of the labour and industrial interests of Ireland. Formally, the League was to be controlled by a forty-eight member council, thirty-two elected by county conventions and sixteen by the parliamentary party. The council never materialised and it was run by an executive which ensured control for the parliamentary wing of the movement and Parnell in particular (Davitt interpreted this arrangement as a 'nominal dictatorship'). In the opinion of Lyons, this marked a transition from the 'proto-revolutionary' character of the 1879 League to an organisation dominated by parliamentarians and committed to constitutional action.[7]

This focus was premised upon, and facilitated by, the evolution of party discipline. The party of Butt and Shaw had been a loose coalition of members with little central control. After gaining the chairmanship in 1880, Parnell had introduced a pledge binding members to the principle of obedience to majority rule. In 1885, after a series of by-election victories which had reinforced Parnell's standing, a second and stronger pledge was introduced. This was a condition of seeking election for the party, rather than a post-election pledge, and bound the candidate to 'sit, act and vote with the Irish Parliamentary Party'. The one exception to this was the case of Captain O'Shea, who refused to take the pledge when contesting the Galway by-election of 1886. It is most likely that Parnell backed the candidature of the unprincipled and generally unpopular O'Shea for fear of the latter publicising the affair of Parnell and his wife Katharine which had begun in 1880.

As detailed below, this relationship was later to be Parnell's nemesis, and the opposition to O'Shea's candidature by many of his party, and in particular Timothy Healy, was later to prove costly. However, it is an indication of his dominance in this period that he could ride roughshod over the objections of many leading members of his own party. With hindsight, it is possible to see that various factors, such as the revival of land agitation, the failure of the Home Rule strategy and jealousies within his party, had the potential to undermine Parnell's position. Yet in 1886 Lyons opines, 'he had behind him virtually the whole of articulate Irish nationalism at home and abroad'.[8] This included Irish-America and the Catholic hierarchy, the latter having been reassured by the decline in Fenian influence within the Land League, Parnell's volte-face over the atheist MP Charles Bradlaugh, and his opposition to financial support for the religiously mixed Queen's Colleges in 1883. By 1886, Church–party relations were therefore much improved compared with the position in the early 1880s.

The 1886 Home Rule Bill

It appeared that the policy of constitutional agitation was to prove fruitful when Gladstone's Liberal administration introduced a Home Rule Bill (officially entitled the Government of Ireland Bill) in 1886. This episode has been the subject of comprehensive study and only a basic outline can be given here. A few preliminary comments should be made. First, it seemed that Parnell had luck to supplement his tactical acumen and, at this time, skill in 'balancing' the nationalist factions. Franchise reform in 1884 had boosted the position of the Home Rule Party, which had won eighty-six seats (eighty-five in Ireland and one in Liverpool) in the election of late 1885, leaving only Dublin and parts of Ulster outside its control in Ireland. This figure was exactly the difference between the Liberals and Tories in the Commons, thus giving the Home Rule Party the balance of power. Second, Gladstone had undergone a 'conversion' to Home Rule and became convinced that it was a necessary measure to avert revolution or at least social upheaval. With the lack of a 'liberal centre' in Ireland, Gladstone had come largely to rely upon Parnell's analysis of the social and political conditions of Ireland. Whether one accepts the belief that Gladstone was driven by moral considerations, or more by *realpolitik*, his conversion was both crucial and atypical of his party – much of which was lukewarm in its support, with some leading members (notably Chamberlain) actively hostile. However, such was Gladstone's standing that he managed to retain the support of the majority. Third, this marked an important shift in British politics. Up until this point, it was by no means clear that the Liberals were likely to deliver any more to Irish nationalists than the Tories. The former had frequently introduced coercive legislation and, in the previous year, the latter had introduced plans for the reform and democratisation of local government which Parnell had rejected as insufficient since a Dublin legislature was a minimum demand.

It will be discussed further in the final section how Parnell and nationalists viewed the different possible constitutional options between Great Britain and Ireland; what is interesting to note here is that much of the planning of the Bill and its provisions came from Gladstone, with few constructive ideas emanating from the Home Rule Party. It is as though devotion to the idea of Home Rule had blinded the Irish party to deep thought about the 'nuts and bolts'.

The Bill was introduced in April 1886. The Dublin parliament was to have 307 or 309 seats (depending on university representation). The Upper House was to have 103 members, 28 of whom were in the Westminster House of Lords, with 75 to be elected on a restricted property franchise, while the Lower House was to have 204 or 206 seats. The principal excluded powers (that is, those which remained in the hands of the imperial parliament) were defence, diplomatic matters, colonial matters, customs and, in the short term, policing. It was envisaged that Irish representation would cease at Westminster; Gladstone favoured its retention but thought it impractical and a possible source of conflict.

Irish dissatisfaction focused on three main areas. These were the retention by Westminster of customs and policing powers, the size of Ireland's imperial contribution (which the Home Rule Party felt excessive) and the relative influence of the Upper House in being able to veto legislation. Whether these objections could have been overcome is uncertain and, of course, hypothetical. However, the question of the imperial contribution, the retention or not of Irish MPs and the complexities of the Land Bill which was to be introduced concurrently all seemed likely to be crucial stumbling-blocks. Gladstone, who had foreseen such difficulties, announced at the end of May that if the Bill were passed on second reading it would be reintroduced with amendments in the autumn. In many ways, this would be the worst outcome for Parnell, since the more the minutiae of the proposal were examined, the more likely were divisions within the party which he had both united and had come to dominate. At this time, Parnell resorted to one of his favoured tactics when faced with being 'pinned down' to positions which did not suit him – evasion and inaccessability.

The rebellion of thirty Liberal Unionists in the Commons ensured the Bill's defeat in June 1886 and, had this not occurred, it would have fallen in the House of Lords. (As well as the problems alluded to above, the question of Ulster opposition to Home Rule would have had to have been addressed, and this will be returned to in the final section.) It has been claimed that the Bill's failure did not damage Parnell's position and may well have enhanced it. As O'Day argues, the more likely the Bill was to fall the more fully it could be supported without having to worry about party splits and the problems of detail and implementation.[9] Also, two important developments had taken place which, despite manifold problems, were to be maintained over the next thirty-odd years. First, one of the two major political parties in Britain had become converted to Home Rule, albeit at some cost. Second, after 1886, self-government had become more clearly defined as a Dublin assembly with legislative powers; before then, a more limited and circumscribed form was generally envisaged, such as extensive local government or a central body with limited legislative powers.

One further outcome of this episode must be highlighted. The Liberal conversion effectively ended the strategy of 'independent opposition' which Parnell had fostered in the period when the discipline of the party was being increased. Any tactic of 'playing one off against the other' was now redundant, as the two parties had struck their positions on Home Rule. It has been argued that this loss of independence was no great sacrifice since the Home Rule Party was largely supportive of the Liberals anyway in broad ideological terms. However, the question of the relationship with the Liberals was to re-emerge in stark relief at the time of the split in 1890–91.

The Liberal alliance in the late 1880s

The emphasis on the Liberal alliance – the 'Union of Hearts' – was central to the Parnellite strategy for the years after 1886 and helps to explain his cautious attitude to revived agrarian agitation in this period. In October 1886 the 'Plan of Campaign' was launched; the main tactic of this was to encourage tenants to withhold excessive rents and use the money to provide a fund to fight cases of eviction. This was, over the following years, to cause friction between Parnell and the leading members of the campaign, Dillon and William O'Brien. Although Parnell supported in principle the aims of the campaign, in addition to the possible adverse effects on the Liberal alliance, his own distaste for the violence that existed around the margins of such a campaign, the risk of provoking clerical disapproval and doubts that the tactics of the campaign were the best use of limited funds were factors in Parnell's passive role in the campaign.

Parnell was able to adopt such a strategy because his position as nationalist leader seemed unassailable. Despite talented deputies within the party, he had a stature within it and in Ireland with which no one at this period could seriously compete – in part because they did not 'straddle' the parliamentary and extra-parliamentary wings as Parnell did. This would explain why O'Brien and others were quiescent after being implicitly criticised by Parnell in his speech to Liberals at the 'Eighty Club' in 1888.

In the latter years of the 1880s Parnell often became increasingly elusive and withdrawn from the public eye and was absent from Ireland for long periods. This was related to a number of factors, including poor health and his liaison with Mrs O'Shea of south London. Also, as in earlier periods, it suited Parnell tactically to withdraw if his presence might force him to clarify attitudes and positions when silence or a degree of ambiguity might better serve him in the attempt to 'balance' nationalist forces. In the short term, at least, this seemed only to strengthen his position, as his aloof and elusive nature bolstered the mystique of his leadership. His stature was reinforced by the outcome of the Special Commission (September 1888–November 1889) set up to inquire into the relationship between agrarian agitation and the constitutional nationalist movement. Although Parnell failed to prove conclusively his lack of involvement in the advocacy of illegal activity, the

Commission did prove that the supposed letter from Parnell to *The Times* of April 1887 – supporting the murder of Burke, the Under-Secretary for Ireland in Phoenix Park, Dublin in 1882 – was indeed a forgery intending to discredit him.

The parliamentary focus of Parnell is given priority in this period, a strategy premised on the belief that the return of a Liberal government would produce Home Rule. To this end, discussions took place with Gladstone in 1888 and late 1889 in an attempt to address some of the detail and practicalities of such a policy which had been underdeveloped in 1886. However, it should be noted that the Westminster focus was contingent on such an outcome. In a speech in May 1889, Parnell forcefully emphasised the conditional and provisional nature of Irish attendance at Westminster. This can be seen as another example of 'balancing', as he had had to stress his moderation and distance from land agitation when giving evidence to the Special Commission. But it also underlined a consistent theme in Parnell's rhetoric that Irish representation had always to be on guard against the corrupting and debilitating influence of Westminster politics.

The fall of Parnell

In December 1889 Captain O'Shea filed a divorce petition naming Parnell as co-respondent, the event which was to precipitate Parnell's fall. The details of the relationship are beyond the scope of this chapter, though it may be worth noting that O'Shea and many others had known of the affair for some time and that he only filed for divorce after the death of Katharine O'Shea's aunt, from whose estate he hoped to benefit. In November 1890 a decree nisi was issued, uncontested by Parnell. Initially it seemed that Parnell would survive the scandal since the Catholic Church was sensitive to accusations of political interference. It was hoped by the Catholic hierarchy that the party would repudiate Parnell, with Thomas Croke (Archbishop of Cashel) claiming that Parnell's temporary retirement from the leadership would be sufficient to defuse the situation. Gladstone also initially deemed it a matter of private morality.

However, grass-roots Liberal opinion quickly moved against Parnell. In late November, Gladstone claimed that his own leadership – and therefore ability to promote Home Rule – would be rendered 'little better than a nullity' if Parnell remained leader.[10] This was crucial in the later Home Rule Party meetings; since Parnell had set much store on the Liberal alliance if his continued leadership jeopardised it, this was a powerful weapon for opponents seeking to replace him. Parnell reacted angrily to what he perceived to be unwarranted interference in an independent party's affairs and, on 28 November, issued a manifesto entitled 'To the People of Ireland' in which he attacked Gladstone's interference, gave details of the Home Rule settlement he and Gladstone had supposedly agreed in December 1889, and accused Morley of planning to offer the post of Chief Secretary of Ireland to a member of his party in the next Liberal administration, thus undermining the principle of 'independent opposition'.

What was or was not discussed or agreed in the talks of December 1889 is less important than the fact that the Liberals were angered at both the publication of details of confidential discussions and Parnell's interpretation of them, while the manifesto is an indication that Parnell hoped to appeal to the country over the heads of the party in his battle to remain leader.

Parnell had been re-elected as Party Chairman on 25 November, but a second five-day meeting was held at the beginning of December. His position had weakened in the interim as five of the six party members on a USA delegation telegraphed a call for his resignation, including the prestigious and respected O'Brien and Dillon. The debate in the second meeting largely focused on the political implications rather than the morality of Parnell's long-standing relationship with a married woman. For the 'anti-Parnellites', the breach with the Liberals meant Home Rule would be jeopardised if he did not resign. For his supporters, the unacceptability of Liberal 'dictation' was invoked. Parnell offered to resign if the Liberal leadership responded satisfactorily to concerns over land reform and control of the police in the event of Home Rule, but Gladstone refused to enter into discussions until the leadership question was resolved.

Of the members in attendance, forty-five left to convene a further meeting under the chairmanship of Justin McCarthy, while twenty-six supported Parnell. Significantly, virtually all the most notable members fell into the 'anti-Parnellite' camp. Parnell still considered himself the legitimate leader as he had not formally been defeated in a vote on the chairmanship. In addition to having minority support within the parliamentary party, the hierarchy denounced Parnell in early December and the balance of forces appeared to be turning against him (as indicated in the defeat of his candidate in the Kilkenny by-election in which the influence of clerical opposition was significant).

Parnell's position was not irretrievable, as attempts were made by leading figures to salvage party unity and there was a series of negotiations between Parnell, O'Brien and Dillon in France which ended in February 1891. Both of the latter also wanted a settlement since they feared that both clerical influence upon – and sectarian elements within – the party were likely to increase if the split were not healed. Included in the conciliatory overtures to Parnell were offers of a role in Home Rule negotiations, leadership of the National League, the retraction of the bishops' attack and Gladstone's acknowledgement of the precipitate publication of his 'nullity' letter. It is unclear to what extent, if at all, Gladstone would deal with Parnell if he were no longer *de facto* leader of the party.

In any case, the negotiations failed. There are two basic positions concerning Parnell's attitude to the talks. The first is that he was not seriously entertaining the proposals and, in effect, was 'playing for time' while hoping to open divisions in the party. The second is that he was sincere in negotiation and close to acceptance, which may have allowed him to reclaim the chairmanship after a temporary resignation. His final rejection has been explained in terms of pride and stubbornness, motivated by an unwillingness to compromise, but also as a more considered strategy (this, at least, was the view of Bull).[11] The latter was premised upon growing doubts about the success of the existing arrangement with the Liberal Party and the belief that his status would allow the forging of a new nationalist organisation if required.

Parnell fared badly in the months leading up to his death in October 1891. By July his candidates had lost two more by-elections (in North Sligo and Carlow), O'Brien and Dillon had moved close to a commitment to the 'anti-Parnellite' faction, and a unanimous resolution of bishops and archbishops called on the people to repudiate his leadership. The period of the split and after was characterised by the theme of 'independence' – independent opposition being the fundamental strategic premise of Parnellism, underpinning the attack on his opponents who had accepted 'dictation' from both the Liberal Party and the Catholic Church. In terms of support, Parnell was not totally isolated as the Fenian movement sided with him, partly because he symbolised opposition to the conformism of the Catholic hierarchy and Gladstone's liberalism. There is little indication that Parnell's views changed significantly in this period; he looked to Fenian support without rejecting constitutionalism or endorsing their physical-force politics. This period is also marked by an appeal to labour. This did not, however, amount to a conversion to radicalism or a class-based view of politics; according to Callanan, his labour programme was 'ruthlessly subordinated to his political purpose, as part of his strategy to redress the increasingly conservative configuration of power within nationalism'.[12]

Parnell's premature death, probably of pneumonia complicating kidney failure, renders hypothetical the question of whether he could have staged a 'comeback'. Yet it is likely that this could only have been achieved had he accepted some form of rapprochement with the other faction of the party. Given the status of those within it, and its support from important social forces within Ireland (especially the Catholic hierarchy), it seems unlikely that a new and autonomous organisation would have gained ascendancy in the nationalist movement.

Legacy

Parnell's political ideas

As the preceding section has been principally chronological, the start of this section will consider in a little more depth the important themes of Parnell's political ideas. It was outlined above how Parnell believed that land reform and some form of self-government were interlinked, a process which would allow the landlord class to identify with the nationalist movement. However, the precise form of the envisaged relationship between Ireland and Britain remains elusive. Several factors help to account for this. First, Parnell had to appeal to different audiences so it is unsurprising that there appears to be a lack of consistency in his declarations concerning the relationship. Second, a certain vagueness about the relationship was not unique to Parnell; the precise meaning of 'Home Rule' seems curiously underdeveloped among many of its supporters in both Britain and Ireland. Third, as Parnell himself said, a final and immutable relationship between the two countries was not his to define, since future nationalist leaders and the British government might wish to develop and refine it further. In relation to this question, and of political ideas in general, it is worth noting here that Parnell was not overly concerned with theorising and recorded no systematic collection of his political ideas. He was principally an active politician, more concerned with practical gains to be made within the constraints and contexts in which he found himself.

The importance of context is revealed when two of Parnell's more 'extreme' speeches are considered, 'extreme' here meaning those that anticipated or advocated the greatest separation from Britain. While on an American fundraising tour in 1880, he gave a speech in Cincinnati which was reported as including the sentence: 'None of us, whether we be in America or in Ireland, or wherever we may be, will be satisfied until we have destroyed the last link which keeps Ireland bound to England.' In March 1891, in a speech in Meath, he foresaw the day when he might address his audience as the men of republican Meath rather than the men of that royal county. Although its tone was undoubtedly separatist, there remains much doubt as to whether Parnell used the phrase 'last link'. But the important point is that the American audiences on this tour, or significant elements of them, held strongly separatist and Anglophobic sentiments to which Parnell had to appeal. The more 'republican' strand in his rhetoric recurred at the time of the split, and a recent study of the period has dismissed the Meath speech as hyperbole.[13] At the time of the split Parnell was engaged in a bitter attack on the Liberal Party while attempting to rebuild support in Ireland 'over the head' of his party, and this would help explain his more separatist rhetoric.

Most commentators argue that Parnell's republicanism should not be overemphasised and was atypical. More representative of his ideas was the maintenance of a link with Britain via the Crown, but with a Dublin parliament having extensive powers. As remarked above, Parnell frequently invoked the idea of Grattan's parliament of 1782–1800 because of its symbolic significance as the last legislature that Ireland had enjoyed. However, this was a somewhat inaccurate reading of that parliament since its independence was limited as its executive was outside its control and not independent of Westminster. Despite the lack of clarity of detail surrounding the Home Rule proposals of 1886, it seems clear that Parnell envisaged a degree of independence that surpassed that of Grattan's parliament, while the Tory offer of reformed local government was also deemed inadequate.

Any attempt at defining what Parnell 'really' wanted in terms of the constitutional relationship is chimeric, because it cannot be demonstrated that he had a fixed notion. Lyons has made the valuable point that, rather than being evolutionary, his thinking can be seen as circular, with the more 'extreme' positions being held early in his career; for example, when he attacked Butt's federal ideas or later, at the time of the split. In the intervening period, especially the late 1880s, a less extensive form of Home Rule appeared acceptable.[14]

In the area of broader political ideas and sentiments, parliamentary Liberalism and the ideas of the American revolution were significant influences on Parnell. An important element in these was the stress on the importance of local representation and close links between the electorate and their representatives. British rule in Ireland lacked this organic linkage and thus resorted, typically, to a mixture of corruption and coercion. So, while Parnell was a nationalist, his desire for reform also embraced principles of a universalist and pluralistic Liberalism in which responsiveness to public opinion and a distrust of the centralised state were important strands. This tradition of thought could also justify the use of violence in resistance to tyranny, or unjust government, which allowed Parnell's defence (though not advocacy), of Fenian activity. It may be argued that Parnell was a relatively rare hybrid of Irish nationalist and the Anglo-American constitutional tradition.

Success or failure?
With a century's hindsight, how is one to judge Parnell's legacy? The dramatic nature of his fall quickly saw him absorbed into nationalist mythology and 'claimed' by a diverse group of individuals. Yeats invoked him as a representative of the secular and pluralistic tradition in nationalism, marginalised by reaction and clerical domination. Connolly and Pearse, somewhat fancifully, linked Parnell to a separatist tradition which they later promoted through insurrection in 1916.[15] Parnell's critics, however, can point to failures and gaps in his career which left many problems unresolved. For example, having set much store on the Liberal alliance, his failure to resign – when his own actions had made that alliance untenable – led to the division in the parliamentary party that was to remain unhealed until 1900. Foster has argued that both the 'turning away' from politics after 1891 (towards the two currents of cultural nationalism) and the revival of the 'physical force' tradition have been exaggerated, but the prospects for Home Rule were undeniably weakened.[16] Parnell also underestimated the depth of opposition from Ulster Unionists to Home Rule and, while it may have been beyond anyone's ability to fashion a settlement acceptable to them, such opposition merited a more serious consideration than Parnell offered. Lyons has given examples of other important and potentially contentious areas that any future Home Rule government would have to address, including those of the role of religion in education and Church–state relations. To all these, Parnell gave insufficient attention.[17]

However, the evaluation must be balanced by the more positive aspects of his legacy. Although the party cause suffered in the last decade of the century, Parnell created both a disciplined and organised parliamentary party at Westminster and moulded a system of constituency organisation through the Irish National League within Ireland. Without such a structure Home Rule could not have been promoted and finally passed in 1912. It remains, of course, a matter of conjecture when, and in what form, it would have occurred without the rising of 1916. The conversion of Gladstone, and his reliance on Parnell for an assessment of Irish policy, ushered in an era in which a principal British party became converted to the principle of Home Rule and remained so; this in itself is sufficient to establish his historical standing.

Three other contributions supplement this. Perhaps the most important is the passage of the 1881 Land Act, which marked the start of a long process by which land tenure in Ireland was revolutionised. This was to culminate in the end of Anglo-Irish dominance, a changed social structure in Ireland and the gradual elimination of widespread social distress. All this was made possible by the second contribution: Parnell's tactical skill in this period of uniting and 'balancing' the disparate sections of Irish nationalism. Finally, Parnell had shown the potential of democratic participation and engagement in the parliamentary arena. This was to have a lasting influence on the form of the future Irish state, particularly in the face of competing strategies and ideologies.

Chronology

1846	birth of Parnell in County Wicklow
1874	ineligible to stand as candidate in Wicklow; loses by-election in County Dublin
1875	wins Meath by-election
1876	joins campaign of parliamentary obstruction
1877	elected President of Home Rule Confederation of Great Britain
1879	'New Departure'
1879	Irish National Land League founded: Parnell President
1880	elected Chairman of Irish Parliamentary Party
1881–82	imprisoned in Kilmainham
1882	Kilmainham Treaty
1882	Irish National League founded: Parnell President
1885	Eighty-six nationalist MPs returned in general election
1886	Gladstone introduces Home Rule Bill; later defeated in the House of Commons
1886	'Plan of Campaign' begins
1888	Special Commission established
1889	forgery of Parnell letters exposed; conclusion of Special Commission
1889	Captain O'Shea files for divorce
1890	Parnell re-elected Chairman of party; issues manifesto 'To the People of Ireland'

1890   split in party; majority of MPs join 'anti-Parnell' camp
1891   negotiations between Parnell, Davitt and O'Brien in France broken off
1891   marriage to Katharine O'Shea
1891   Parnellite candidate loses third by-election since split
1891   death of Parnell at Brighton

Notes

1 P. Bew, *Charles Stewart Parnell* (Dublin, Gill and Macmillan, 1980), p. 5.
2 R. F. Foster, *Charles Stewart Parnell: The Man and his Family* (Hassocks, Harvester Press, 1976), p. 133.
3 For a useful diagrammatic representation of these forces see C. C. O'Brien, *Parnell and his Party 1880–90* (Oxford, Clarendon Press, 1957), p. 37.
4 F. S. L. Lyons, *Charles Stewart Parnell* (London, Fontana, 1978), p. 76. First published in 1977 by William Collins.
5 Bew, *Parnell*, p. 13.
6 O'Brien, *Parnell*, p. 72.
7 Lyons, *Parnell*, p. 237.
8 Lyons, *Parnell*, p. 341.
9 A. O'Day, *Parnell and the First Home Rule Episode 1884–87* (Dublin, Gill and Macmillan, 1986), p. 199.
10 Lyons, *Parnell*, p. 491.
11 P. Bull, 'The fall of Parnell: the political context of his intransigence', in D. G. Boyce and A. O'Day (eds), *Parnell in Perspective* (London, Routledge, 1991) pp. 129–47.
12 F. Callanan, *The Parnell Split 1890–91* (Cork, Cork University Press, 1992), p. 298.
13 Callanan, *The Parnell Split*, p. 212.
14 F. S. L. Lyons, 'The political ideas of Parnell', *The Historical Journal*, 16:4 (1973) 774.
15 Lyons, *Parnell*, p. 608.
16 R. F. Foster, *Modern Ireland 1600–1972* (London, Penguin, 1989), pp. 431–46. First published in 1988 by Allen Lane.
17 Lyons, *Parnell*, p. 623.

Further reading

Before more scholarly reappraisal gradually developed, Parnell's life was the subject of works by journalists, associates and members of his family. Many of the earlier works are partisan and unreliable and an interesting account of the evolution of the literature is D. George Boyce, '"The portrait of King is the King"; The biographers of Charles Stewart Parnell' in D. George Boyce and A. O'Day (eds) *Parnell in Perspective* (London, Routledge, 1991), pp. 284–309. The best short biography is Paul Bew, *Charles Stewart Parnell* (Dublin, Gill and Macmillan, 1980), reprinted in 1991, and the standard full-length work is F. S. L. Lyons, *Charles Stewart Parnell* (London, William Collins, 1977). Two more specialised works are recommended for the context they provide: R. F. Foster's history of Parnell's family and the Wicklow heritage in

Charles Stewart Parnell: The Man and his Family (Hassocks, Harvester Press, 1976), and Conor Cruise O'Brien's *Parnell and his Party 1880–90* (Oxford, Clarendon Press, 1957) provides a detailed study of the evolution of the parliamentary party and Parnell's role within it. Two good edited collections were published to mark the centenary of his death which also help to locate Parnell among other movements and groups of the period and examine aspects of his thought in greater detail: D. George Boyce and A. O'Day (eds) *op. cit* and D. McCartney (ed.) *Parnell* (Dublin, Wolfhound Press, 1991). Although perhaps too detailed for the general reader, the dramatic last year of Parnell's life is the subject of two books: F. S. L. Lyons' *The Fall of Parnell, 1890–91* (London, Routledge and Kegan Paul, 1960) and F. Callanan, *The Parnell Split 1890–91* (Cork, Cork University Press, 1992).

Robert, 3rd Marquess of Salisbury

Hugh Cecil

Background

Lord Robert Arthur Talbot Gascoyne-Cecil, later 3rd Marquess of Salisbury, was born on 3 February 1830, the third son of James, 2nd Marquess of Salisbury. The family owed its aristocratic position to the careers of William Cecil, 1st Lord Burghley, Chief Secretary to Elizabeth I, and his second son, Robert Cecil, 1st Earl of Salisbury, who served both Elizabeth and James I in that capacity.

The Robert Cecil examined in this chapter had a most unhappy childhood. His beloved mother died when he was nine. His father, though able and enlightened, was overbearing, particularly to his children. Precociously intelligent and unathletic, Robert was bullied at school. He went on to Christ Church, Oxford University, broadened his religious education and became Secretary and Treasurer of the Oxford Union, but left early because of poor health, with only fourth class honours. On doctor's advice, he undertook a two year world tour which strengthened his physique and taught him much of the unedifying as well as the impressive aspects of British colonial life. Back in England in 1853, he gained a Fellowship of All Souls' College, one of Oxford's highest intellectual distinctions, and was elected as MP for the family borough of Stamford, Lincolnshire.

Four years later, he fell in love and married Georgina Alderson, the daughter of an Exchequer Court judge. His father objected, for 'Georgie' had little money. Of Robert's two elder brothers, one had died in infancy; and as long as the other (who was unmarried and sickly) lived, Robert had no expectations of wealth to finance what his father hoped would be an outstanding political career. Georgina had more important assets – cheerfulness, intelligence and energy. The young couple shared a robustly ironical view of the world and thought alike on religion and politics. Ambitious for her husband, she 'put him on the rails', as one friend put it, 'and drove him', thus ending fears that he was too neurotic to succeed.[1]

For several years, from 1859, Robert supported his wife and growing family partly through writing for the *Saturday Review* and the *Quarterly Review*. The 630-odd articles he wrote then and, more occasionally, later, provide a comprehensive statement of his political beliefs, expressed in a concise, witty style;[2] but he was relieved to be able to give up this journalistic grind when his brother's death in 1865 left him heir, with the title of Lord Cranborne, to his father's peerage and seat at Hatfield House, Hertfordshire, an estate of more than 3,000 acres. He also inherited extensive and valuable properties elsewhere, notably in Liverpool, Dorset and the West End of London.

Robert Cecil was a High Anglican, as fervent as Gladstone. Highly strung and from youth a prey to depression, he had a profoundly disillusioned view of human life; but, as with the French theologian, Pascal, this was balanced by an immensely strong and single-minded religious faith which saved him from despair.[3] His religious beliefs were rooted in his upbringing and also in an early and intense spiritual experience. They lay at the core of his outlook. A principal tenet of his Conservatism was that the established Church was fundamental to the national existence.[4] In this, as in other views, he was consistent throughout his life.

Apprenticeship

During his twelve years on the Tory backbenches, Robert made his mark as a brilliant, controversial speaker, often accusing his own party leadership of betraying its principles. He blamed Disraeli for their almost total failure from 1846 to 1866 to capture what Cecil considered the large, naturally Conservative vote in the country. Describing Disraeli as 'the grain of dirt that clogs the whole machine',[5] he attacked the Tories for making misguided alliances with various Commons radicals, to court the masses and gain temporary anti-Whig majorities. The only result, in Cecil's view, had been to promote democracy at the expense of the traditional ruling class, while failing to outmanoeuvre the Whigs.

In religious affairs, he took a stronger line than most, mercilessly challenging the demands of the Nonconformist militants for greater fairness of treatment and warning his party that these were the prelude to a general assault which would culminate in the disestablishment of the Church. Over finance, he attacked Gladstone's 1860 budget, putting a penny on the income tax, as demonstrating the now dominant desire of governments to placate the masses at the expense of the propertied classes.

Above all he protested against large-scale parliamentary reform, feeling that a satisfactory balance had been reached in 1832 between the masses and their natural leaders, who held the bigger stake in the country in terms of wealth and expertise. He feared that if the working classes were given a vote out of proportion to their stake in the country, they would simply, in their ignorance, be persuaded to use their new power to plunder the minority, propertied class, leading to victimisation and an inevitable decline in national leadership. The true guarantee of freedom lay 'more in the equilibrium of classes than in the equality of individuals',[6] since such an arrangement afforded property and personal rights a better protection. Having vigorously opposed Gladstone's Reform Bill of 1866, he was naturally horrified in 1867 when, after ousting the Liberals, the Disraeli–Derby Conservative administration introduced a Bill giving an even wider franchise. By this time a member of the government, he resigned with two other colleagues, though without attempting to organise a general revolt.

After his father's death in 1868, he became Marquess of Salisbury (as he will henceforth be called in this chapter). He felt bitterly that Disraeli was a traitor to Conservative principles and it was not until 1874 that he agreed to work with him, resuming his earlier post as Secretary of State for India. Here, his penetrating ministerial judgement was the produce of indefatigable study. Unable to forget the Indian Civil Service's inhumanity and incompetence over the 1866 Orissa famine, he consistently pressed for a famine code of practice, only adopted in 1880 after a string of similar disasters. His caution in restraining Lord Lytton, the Viceroy, from military action against Afghanistan, was subsequently justified by the reverses following the 1878–79 Afghan campaign.[7]

His comprehensive understanding of world politics drew him closer to Disraeli over the Eastern Question of 1876–78. Both claimed that the policy of the allegedly 'fumbling' Foreign Secretary, Lord Derby,[8] was insufficiently assertive to check Russian ambitions, avert the break-up of the Ottoman Empire or prevent what Salisbury feared would be 'the greatest war of the century'.[9] Salisbury represented Disraeli at the Constantinople Conference in 1876. As Foreign Secretary from March 1878, he secured for Britain a precarious influence over Turkey to prevent it from endangering the fragile peace established at the Berlin Congress in June.

Limelight

Disraeli, whose government fell in 1880, died in 1881. Thereafter, the Conservative Party was led by Sir Stafford Northcote in the Commons and by Salisbury in the Lords. Despite the disadvantage of leading from the Lords, Salisbury was by far the most formidable of the two, in both personality and intellect. He and Northcote were agreed in trying to strengthen their party's base by winning over disaffected Liberal members. Northcote, however, was continually under attack from a prominent and irreverent Tory group, 'the Fourth Party',[10] and his authority quickly declined. It was Salisbury who led his party in the bipartisan discussions on the redistribution of seats which accompanied the Liberals' Franchise Reform Act of 1885; and, when Gladstone's government resigned in that same year, it was Salisbury who headed the new Conservative administration, combining the Prime Minister's office with that of Foreign Secretary (as he was to do, save for one brief period in 1886, until after the election of 1900). Thus he reinforced his great diplomatic expertise by adding to it the authority of national leadership – invaluable at a time when Britain's prestige and influence had plummeted under Gladstone. Salisbury's minority 'caretaker' government lasted only eight months (1885–86). Its main achievement, thanks to his firm stance on the Near-Eastern crisis of 1885–86, was to begin the restoration of Britain's international reputation.[11]

In February the Liberals returned to power, albeit with a smaller majority. Gladstone's conversion to Irish Home Rule, however, split his party irrevocably and ninety-three Liberals – including the powerful radical Joseph Chamberlain – voted with the Conservatives in the parliamentary division of June 1886, championing Ireland's continued legislative union with Britain. In the general election that followed, 78 of these dissidents were returned to parliament alongside 316 Conservatives; with these they joined forces in supporting a minority Conservative government to keep out another Gladstone administration.

Yet Salisbury's majority was at first insecure, given the wish of many Liberal Unionists to return eventually to the Liberal fold. It was a while before the Tories could rely on Liberal Unionist support save 'on the most general measures',[12] and before they could achieve the solid alliance which, against the odds, endured, and which was formalised in the final merger of their organisations in 1911.

Salisbury felt no mystique about his party, or the party system, believing gloomily that most politicians were more concerned about honours and power than principles. Aloof and preferring to be with his family at Hatfield, he gave a misleading impression of being somehow above party management. In fact, he was in constant touch over strategy with Richard Middleton, the chief party agent.[13]

The greatest threat to his leadership came from Lord Randolph Churchill, one of the party's best orators. Normally patient, Salisbury was exasperated by Churchill's changing moods and opinions. Young, brilliant and crudely ambitious, Churchill had adopted the cause of 'Tory Democracy', a nebulous concept involving populist legislation for a changing society and deference to the views of the National Union of Conservative Associations (the umbrella body for constituency Tory parties, formed in 1867).

Churchill, the proclaimed darling of the National Union, had exploited its desire for greater influence on Conservative policy, including the election of party leaders (an arrangement from which Churchill hoped, before long, to profit). Salisbury, however, had temporarily outmanoeuvred him by limited concessions which satisfied the National Union. Later, in December 1886, Churchill, as Chancellor of the Exchequer and Leader of the House of Commons, tried to bully him into coercing fellow ministers over the defence estimates by offering his resignation – reckoning on Salisbury being afraid that the loss of so vital, irreplaceable and popular a minister would cause a national uproar. Salisbury called his bluff, appointing George Goschen (an able Liberal Unionist turned Tory), and Churchill found himself without the support in the country he expected. His fall was total, with all attempts at a comeback (lasting until 1893) ending in failure. It demonstrated that nationally and in parliament the Tories now recognised Salisbury as having restored their reputation as a party of government. In these circumstances, the National Union had no wish to rock the leadership boat.[14]

From December 1886 Salisbury, while remaining Premier, resumed the Foreign Secretaryship. The international situation was dangerous, with war threatened between France and Germany and the 'scramble for Africa' now complicating relations between the powers almost as much as the Eastern Question; and although Germany was still wisely guided by Bismarck, the death in 1888 of the old Emperor, the fatal illness of his successor and the unstable character of his grandson, Wilhelm, made the future uncertain: 'I can see the sea covered with white horses',[15] Salisbury told his younger daughter. With advancing technology, too, defence costs put an ever-increasing strain on national resources.

Salisbury steered a path between total isolation on the one hand and entangling commitments to fight for foreign powers on the other. In his view democratic government ruled out such binding alliances, but he compromised through limited, though still risky, secret agreements with Austria and Italy in March and December 1887, to safeguard the *status quo* against possible Russian and French threats in the Mediterranean. He failed to achieve agreement with France over British withdrawal from Egypt, to cure, as he hoped, a running sore. However, he induced the Italians to sign a demarcation treaty in East Africa freeing Britain to reconquer the Sudan and gain control of the Upper Nile. Meanwhile, he cultivated better relations with Germany, assuring her of co-operation in preserving the *status quo* and obtaining concessions in East Africa, while still avoiding any commitment to join her in a quadruple alliance. The British Navy was strengthened through the Naval Defence Act of 1889, though closer Russo-French ties in the early 1890s left the British Admiralty uncertain of its ability to take on the Russians at the Straits and the French in the Mediterranean simultaneously. Even so, Britain now stood far higher internationally than after her Sudanese and South African defeats under Gladstone.[16]

The Irish Question dominated home affairs. The Irish Secretary, Arthur Balfour, with the sometimes reluctant approval of his uncle, Salisbury, applied the Tory policy of 'coercion and conciliation' to reconcile Ireland to the Union. This involved tough measures against violence, some sacrifice of landlord interests and an imaginative perception of the problems of an undeveloped country.[17] For a while, until the downfall of the Irish Nationalist leader Parnell in November 1890, the Irish Nationalist MPs 'campaign of disruption' in parliament made the normal passage of legislation impossible;[18] but even during the worst parliamentary turmoil, of 1887, measures on allotments and protecting miners at work went through, while more important reforms followed: the Local Government Act of 1888 set up a new elected county council system, ending local government in the counties by magistrates at the Quarter Sessions; in response to the depression in farming, another Act established a Board of Agriculture. Further legislation addressed problems of working-class housing, cruelty to children, the defrauding of customers in shops and corruption in public services. In the calmer waters after 1890, the Tithes Bill, held up for three years, was finally passed, making landowners rather than occupiers responsible for tithe payments, as was the Education Bill of 1891, establishing free elementary education in denominational and state schools. Salisbury was anxious that the reform programme should not lose its momentum, because it was popular and won support from the Liberal Unionists and because in some cases, such as housing, he had given it real thought.[19]

It was an exhausted Conservative government which went to the country in 1892 and despite its achievement – no mean one considering its insecure position over the previous six years – it was defeated by the Liberals, who returned without an overall majority, led by Gladstone with Lord Rosebery as Foreign Secretary.

In Opposition, Salisbury headed a successful campaign against Gladstone's last effort at Irish Home Rule, showing himself, as on other occasions, to be a powerful popular orator. Although he counted on an almost entirely Unionist House of Lords to throw out the Bill, he was anxious to present the best possible case so that the Lords' claim to represent the nation could not be faulted. Thereafter he worked hard to cripple Liberal legislation; but, lest it could be argued that the Upper House had only its own interests, rather than the nation's, at heart, he was careful not to use the Lords to crush Sir William Harcourt's Death Duties Bill, precisely because he saw the measure as directly threatening the aristocracy.[20]

After the Liberal administration petered out in the summer of 1895, the Unionists won an overwhelming victory at the polls. The Conservative–Liberal Unionist coalition, led by Salisbury, was now firmly forged and, at last, there was a major Liberal Unionist presence in the Cabinet, including Chamberlain at the Colonial Office, Devonshire as Lord President (having refused the Foreign Office) and Landsdowne in the War Office. The Chancellor of the Exchequer was the Conservative, Sir Michael Hicks Beach.

In Cabinet, Salisbury never exercised the same degree of control as Disraeli, frequently letting matters be decided by a small majority of votes, against his own opinion. With colleagues, his manner was 'kindly sarcastic' but always frank and fair.[21] However, he particularly disliked wrangling with the Treasury over expenditure and listening to the military experts of the War Office (if allowed full scope, he said, they would insist on garrisoning the Moon to ward off an attack from Mars).[22] Most of all he loathed the business of promotions and appointments, both because it revealed fellow politicians at their most unattractive and because of the injured feelings it involved.

At home, Salisbury gave Church policy his highest priority, choosing bishops carefully so as to provide exemplary leadership, without provoking internecine conflict over such sensitive areas as Church ritual. He believed that society could not survive without a Christian moral order underpinning it and tempering, in a democratic age, class hatred and envy.[23] By 1895, while still fearful of potential Socialist agitation, Salisbury and Conservative colleagues (as opposed to Chamberlain) were against spending much more money on social reform, and were relieved that their electoral success made this less urgent. Even so, many laws were passed reflecting concern about social conditions: Acts to improve the environment of shop assistants, cotton operatives and miners; amendments to the Factory Acts; and, in 1899 and 1900, improved regulations governing working-class housing. The Workmen's Compensation Act of 1897 broke new ground. The most important measure that was mooted, which might have provided old-age pensions for workmen over seventy, foundered because of Boer War expenditure.[24] In Ireland, the government's 'conciliation' involved extensive intervention, including loans to facilitate land purchase by peasantry from British landlords.

In foreign affairs, Salisbury resumed his task of diminishing areas of friction, though the three year interruption of his control meant that he never regained fully for himself or for Britain, that mediatorial authority which was built up unobtrusively between 1886 and 1892.[25] He agreed, unwillingly, to settle by arbitration a boundary dispute between Venezuela and British Guyana, which USA considered a Monroe Doctrine matter. The result, favouring Britain, placated the US President and though Salisbury was well aware of the limitations of an arbitration tribunal in solving an international issue, he was anxious in general to use any effective alternative to force. He was profoundly distressed by the carnage of war, but also aware of the social threat that big defence budgets presented: Harcourt's Death Duties had been enacted to pay for increased naval armament. The richer landowning class, to which he belonged, would bear the brunt of the burden, and as its wealth was eroded, so its influence would decline.[26]

Meanwhile, Salisbury's support for Turkey was strained to the limit by the massacres, between 1894 and 1897, of thousands of Armenian Christians; so much so that he invoked the old Concert of Europe for collective action by the Powers to force the Turks to reform; but he found France and Russia as unwilling to join in defending the Armenians as his own Cabinet was to support his suggestion of British naval action against Turkey. He now saw nothing in principle against bargaining over the future of the Turkish Empire with Russia; but while he admitted that Britain's past anti-Russian policy might have been a mistake, he still felt it would be a great blow to his country's interests if Russia were allowed to take Constantinople and gain control of the Eastern Mediterranean. Meanwhile, the Austrians began to insist, as a condition of renewing the Mediterranean Agreements, that Britain should undertake a definite commitment to fight to defend Constantinople against Russia. Because Salisbury, no longer feeling that his country had the naval capacity or the will to honour such a pledge, refused, the Agreement lapsed. Relations with Russia remained uneasy, particularly over its ambitions in China, and Salisbury proceeded cautiously, though not weakly, successfully avoiding hostilities with Russia and with Germany which was also developing Far Eastern interests.[27]

In the end he abandoned the policy of safeguarding Britain's position in Asia by propping up the Turkish Empire, in favour of defending the route to India via Egypt and the Suez canal. He accepted the need to defeat the forces of Mahdism which, since the early 1880s, had posed a threat to Egypt. In 1898, Sir Herbert Kitchener completed his successful Sudan campaign in time to thwart a French expedition, lately arrived at Fashoda from West Africa, to secure the Upper Nile for France. Britain and France seemed close to war, but Salisbury's skilful handling defused the crisis and thereafter relations with the French improved as colonial differences were settled.[28]

Salisbury was infuriated by Germany's activities in Africa, which included seeking concessions from Britain in return for German non-interference in Britain's South Africa affairs. He resisted Berlin's pressure for an agreement but, much to his regret, conventions were signed with Germany during his temporary absence from the Foreign Office in 1898, including a discreditable secret arrangement about the possible future disposal of the Portuguese African colonies. Kaiser Wilhelm II's obsession with matching British naval power led, in 1899, to tension over Samoa, where Germany wanted a coaling station. Again Salisbury would have preferred to resist German demands for a partition of the Samoan archipelago, but let himself finally be overruled by his Cabinet. Already, the Kaiser had complained about Salisbury to Queen Victoria. The Queen, however, who was more devoted to the fatherly Salisbury than to any other of her Prime Ministers since Lord Melbourne, rebuked her grandson. Salisbury, hearing that the Kaiser now referred to him as 'my enemy', commented: 'I must console myself with thinking that five years ago he hated Rosebery nearly as much as he hates me now.'[29]

As the century closed, Salisbury's hold on foreign affairs was believed by many, particularly imperial enthusiasts, to be slipping. Lord Curzon, Viceroy of India, felt Salisbury was feeble with Russia over its ambitions in Persia and China: 'Curzon always wants me to talk to Russia as if I had five hundred thousand men at my back and I have not', complained Salisbury.[30]

Although Salisbury had presided over massive annexations in Burma and Southern, West and East Africa, he was known not to share the mood of 'New Imperialism' celebrated by Rudyard Kipling, which went with notions such as the Cape to Cairo Railway ('a curious idea' in Salisbury's view)[31]. However, he was genuinely convinced that the Empire did bring civilisation and justice, even if its authority rested ultimately on force; and while he regarded 'damned nigger' attitudes among whites in British India as one of the greatest threats to long-term British rule there, he was opposed to Indian independence or the idea of 'Africa for the Africans'.[32]

Among those impatient with his chief was Joseph Chamberlain whom Salisbury checked when he trespassed on to Foreign Office ground in seeking an alliance with Germany, in which Salisbury saw no advantage. He firmly believed that no minister should interfere in the work of another's department. Unfortunately, by the same token, he himself would not interfere, save when consulted, with Colonial Office matters, such as Chamberlain's South Africa policy, of which even 'Great Joe' began to lose control. From 1899 to 1902, Britain's military resources were locked up in a struggle with a tough, well-equipped, but very small, army of Boer South African farmers, whose resistance made other countries aware of how vulnerable British imperial power really was. The crucial Cabinet decisions were made in the summer of 1899, when Salisbury's wife was dying and he was too distracted to criticise them effectively. After an illusory victory over the Boers in the summer of 1900, the Unionist Alliance went once more to the polls to cash in on war popularity.

The result, which benefited from the divisions within the Liberal Party over the war, was much the same as in 1895, giving the Unionists a substantial majority. Salisbury formed a new government. He was persuaded by his doctors to leave the Foreign Office, but was publicly criticised by a Tory MP and veteran party servant, C. G. T. Bartley, for having given too many ministerial posts to friends and relations of the Cecil family.[33] Salisbury remained Prime Minister until a peace treaty had been signed with the Boers in May 1902. Worn-out and ill, he would have been glad to leave earlier, but feared that this might have been interpreted as a quarrel with his Cabinet over war and other policies, which would have enheartened the nation's enemies.

In truth, he was unhappy about new departures in foreign policy. He failed to discourage his successor, Lansdowne, from concluding the Anglo-Japanese Alliance, binding the two countries to come to one another's defence if ever either found itself at war with more than one power. In Salisbury's view, this went well beyond what a democratic state could honestly promise.[34]

Salisbury died in 1903. His regime had been popular. As both an old-fashioned patrician and an industrious professional, he was widely trusted. His massive presence, bearded, grand but unflamboyant, embodied the reliability and long-standing success which, as much as more recent commercial and imperial triumphs, were central to Britain's identity in the late nineteenth century.

Legacy

Lord Salisbury was one of the most successful Conservative leaders: his four administrations lasted fourteen years in all. What effect did his leadership have on the party and on the nation?

In foreign affairs, largely through his efforts, British prestige remained high in an uncertain period. His aim had always been to maintain this while preventing minor incidents building up into crises. However, his own self-deprecating rhetoric has given a somewhat misleading picture of his achievement, as when he likened his foreign policy to punting down the river of events, occasionally putting out the pole to avoid collisions with the bank. His own prodigious industry certainly belies any notion of drift: often he was at his despatch boxes until 2 a.m. He had learned not to trust his experts without question, and before considering their opinions he mastered a subject thoroughly. For the width of his view and the depth of his learning he far surpassed Lansdowne, let alone the pre-war Liberal Foreign Secretary, Grey. This contrast was indeed so profound that it makes little sense to speak of continuity between his policy, of commitments limited strictly to certain areas, and the 'entente' policy of his successors.

Lansdowne's Foreign Secretaryship spelt the end of the policy by which Salisbury, with finesse and toil, had done so much to preserve a precarious peace over the previous fifteen years. In one respect, however, Salisbury's influence lived on: his public speeches expressing the hope that judicial arbitration might become increasingly a substitute for 'the cold cruel arbitrament of war' and that closer collective action by the Powers might prevent aggressive outbreaks, fired the idealism of his son, Lord Robert Cecil, a statesman less sceptical by temperament and the chief British architect of the League of Nations.[35]

On Ireland, the Salisbury–Balfour policy undoubtedly brought a quarter-century of peace and improvement to Britain's troubled colony until 1916, though it could not eradicate Irish national aspirations, the endurance of which both men underestimated.

To his party, Salisbury contributed significantly. First, in the area of social policy: it is often said that his administrations were simply putting the reformist vision of Disraeli into practical shape. Salisbury needed little such inspiration. Although he left the formulation of the legislation to others, he was genuinely concerned about the 'terrible individual and social suffering';[36] and he was never doctrinaire against state intervention. However, because the Conservative reforms were introduced pragmatically and not in a spirit of class warfare or as part of a defined programme, Salisburys administration has been seen as unresponsive to social problems. Some historians have alleged that Salisbury failed to react adequately to the crises of the cities, of agriculture, of poverty.[37] It is true that no *Ministry* of agriculture was set up in response to the widespread problems of farming in the late nineteenth century, only a 'Board'; and there was no commission on the Poor Law to revise the inadequate system which had operated since 1834; nor was there any comprehensive effort at town planning; and to this day the Liberal governments between 1906 and 1914 are credited with a more imaginative and generous social programme than any of Salisbury's administrations. However, the sheer volume of social legislation between 1886 and 1902, and measures such as the provision of free elementary education, make a case for arguing that then, rather than the age of Lloyd George, was the real beginning of Britain's Welfare State. It is worth reflecting on the judgement of a radical contemporary, the veteran Chartist, George Julian Harney, in July 1892, on the Salisbury administration that had just ended:

> I look back over sixty years of intelligent interest in political questions and public affairs, and I affirm that the present has been the best administration within that time. There have been epochs when organic changes more important than the County Councils Bills have been enacted. But it does not follow that a Ministry presiding over or inaugurating revolutionary changes must, therefore, have been a better administration than that of the last six years. The most notable of organic changes was the Parliamentary Reform Bill of 1831–32, the forerunner of subsequent more sweeping changes, but the Reform Bill Administration of 1831–35 was a hard and cruel Administration, best known for the enactment of the New Poor Law, erecting bastilles over the land and barbarously punishing the poor for their poverty, which did more than all other grievances to drive the working people well-nigh to despair.[38]

On the Continent, nearly 30 per cent of German voters chose the Marxist Socialist Party in 1898 (French Socialists were making similar progress), whereas in Britain, only 1.3 per cent of the national vote went to Labour candidates in the 1900 general election. This is a measure of the success which the British Conservative government policies were having in wooing the lower-middle-class and working-class voter.[39]

It had also much to do with Salisbury's second contribution – to party organisation: although he was helped by Gladstone's refusal to retire or give up Home Rule, it was no small achievement – considering the personalities involved and the resentment felt by Conservative MPs at having to make room for former political enemies – to have forged an effective and enduring administration composed of two major elements, Liberal Unionist and Tory. Under Salisbury, the Conservatives became and remained a party of government.[40] Joseph Chamberlain, populist and imperialist, turned out to be one of the coalition's greatest electoral assets, despite the anxiety he caused his leader, and the two men respected each other across great gulfs of temperament and background.[41] The coalition survived the party disunity over

Chamberlain's policy of tariff reform after Salisbury's retirement, which was not along a Conservative/Liberal Unionist fault-line. Moreover, Liberal Unionists, such as Lansdowne and the younger Chamberlains, continued as central figures in the early twentieth century Conservative Party.

Again it has been argued that more, perhaps, through luck than prescience, Salisbury's adroit handling of negotiations over the redistribution of boroughs, in 1884, secured for the party a large middle- and lower-middle-class suburban vote, which was destined to be its mainstay. For these voters and for many from the upper-working-class, the imperial opportunities and limited social reform provided by the Conservatives had great attraction, coupled as they were with an emphasis on respectability, social mobility and protection of individual freedom and property rights from social disintegration or Socialism. In the twentieth century, this support has been a vital prop of what became, under Salisbury, a *national* party. The preservation of these values has been, it is claimed, a bulwark against totalitarianism in Britain.[42]

On party leadership Salisbury also left his mark: by defeating Churchill over the powers of the National Union, Salisbury had made sure that he could promote and appoint ministers without reference to any party caucus, and this, again unintentionally on his part, secured his successors an equal freedom. Less happily, his designation of Balfour as the first of these left a vacillating leader in charge. It is a measure of Salisbury's leadership that he was able to work both with Chamberlain and with Devonshire, whereas neither Balfour nor Gladstone managed to avoid quarrelling with them.[43]

In his writings and speeches, Salisbury provided his party with a body of political thought, in a Burkeian spirit, which qualified the sometimes high-flown claims of Disraeli. On constitutional matters he was less blind to reality than his predecessor, who never appreciated that the days of aristocratic political power were numbered after 1867. Salisbury was no die-hard, and in the *Quarterly* for October 1867, he reluctantly accepted the Second Reform Act, enunciating what was to become a Conservative orthodoxy at least until Margaret Thatcher's leadership in 1979: 'It is the duty of every Englishman, and of every English party, to accept a political defeat cordially, and to lend their best endeavours to secure the success, or to neutralise the evil, of the principles to which they have been forced to succumb'.[44] However, some late twentieth century Conservative supporters, such as the political journalist Paul Johnson, have felt that this doctrine – 'that the drift to the left was a ratchet process and irreversible' – has had a 'pernicious' influence on Tory policy.[45]

Throughout his career, Salisbury was haunted by the spectre of class war; for a long time he underestimated the likelihood of his own party, that of property and traditional political bulwarks, ever enjoying mass popularity. As it was, he felt its success depended on the mistakes of the Liberals: 'I rank myself no higher in the scheme of things than a policeman – whose utility would disappear if there were no criminals'.[46] He did what he could to preserve, without over-asserting, the interests and authority of his class. It can be argued that this was a necessary policy in ensuring a smooth transition from aristocratic, to popular and professional, government.[47]

Reserved and mysterious, Salisbury fits into no clear category: an anti-democrat yet no Wellingtonian reactionary, and liable at times, in one of his occasional 'blazing indiscretions' to betray an impatience with party orthodoxy; an eager amateur scientist who read Latin poetry for pleasure; a humane, though unsentimental, man of deeply rooted traditional religion who was bleakly determinist in modern, Darwinian terms about 'dying nations' being doomed to succumb to stronger ones;[48] a man of great riches, who lived unhedonistically and was so shabbily dressed he was once refused entry to the casino at Monte Carlo.[49] In the late twentieth century he has become a hero to a section of the right-wing intelligensia, his popularity even spawning *The Salisbury Review*, a journal aimed at reflecting his anti-Liberal, independent, no-nonsense but intellectual Conservativism.

Sceptical and pessimistic though Salisbury certainly was, he was not a cynic, though many, including admirers, have thought so. His intelligence was of the heart as well as the head, and he was, above all, a Christian. Defending the American Confederate States against the Union, he nevertheless denounced slavery as degrading. When Kitchener won his victory at Omdurman in 1898, Salisbury spoke with sombre irony about British jingoist satisfaction that 16,000 dervishes had been gunned down by the Anglo-Egyptian force. For years, too, he was tortured by his memory of the 1866 Orissa famine: 'I did nothing for two months', he wrote in 1875, 'and – it is said – a million people died'.[50] These are not the remarks of a cynic.

Chronology

1830	birth of Salisbury
1839	death of his mother
1840	goes to Eton
1848	goes up to Christ Church, Oxford
1850	leaves Oxford, prepares for bar, never called
1851–53	world tour
1853	returned to parliament for Stamford
1857	marries Georgina Alderson
1858–59	Conservative government
1865	death of elder brother, Lord Cranborne; he takes that title
1866	joins Derby–Disraeli Conservative administration as Secretary of State for India. Orissa famine
1867	resigns from government over Disraeli's Parliamentary Reform Bill
1868	Chairman of Great Eastern Railway (until 1872). Becomes Marquess of Salisbury. Fall of Conservative government
1869	Chancellor of Oxford University
1874	joins Disraeli administration as India Secretary
1876	represents Disraeli at Constantinople Conference

1878	Foreign Secretary. Attends Berlin Conference
1880	Conservative government falls
1881	Disraeli dies
1885	Gladstone resigns, Salisbury heads 'caretaker' government as Prime Minister and Foreign Secretary
1886	Liberals resume power but split over Home Rule; Conservatives returned in summer election supported by Liberal Unionists. Salisbury Prime Minister. Challenge and resignation of Lord Randolph Churchill. Salisbury also takes Foreign Secretaryship
1887	Balfour, as Irish Secretary, begins coercion policy. Mediterranean Agreements
1888	Local Government Act. Wilhelm II becomes Kaiser
1889	Naval Defence Act
1890	Anglo-German treaty over African possessions. Fall of Bismarck. Fall of Parnell
1891	Irish Land Purchase Act. Education Act. Agreement with Italy over Africa
1892	general election. Liberals return to power
1893	Home Rule Bill introduced and defeated
1894–6	Armenian massacres
1895	Unionists' victory over Liberals in general election. Venezuela boundary arbitration (decision 1899)
1896	German Kaiser congratulates President of South African Republic on thwarting 'Jameson Raid'
1897	Workmen's Compensation Act. German aggression in China at Kiachow begins crisis. Russia sends fleet to Port Arthur
1898	reconquest of the Sudan. The Fashoda incident. Anglo-German Africa Conventions signed
1899	Boer War begins. Samoa incident with Germany
1900	general election. Salisbury returned for fourth term; gives up Foreign Office. Anglo-German China Agreement. C. G. T. Bartley's public criticism of Salisbury's appointments
1902	Boer War ends. Salisbury retires as Prime Minister. Anglo-Japanese treaty

Notes

1 D. Cecil, *The Cecils of Hatfield House* (London, Constable, 1973), Part 3, ch. 1; Lady G. Cecil, *Life of Robert, Marquis of Salisbury* Vol. I (London, Hodder and Stoughton, 1921), ch. 1.

2 G. Cecil, *Life of Robert*, Vol. ch. 2; M. Pinto-Duschinsky, *The Political Thought of Lord Salisbury 1854–1868* (London, Constable 1967); P. Smith (ed.), *Lord Salisbury on Politics* (Cambridge, Cambridge University Press, 1972); Lord Salisbury, *Essays by the Late Marquess of Salisbury 1861–1864* (London, John Murray, 1905).

3 G. Cecil, *Life of Robert*, Vol. I, ch. 1; H. Cecil's Introduction to R. Harcourt Williams (ed.), *Salisbury-Balfour Correspondence* (Hertford, Hertfordshire Record Society, 1988).

4 E. D. Steele, 'Salisbury and the Church', in R. Blake and H. Cecil (eds), *Salisbury: The Man and His Policies* (London, Macmillan, 1987).

5   R. Stewart, 'The Conservative reaction', in Blake and Cecil, *Salisbury*, p. 94.
6   R. Taylor, *Lord Salisbury* (London, Allen Lane, 1975), p. 18.
7   E. D. Steele, 'Salisbury at the India Office', in Blake and Cecil, *Salisbury*.
8   J. Vincent (ed.), Introduction to *A Selection from the Diaries of Edward Henry Stanley, 15th. Earl of Derby, Between September 1869 and March 1878* (London, Royal Historical Society, 1994), pp. 25–31.
9   G. Cecil, *Life of Robert*, Vol. II (1921), p. 211.
10 R. Blake, *The Conservative Party from Peel to Thatcher* (London, Fontana, 1990), pp. 134–7.
11 G. Cecil, *Life of Robert*, Vol. III (1931), pp. 237–61.
12 Taylor, *Lord Salisbury*, p. 108.
13 R. Shannon, *The Age of Salisbury 1881–1902: Unionism and Empire* (London, Longman, 1996), ch. 11; see also P. T. Marsh, *The Discipline of Popular Government: Lord Salisbury's Statecraft 1881–1902* (Hassocks, Harvester Press, 1978).
14 Shannon, *Salisbury*, pp. 226–35; Blake, *Conservative Party*, pp. 150–59; R. F. Foster, *Lord Randolph Churchill* (Oxford, Oxford University Press, 1981).
15 H. Cecil, 'Lady Gwendolen Cecil', in Blake and Cecil, *Salisbury*, p. 65.
16 C. J. Lowe, *Salisbury and the Mediterranean 1886–1896* (London, Routledge and Kegan Paul, 1965).
17 L. P. Curtis, *Coercion and Conciliation in Ireland 1880–1892: A Study in Conservative Unionism* (Princeton, Princeton University Press, 1963).
18 E. A. Akers-Douglas, 3rd Viscount Chilston, *Chief Whip: The Political Life and Times of Aretas Akers-Douglas: 1st Viscount Chilston* (London, Routledge and Kegan Paul, 1961).
19 Taylor, *Salisbury*, pp. 171–4.
20 3rd Marquess of Salisbury Papers, Hatfield House Muniments, HH/3M/CC; extract from G. Cecil, 'Life of Robert' Vol. V (unpublished).
21 Gloucester County Record Office, Hicks Beach Papers, PCC/69, copy of Lord St Aldwyn's account of Salisbury for G. Cecil.
22 D. Cecil, *Cecils*, pp. 238–9.
23 Steele, 'Salisbury and the Church'.
24 Taylor, *Salisbury*, pp. 159–60.
25 G. Cecil, *Life of Robert*, Vol. IV, p. 408.
26 A. N. Porter, 'Salisbury, foreign policy and domestic finance 1860–1900', in Blake and Cecil, *Salisbury*.
27 J. A. S. Grenville, *Lord Salisbury and Foreign Policy: The Close of the Nineteenth Century* (London, Athlone Press, 1970), chs 4–6.
28 Grenville, *Salisbury*, ch. 10; Taylor, *Salisbury*, pp. 171–4.
29 Salisbury Papers, HH/3M/A/122(15); Salisbury–Frank Lascelles letter, 10 May 1899.
30 Grenville, *Salisbury*, p. 299.
31 G. Cecil, *Life of Robert*, Vol. IV, p. 322.
32 G. Cecil, *Life of Robert*, Vol. IV, pp. 342–3; E. D. Steele, 'Salisbury at the India Office', in Blake and Cecil, *Salisbury*, p. 118.
33 J. P. Cornford, 'The parliamentary foundations of the Hotel Cecil', in R. Robson (ed.), *Ideas and Institutions of Victorian Britain* (London, Bell and Sons, 1967); Shannon, *Age of Salisbury*, pp. 125–7.
34 Grenville, *Salisbury*, ch. 17.

35 R. Cecil, *A Great Experiment* (London, Cape, 1941), ch. 1.
36 E. D. Steele, 'Lord Salisbury and his Northern Audiences', *Northen History*, Vol. XXXI (University of Leeds, 1995), p. 226.
37 D. Southgate, 'Imperium et libertas' in R. A. Butler (ed.), *The Conservatives: A History from their Origins to 1965* (London, Allen and Unwin, 1965), p. 224; R. C. K. Ensor, *England 1870–1914* (Oxford, Oxford University Press, 1960), pp. 353–4.
38 G. J. Harvey, *Newcastle Weekly Chronicle*, 2 July 1892.
39 P. Johnson, *Sunday Telegraph*, 7 June 1987.
40 France, 'Salisbury and the Unionist Alliance', in Blake and Cecil, *Salisbury*, p. 244.
41 Salisbury Papers, HH/3M/CC, ch. 2 of Lady G. Cecil's unpublished 5th vol. of *Life of Robert, Marquis of Salisbury*.
42 Shannon, *Salisbury*, p. 555.
43 France, 'Salisbury and the Unionist Alliance', in Blake and Cecil, *Salisbury*, p. 245.
44 Quoted in Stewart, 'The Conservative reaction', in Blake and Cecil, *Salisbury*, p. 113.
45 P. Johnson in the *Sunday Telegraph*, 7 June 1987.
46 Lady G. Cecil, *Biographical Studies of the Life and Political Character of Robert Third Marquis of Salisbury* (London, Hodder and Stoughton, privately printed, 1949), p. 84.
47 See generally, P. T. Marsh, *Discipline of Popular Government*.
48 Grenville, *Salisbury*, pp. 165–6.
49 Kenneth Rose, *The Later Cecils*, (London, Weidenfield and Nicolson, 1975), p. 46.
50 Taylor, *Lord Salisbury*, pp. 13, 174; Steele, 'Salisbury at the India Office', in Blake and Cecil, *Salisbury*, p. 124.

Further reading

The best biography of Salisbury remains, despite a daughter's bias, Gwendolen Cecil's four volume *Life of Robert* (London, Hodder and Stoughton, 1921–32). However, the two shorter accounts by R. Taylor (London, Allen Lane, 1975) and A. L. Kennedy (London, John Murray, 1953) are useful, and forthcoming works by E. D. Steele and Andrew Roberts promise to be far-reaching studies of his influence upon British politics.

Essential reading on aspects of his leadership are R. Blake and H. Cecil (eds), *Salisbury: The Man and His Policies*, (London, Macmillan, 1987); P. T. Marsh, *The Discipline of Popular Government: Lord Salisbury's Domestic Statecraft 1881–1902* (Hassocks, Sussex, Harvester Press, 1978); and R. Shannon, *The Age of Salisbury 1881–1902* (London, Longman, 1996). On foreign policy, the most original and stimulating work is still J. A. S. Grenville, *Lord Salisbury and Foreign Policy* (London, Athlone Press, 1970), while L. Penson's, *Foreign Affairs under the Third Marquess of Salisbury* (London, Athlone Press, 1962) is important. Valuable general works covering his terms of office include R. Shannon, *The Crisis of Imperialism 1865–1915* (London, Paladin Grafton Books, 1986) and R. Blake, *The Conservative Party from Peel to Thatcher* (London, Fontana, 1990).

Joseph Chamberlain

A man of whom more will be heard.[1]

Jeremy Smith

Background

Joseph Chamberlain was born in London on 8 July 1836, the first son of Joseph Chamberlain senior and Caroline Harben. Both parents were from solid commercial backgrounds. His mother came from a line of brewers and wholesale merchants, while his father managed the family shoe-making business in the City of London, a prosperous enterprise of three generations which had made shoes for Wellington's forces against Napoleonic France. The Chamberlains lived modestly in the middle-class suburb of Camberwell in London, later moving to more comfortable dwellings in Islington when Joe was nine. At fourteen he was sent to University College School, where his intense determination and capacity for hard work won him excellent results in mathematics and modern languages. But instead of university, which Joe had hoped for, he entered his father's business at the age of sixteen to learn the rudiments of commercial practice. Just two years later, in 1854, he was sent to Birmingham as a partner in the screw-making firm, Nettlefold and Chamberlain, in which his father had recently made a substantial investment, and during the 1860s Joe helped transform it into one of Birmingham's most successful industrial enterprises. Through these changing circumstances of Joe's early life, three elements had a particularly profound impact on his character.

The first was the Unitarian religous beliefs of both his parents. Unlike other Nonconformist groups, Unitarians resisted the emotional excesses of the evangelical revival, with its emphasis on 'conversion, activism, Bible and cross',[2] promoting instead a more down to earth and rational creed that was less excitable and which 'valued the ethical teaching of Christianity'.[3]

Such an outlook prescribed a practical, reformist approach to social questions. The under-privileged were not to be spiritually roused, but assisted with temporal schemes that attacked poverty, bad housing, alcoholism and illiteracy. Accordingly, Joe took Sunday School lessons at a Church mission in the East End, when still in his teens and, once located in Birmingham, taught history and English at a charitable evening school. He also established a Working Mens' Institute for Nettlefolds and Chamberlain. Unitarianism equipped Joe with a deep sense of social responsibility and commitment to reform. His religion was 'a practical duty' and 'expressed itself in action',[4] priorities he carried with him into his later career.

A second major influence was family. Joe enjoyed a secure and affectionate family setting that instilled in him a deep personal confidence. His marriage to Harriet Kenrick, in 1860, similarly provided the stability and inner belief to pursue a thriving business career, while her brother William, who later married his sister Mary, became a life-long friend and political confidant. However, Harriet's untimely death in 1863 (and later, in 1875, the death of his second wife, Florence), 'tore Joe from his moorings'[5] and implanted into his character an iciness that he never quite lost. Family ties also helped buttress his commercial activities, as was common with much mid Victorian business. The Kenrick connection brought Joe entry into the extended kinship network of Birmingham's commercial and industrial (and predominantly Unitarian) elite, providing him with vital channels of influence and support for his business operations and, later, his political ambitions.

Finally, the cultural and political atmosphere of Birmingham moulded Joe's political philosophy. The city's long association with 'progressive Dissenting radicalism',[6] dating back to J. B. Priestly in the 1790s, channelled his sense of social responsibility in a radical political direction, as seen with his growing support for suffrage reform, Disestablishment, temperance reform and attacks upon the landed aristocracy. Furthermore, as with other mid nineteenth-century provincial cities, Birmingham witnessed a growing pride in its civic affairs. This 'civic gospel'[7] encouraged urban elites to improve and beautify their environment with libraries, parks and new municipal buildings in an effort to win local standing and unify the urban classes around a common loyalty following the strains of the 1840s. Joe digested this civic ideology, recognising in local government a vehicle for social improvement. Birmingham influenced Joe in another way. The town's industrial make-up, with its preponderance of small workshops all in cut-throat competition, nurtured in him a certain 'hardnosed' business acumen and an efficient, well-ordered mind, what Garvin refers to as his 'all-there-ness'.[8] The competitive atmosphere of Birmingham encouraged Joe's flair for marketing and salesmanship (useful attributes for a future politician), his enormous drive and energy, and a ruthlessness that ensured Nettlefold and Chamberlain not only monopolised the production of screws throughout the Midlands by the 1860s, but was beginning to encroach into the Continental market.

Apprenticeship

The Reform issue, 1866–68

Chamberlain's involvement in politics had been limited to the Edgbaston Debating Society, where he made his name as a sharp-tongued and concise speaker. All this was to change during the upheaval following Palmerston's death in 1865, which catapulted the provincial businessman into politics. The reconstruction of national politics during the Reform crisis of 1866–67 provided Chamberlain with his 'political awakening'.[9] The struggle for reform persuaded him to join the newly formed Birmingham Liberal Association, where he quickly emerged as its leading organiser and most effective speaker. The Reform issue stirred his radical and democratic sympathies, yet his faith in democracy was tempered by a recognition that the new electorate had to be organised, managed, disciplined and, above all, instructed, sharing Robert Lowe's observation of 1867 that 'we must educate our masters'.[10]

Education, 1868–73

Educating the masters provided Chamberlain's springboard into national politics. In 1868 a small group of Birmingham radicals, led by George Dixon, established the Education Society, which by 1869 had evolved into the National Education League and elected Chamberlain as its Vice-Chairman. The League campaigned for a national system of state-financed, non-denominational education to eradicate illiteracy, reduce the power of the established Church and instil political responsibility among the new voters, while simultaneously driving the Liberal Party in a more radical direction. The League was sadly disappointed by Forster's 1870 Education Act, which ignored most of its recommendations, and particularly their demand for non-sectarian religious instruction. The setback galvanised them into a national campaign, with Chamberlain the 'mainspring'[11] of this crusade, channelling the anger of dissenting radicalism (itself more assertive during the 1860s[12]) behind his finely tuned organisation. He worked tirelessly, establishing new branches, raising money and petitions, speaking across the country, mobilising press support (most notably John Morley, the young editor of the *Fortnightly Review*), encouraging non-payment of the School Board rate and threatening sitting Liberal MPs with a challenge if they failed to endorse the League's programme.

Yet the League made little obvious progress and formally ended its campaign in 1873. For Chamberlain it provided an invaluable political apprenticeship, particularly with public speaking and organising local constituency support, important skills in the more 'democratic' political environment after 1867. His campaigning also won him national prominence and respect within high-political circles, catching the attention of Gladstone and earning the friendship of Sir Charles Dilke. This latter connection helped broaden

Chamberlain's still rather provincial radical horizons towards a wider agenda, sponsoring the so-called 'four fs' (free schools, free land, free Church and free labour) and even a brief flirtation with republicanism, as well as reinforcing his determination to rid the Liberal Party of its conservative, Whig elements.

Limelight

Mayor of Birmingham, 1873–76
Chamberlain used his newly won eminence as a fiery provincial radical to gain a seat in parliament. However, his first encounter proved bruising. Despite promises of a seat at Sheffield he failed to secure the nomination. The rebuff, along with the Liberal collapse at the 1874 election, refocused his attentions on to the local political arena. Since 1869 he had been a town councillor and member of the School Board. Following poor local election results in 1872, he took charge of organising Liberals in Birmingham, mobilising party associations and forging alliances with local labour leaders and the Birmingham Trade Council. These changes enabled the Liberal Party to sweep the board at the 1873 local elections and laid the foundations for the Chamberlainite domination of Birmingham for the next forty years. Joe was now offered the Mayorship and characteristically turned what was regarded as a rather colourless office to his own spectacular advantage, beginning 'the most outstanding Mayoralty in English history',[13] and perhaps the most successful phase of his whole career.

Chamberlain directed his energies to improving conditions in Birmingham. He promised that 'the town will be parked, paved, assized, marketed, Gas and Watered and improved',[14] and within three years drains were laid, slums cleared, improvements made to the supply of gas and water, the city centre reconstructed, hugh thoroughfares built, libraries, and parks provided and a magnificent town hall erected. His constructive reforms drew upon the civic ideology assimilated in the 1850s, his desire for practical social improvement and the business methods learnt at Nettlefold and Chamberlain. Some historians have been less generous, arguing that his improvements owed much to the buoyant economic climate and the rush of enabling legislation of the early 1870s, and simply emulated developments undertaken in other British cities. Chamberlain was, according to this representation, 'less a pioneer than a typical exponent'.[15]

On the other hand, the grand scope of Chamberlain's vision showed a boldness and drive few others could match. Neither did he shrink from intervening in the economy to implement this transformation, methods he deemed necessary but which contravened the free-trade prejudices of many and fuelled taunts that he was a municipal Socialist. And regardless of whether, in terms of municipal reform, Chamberlain was original, he certainly 'sold' his achievements far more effectively than others, revealing his genius for populist, democratic politics. Above all, Chamberlain's Mayoralty represents what Marsh calls the 'entrepreneur in politics'. Birmingham was a failing and underdeveloped resource that he turned into a flourishing enterprise through shrewd investment, rigorous management and sound finance, although, like any entrepreneur, he tended to be a disciplinarian and something of a control freak.

Parliament and the National Liberal Federation, 1876–80
Chamberlain's success as Mayor and the financial independence brought about by his retirement from business in 1874, finally helped lift him into parliament, acquiring the Birmingham seat in 1876 from his friend, George Dixon. The jump from provincial radical to national politician was not easy. Chamberlain's power was confined to Birmingham and he himself was associated, somewhat narrowly, with the education issue. Within the clubby Westminster atmosphere he found himself marginalised and forced to play second-fiddle to the radical, Sir Charles Dilke. Chamberlain remedied this by constructing his own power base outside parliament where his authority and popularity stood much higher. In 1877, helped by William Harris and Francis Schnadhorst, he established the National Liberal Federation as a central forum for local Liberal associations to discuss policy and co-ordinate operations. He publicised the federation as a democratic body that would 'organise and speak for grass roots opinion'.[16] Yet few doubted that, behind the democratic shroud and introduction of caucus-style machine politics, lay a vehicle designed to promote Chamberlain as the leader of popular radicalism, one that would regiment provincial Liberalism under his control as 'an instrument against the parliamentary leadership',[17] and which would assist him in radicalising the Liberal Party.

Chamberlain also acquired influence by playing the political game at Westminster. His lucid and combative manner of speech quickly won the 'ear' of the Commons, while the occasional radical outburst gained him useful notoriety. He also gave leadership to a small group of radicals which attacked opponents on both sides of the House and, at various moments, forged tactical alliances with the Irish MPs. As a result of such nuisance-making, Chamberlain was able to lay claim to a seat in Cabinet when the Liberals returned to government after the 1880 election victory, which Gladstone duly conceded by offering him the Board of Trade.

Board of Trade, 1880–85
Gladstone hoped the Board of Trade would 'muzzle'[18] Joe in the same way it muffled Bright in 1868. Unfortunately for the Prime Minister, Chamberlain used his new position, in conjunction with the National Liberal Federation, to drive the government in a radical direction. Initially, this was evident over Ireland, where he recommended conciliation through land reform, devolved local government and the avoidance of coercion as suitable measures to meet

the upsurge in social unrest. Then, from early 1883, with the spread of Socialist ideas and the rediscovery of poverty following several high-profile social investigations, Chamberlain expanded his radical initiative with a wide-ranging domestic programme; what he recommended to Dilke as 'a new departure in constructive radicalism'.[19] In fact his new departure, which consisted of franchise reform, county government reform, free education, and the extension of tenant rights, allotments and smallholdings, had much in common with the 'four fs' agenda of 1873 and Randolph Churchill's recent venture into Reform politics with his Tory Democracy pitch. It also resembled old Radicalism's historic assault on 'privilege, traditionalism, and the irresponsible social power of "sinister interests"',[20] as witnessed by Chamberlain's infamous attack at this time on those 'who toil not, neither do they spin'.[21]

Following the 1884 Reform Act, which extended household suffrage to the counties and enlarged the electorate to nearly 6 million, Chamberlain beefed up his rag-bag of new and old radical policies by including vague references to higher, graduated taxation, the compulsory purchase of land for smallholdings, and hints of a campaign against the powers of the House of Lords. The specific details of what he now called his 'Radical (Unauthorised) Programme' were less important than 'the accompanying hype',[22] which Chamberlain played up during 1885 with dynamic appeals from the platform and a series of articles in the *Fortnightly Review*, later published as a book. His project was to enthuse and direct the newly enfranchised democracy behind the Liberal Party and away from Socialism and labour politics, while advancing his role as the people's champion.

Many viewed this campaign as little more than a pragmatic bid for the support of the agricultural labourers with promises of land ('three acres and a cow'). Others believed it was an implicitly conservative strategy, offering social palliatives to preserve property and the existing social order; in his own words, 'what ransom will property pay for the security which it enjoys?'.[23] The Tory leader, Lord Salisbury, considered Chamberlain's proposals as Socialist spoliation that aimed at inciting the masses against the classes. Richard Jay, however, has placed it within a longer radical trajectory of 'harness[ing] the legitimate grievances of the "People" to the conventional ideologies of the Liberal left'.[24]

From politician to statesman, 1886

The full impact of Chamberlain's Radical Programme was upstaged by Gladstone's adoption of Home Rule late in 1885. Chamberlain opposed the scheme despite earlier moderation on Irish issues, but nonetheless decided, perhaps unwisely, to join Gladstone's third ministry under the impression that he could temporise the scheme as it took legislative shape. When it became clear at the end of March that Gladstone could not be diverted from the purity of his mission, Chamberlain resigned from the Cabinet.

Circumstances now threw him into a pro-Union alliance, alongside Lord Hartington and his followers and the entire Conservative Party, which on 9 June 1886 destroyed Home Rule by 341 votes to 311. Gladstone requested an election, eager to crush this 'unholy' Unionist association, but only succeeded in smashing his own party and forcing Liberal Unionists into a more enduring compact with Conservatives that dominated government for the next twenty years.

Chamberlain's actions during this confused period suggest a political somersault of quite breathtaking magnitude. By late 1885 he was the leader of popular radicalism, sympathetic to Irish grievances and a champion of Nonconformity who gloried in his attacks on both Whigs and Tories. By July 1886, Chamberlain was estranged from most of his radical allies, a vigorous opponent of Gladstone who, in alliance with the Whigs, supported a Tory government which upheld the established Church. Closer inspection, however, reveals a more consistent course. For one, Chamberlain had never supported Irish self-rule. Back in the 1860s, John Morely recognised he 'was never a Home Ruler';[25] the furthest he would go in appeasing Irish claims was devolved local government. His objection lay in a deep veneration for Britain's imperial mission, a sentiment garnered from Dilke and representing a sort of 'Palmerstonian' Radicalism, or what one historian has called a 'Radical Imperialism'[26] that separated him from mainstream radicals and their 'little-Englander' beliefs. Perhaps, then, Chamberlain's actions in 1886 had a logic and constancy after all. They certainly suggest he had more in common with his new political partners than was once thought. Union and Empire provided vital common ground between Chamberlain, Hartington and Salisbury, which facilitated a relatively smooth existence for the Unionist alliance.[27] Moreover, Chamberlain believed Home Rule was irrelevant, if not positively harmful, to both Britain and Ireland. What Ireland urgently needed was development of its resources, not political meddling. Britain desperately required a programme of welfare reform, not anachronistic constitutional wrangles.

Into the wilderness, 1886–87
Chamberlain's prospects in the new political landscape were at best unclear and at worst rather bleak. What role, for example, would he undertake in the new alliance? How would he preserve his reformist reputation in a predominantly Conservative political combination? Initially he sought reconciliation with the Liberal Party (believing most shared his scepticism of Home Rule and were keen to ditch the 'Grand Old Man' following the election catastrophe) but with little success. He then attempted co-operation with Randolph Churchill and his progressive Conservatives. Churchill and Chamberlain endeavoured to attract the newly enfranchised electorate behind a centre party by offering a number of reforms – such as allotments and smallholdings, and Workmen's compensation – in opposition to the Gladstonian Liberal rump and a reactionary, Salisburian clique. This would have

returned politics to a Palmerstonian-style 'centrism' that had existed during the 1850s and 1860s but, unfortunately, Churchill was an erratic partner whose hasty resignation from the Exchequer in December 1886 brought the manoeuvre crashing to the ground.

Liberal Radicalism to Radical Unionism, 1887–88

With Chamberlain's career at rock bottom it was Salisbury who offered salvation by suggesting he lead a delegation to negotiate a fishing dispute between Canada and the USA. Chamberlain accepted, travelling to the new world in October 1887, where over the next six months he was both personally and politically rejuvenated. He found a new wife, Mary, from among New York's elite, whose aristocratic manner eased Joe's assimilation into the new blue-blooded environment he now inhabited. More significantly, his involvement in a major international arbitration strengthened Chamberlain's appreciation of Britain's imperial domains.

Chamberlain's interest in Empire centred upon an economic judgement that it could revitalise Britain's commercial position in the face of America's (and Germany's) huge industrial power. He regarded Britain's sprawling territories not as millstones but as 'undeveloped estates' that with investment and management could open up huge markets for British goods, stimulating domestic economic activity with the benefit of rising profits and stable markets. Sustained economic growth with rising employment, higher wages and revenue for social reforms also enabled him to claim a certain continuity with his earlier radicalism: namely a concern to improve conditions for the poorer sections of society, that ran through his involvement in education, municipal government, radical domestic reform and now imperial development. Empire, then, was a bridge across the chasm of 1886 and the new focus for his restless, modernising and radical instincts.

'Proud to be called a Unionist', 1888–92

On his return to Britain in 1888, Chamberlain began to popularise his Radical Unionist ideas to carve for himself a separate identity within the Unionist alliance, distinct from the negativism of Lord Salisbury and the conservative approach of Lord Hartington. Significantly, Radical Unionism resembled Disraeli's Empire and social reform platform of the 1870s and Churchill's Tory Democracy of the 1880s, two legacies that were currently celebrated by the burgeoning Primrose League movement. These similarities earned Chamberlain a pivotal role inside the Unionist alliance, mediating between the various political factions – a position he strengthened in 1891 on taking the leadership of Liberal Unionists in the Commons. Chamberlain could now exercise real leverage over the Conservative government which he was keen to exploit to sustain his radical, populist image in the country. Hence he claimed, somewhat unreasonably, credit for pushing through such progressive legislation as the County Councils Act in 1888 and the Smallholdings Act of 1892.

However, his influence should not be over-rated. Salisbury was always an unlikely reformist Prime Minister, with most of his ministries' legislation circumscribed by voluntarist clauses and simply extending established precedents. With limited support in the Commons, Chamberlain lacked parliamentary clout and was heavily reliant upon Conservative goodwill, forcing him to blunt his earlier radicalism and duck more controversial questions such as education reform. Such weakness also impelled him to build up another nation-wide organisation – the Liberal Unionist Association – in order to construct for himself an alternative power base. And among Conservative backbenches and constituency associations, Chamberlain remained deeply distrusted, regardless of the Disraelian undertones to Radical Unionism.

Unionist leader, 1892–95
The period of Opposition following defeat of the Unionist government at the 1892 election marked Chamberlain's ascent to the top rank of national leaders. This owed something to the return of Home Rule from 1893. Chamberlain defended Unionism's initial *raison d'être* with an intensity and vigour that raised his public profile enormously. It owed more, however, to the growing relevance of Radical Unionism following the stagnation of British trade during the mid 1890s, a result of foreign tariffs and intense competition that hit profits and increased unemployment. Falling profits moved some industrialists to agitate for controls on imports. Persistent unemployment prompted the formation of new working-class political organisations looking to secure their own interests, as with the I.L.P in 1893. Chamberlain's ideas on Empire and social reform, which he refined and extended during this period, provided Unionism with a coherent response to these tensions.

His ideas on social reform met some of the demands of labour – such as the limitation of hours, restrictions on immigration and old-age pensions – in the hope of wooing the working classes away from independent 'class' politics and fastening them to the existing political system. They were also aimed at the middle classes on the grounds that by giving a little you save a lot; preservation of property and the economic order depended on thwarting class politics with social reform. With Empire, Chamberlain argued for a Commercial Union between the colonies and mother country, with high import duties (tariffs) against foreign competition; in other words a British *Zollverein*. This, he hoped, would expand intra-imperial trade that would, among other things, benefit the interests of both capital and labour.

Little of this was original. Chamberlain's social policies were, in essentials, what he had recommended back in the 1860s, and ideas for reorganising the Empire were already widely voiced in certain political circles and echoed the protectionist Fair Trade Movement of the 1880s and 1890s. Yet these elements equipped Radical Unionism with a broad electoral appeal that helped the Unionist alliance capture the support of a wide variety of constituencies at their stunning election victory in 1895.

Colonial Secretary, 1895–1903
Chamberlain planned a nation-wide campaign for the 1895 session to advertise support for old-age pensions and Workmen's compensation. However, events overtook him when the Liberal government collapsed in June 1895 and Salisbury was invited to form a ministry. Liberal Unionists for the first time entered a Tory government, with Chamberlain requesting (to Salisbury's considerable surprise) the Colonial Office, up until then a backwater ministry. Yet the portfolio furnished Chamberlain with an arena for his restless energy and constructive ideas, one that avoided more domestically oriented ministries where his radical views might have alienated colleagues.

Chamberlain brought a dynamism to colonial affairs, in contrast to the rather stuffy atmosphere of the Colonial Office. His dynamic 'constructive Imperialism'[28] was more appropriate to the hostile international atmosphere of the 1890s and, with mounting public sympathy for nationalism and Empire, once again showed his populist flair. Chamberlain had long believed that survival of the existing economic order could only be achieved through sustained economic prosperity which, in a world of colonial expansion, would only come from consolidating Britain's imperial interests. In this Darwinian frame of mind he was initially attracted to the idea of a grand alliance with Germany and America in a sort of Anglo-Saxon-Teutonic empire, a venture firmly thwarted by an increasingly Francophile foreign office.

More seriously, Chamberlain urged consolidation of the British Empire through expansion into new regions of Africa, while more loosely held territories were placed under firmer control. Imperial resources were to be cultivated and managed.[29] The government would thus facilitate investment into new cash crops and harbours, and help in the construction of railway networks. These all required British labour, skills and material (iron, coal, rolling stock etc.) in the short term, and once the new infrastructure was in place British trade would sustain the new native markets. Chamberlain also pushed for stronger links with the Dominions by regular Colonial Conferences and, more radically, advocating a Commercial Union for the Empire based upon free trade between its composite parts and raising protective tariffs against foreign powers.[30] Few Dominions were willing to expose their fledgling industries to competition from Britain, and even the slightest mention of tariffs took him well beyond what the Cabinet, the press, the Civil Service and the Unionist alliance were willing to tolerate.

By 1897, entrenched free-trade opinion within the British Establishment effectively thwarted Chamberlain in his plans for a British *Zollverein*, well before his attention was diverted into a series of imperial emergencies. The emergency to break in 1897 concerned events surrounding the Jameson

Raid in South Africa late in 1895. The raid was a bungled attempt to destabilise the Transvaal government under Kruger, as a prerequisite to consolidating Britain's hold over southern Africa and seizing control of valuable mining operations on the rand. Although intimate with plans of the enterprise, Chamberlain managed with great nerve to extricate himself, leaving the officials on the ground (chiefly Dr Jameson and Cecil Rhodes, Chairman of the British South Africa Company) to carry the blame – what Jay has called 'a superb, if disgraceful, exercise in political survival'.[31] But perhaps the most important consequence of the raid was that it foreshadowed the more famous imperial emergency of his secretaryship, the South African war of 1899–1901.

'We shall be quite a match for the Boers':[32] Joe's war, 1899–1901
The roots to the South African war also lay in Chamberlain's growing paranoia for uniting Britain's territories in South Africa and seizing the rich mining prospects of the Transvaal. Chamberlain pursued these aims through discussions with Kruger between 1896 and 1898, but without success. Unfortunately, the British High Commissioner, Sir Alfred Milner, was less patient and came to see war with the Transvaal as the only way of furthering British interests. From 1898 he began manoeuvring the Transvaal into war.

Conflict broke out in 1899 and, after some highly embarassing defeats, Britain finally triumphed in 1901. War and then victory raised patriotic sentiment inside Britain and brought the Colonial Secretary national popularity. Unionists were quick to milk this with a 'khaki' election in 1900 at which they won a massive landslide. 1900 marked the high point in Chamberlain's career, with some even speculating (rather groundlessly) that he would succeed the ailing Salisbury as Prime Minister. Yet the war's real significance for Chamberlain was that it left Britain humiliated and financially overstretched. Desperate for cash, the Treasury was forced to consider alternative sources of income to meet its debt commitments (i.e. extra taxation) and, even more controversially, to sideline plans for expensive welfare programmes – particularly old-age pensions – in which Chamberlain had invested much personal credibility; a situation one historian has described as 'Joe's war putting Joe's pensions at risk'.[33] Ignoring welfare commitments undermined Chamberlain's popular radical image, and was politically dangerous since the war had renewed public interest in social reform after displaying the physical weaknesses of recruits from urban areas.

With war hysteria having worn off by 1902, these consequences came into focus and generated a sharp loss of support for the Unionist government. A series of by-election losses was compounded by a conspicuous failure to check the surge in independent working-class politics following the formation of the Labour Representation Committee in 1900. Against this backdrop, Chamberlain, from spring 1903 onwards, returned to his earlier thinking and advocated tariffs as a method for building an imperial

Commercial Union to solve all the financial, welfare and political problems facing the country and party.

Chamberlain's last crusade: tariff reform, 1903–06
Chamberlain outlined his tariff reform programme in a series of speeches early in 1903. The programme represented a distillation of ideas currently being espoused by imperialists and ones Chamberlain had promoted, rather fitfully, since the mid 1880s. Tariffs would be imposed on a range of goods entering the British market but substantially lowered (even removed) against goods from the Empire. This would encourage the economies of Britain and her territories to 'cross-fertilise' (Imperial Federation) which over time would foster closer defensive and cultural ties. Behind these tariff walls, British industry and agriculture could shelter from international commercial competition and the ups and downs of the trade cycle, and so stabilise domestic levels of employment, commercial profits and general economic activity. This represented a 'producer's alliance' that responded to the grievances of both capital and labour and, by encouraging recognition of their common interests, diminished the appeal of class politics. In addition, revenue from tariffs on foreign goods could finance social reform measures, and in particular old-age pensions, without taxing the better-off (and predominantly Unionist-voting) sections of society.

Tariff reform, as Chamberlain packaged it, was 'a single policy to solve a multitude of problems',[34] a panacea to arrest Britain's economic decline, consolidate the Empire, win back working-class voters with stable employment, engender cross-class co-operation and preserve the existing economic order. Tariff reform, therefore, drew upon the concerns he had pursued throughout his career. And as with his other campaigns, he sought to promote his cause from the public platform and by organising at the constituency level.

Unfortunately for Chamberlain, he was unable to capture the country or even the Unionist alliance. Powerful financial and commercial interests regarded protection as economically regressive. This inspired a solid body of Unionist 'free-traders' to resist adoption of the policy. Tariff reform also proved vulnerable to the Liberal cry of 'dear food' (to protect British agriculture tariffs would be needed on incoming foodstuffs), a sensitive issue in working-class communities that contributed to the devastating Unionist election defeat in 1906, where they won just 156 seats. But the biggest blow to the tariff reform campaign was the debilitating stroke Chamberlain suffered in July 1906 that removed him from active politics. A lifetime of unquenchable energy and hard work had finally caught up with him just days after his seventieth birthday. And although Chamberlain continued as MP for Birmingham and still 'cast a long shadow over the Unionist party',[35] and over his son, Austen, in particular, British politics had lost its brightest star. He died a paralysed and broken man just months before the Great War in 1914.

Legacy

Chamberlain's career was marked by disappointment. For all his impressive abilities he never rose further than Colonial Secretary. His great campaigns for education, the radical programme of 1885, Imperial Federation and tariff reform ended in defeat. And despite his constructive rhetoric and grandiose visions, he steered little practical legislation on to the statute book. Such considerations have prompted one historian to write, 'there lies [on Chamberlain] an aura of failure – a sense of grand plans and ambitions, stridently promoted, and subsequently abandoned or brought to nothing'.[36] Furthermore, Chamberlain was no original thinker, rather 'an intellectual magpie', using and discarding ideas that were already common currency.[37] Nor was he a moral force in politics (unlike Gladstone or even Baldwin); most observers judged him a conspirator dedicated to political intrigue rather than conviction. These conclusions suggest a character of relatively slight historical consequence.

What, then, was Chamberlain's importance? A clue to this is provided by the fact that, Churchill aside, he is perhaps the most biographised of modern politicians, all the more unusual given that he was never Prime Minister. This concentration is based primarily upon his being what Clarke has described as 'the first modern politician'.[38] His energy, dynamism and style clearly pre-empt twentieth-century political forms, and were copied by the likes of Lloyd George and Churchill. He was a master of political organisation, practised in the low political arts of organising local bases of support, rallying opinion, raising funds, building up constituency associations and manipulating the electoral register. His platform style allowed him to 'appeal to the average elector which no-one else could do' by rejecting more common techniques of moral righteousness and rhetorical cleverness in favour of directness, clarity and aggression.[39] In all these respects, Chamberlain was the first politician to be fully comfortable with the increasingly democratic political system.

Comfort with democracy did not mean subservience to it, and running through Chamberlain's career was the conviction that the new democracy had to be organised within the existing political system, through bodies such as the National Education League, the National Liberal Federation and the Tariff Reform League, or around programmes and manifestos. It meant directing voters towards causes that bridged social divisions and avoided class issues, as with union with Ireland, Empire and welfare, and defence of the nation. Conversely, government and the political system had to be modernised to absorb the new democracy, away from its aristocratic origins and into a mechanism appropriate to a mature industrial society, one which would recognise middle-class interests and alleviate popular grievances. He approached government as he did business; to stay afloat, the enterprise had to be rationalised by discarding redundant parts (landowners) and extending the more productive areas (i.e. industry). Reform, however radical, was to renovate existing society, not to uproot it or throw it over as his political opponents thought.

By organising democracy and reforming the political system, Chamberlain sought to preserve middle-class property and the economic order against the threats from Celtic nationalism, economic discontent, Socialism, independent working-class politics and the loss of Britain's economic supremacy. Education schemes were designed to foster a skilled, efficient workforce. Reforms to improve the condition of the people would undercut the attractiveness of Socialism. Empire and tariff reform would maintain economic prosperity. Chamberlain's radicalism sought to uphold middle-class wealth and was premised upon the rather conservative impulse of reform to conserve. He was particularly concerned with reforming aristocratic and landed privileges, which he deemed positively harmful to the economic order.

Chamberlain's modernity also originated in his almost prophetic quality of espousing the themes which would come to dominate twentieth-century Britain. Class-based politics, mass political parties, welfare, global trading associations, imperial relations, economic decline, education and the role of the state were all pronounced upon by Chamberlain from the 1880s onwards. Two areas in particular underline his importance in this respect. First, Chamberlain was the first national political figure to think the unthinkable and question *laissez-faire* assumptions by expressing collectivist sympathies and a willingness to use the state to accomplish his various reforms, an inclination that pre-figured the direction of British government for the next seventy years. Second, Chamberlain was the first to perceive that Britain's economic prosperity depended on it being at the 'centre of an economic, geographical and political association which was much wider than the British Isles'.[40] For Chamberlain this association was the Empire. After 1945 it was Europe and the European Community. All Conservative leaders up until Mrs Thatcher have followed in this Chamberlainite assumption concerning Britain's place in the world. Chamberlain's historical importance, therefore, lies more in what he said for the future rather than what he achieved in his own day.

Chronology

1836	born July in Camberwell, London
1852	enters father's firm
1854	moves to Birmingham, joining Nettlefold and Chamberlain
1861	marries Harriet Kenrick
1863	Harriet dies in childbirth
1865	joins the Birmingham Liberal Association
1868	marries Florence Kenrick
1869	Vice-Chairman of National Education League; elected a town councillor
1870	Forster's Education Act introduced

1873	elected Mayor of Birmingham
1874	Liberal defeat at the general election, retires from business
1875	Florence dies
1876	becomes MP for Birmingham
1877	launches the National Liberal Federation
1880	Liberal victory at the general election, Chamberlain made President of the Board of Trade
1881	supports the Irish Land Act
1882	helps negotiate Kilmainham pact with Parnell. Seaman's Wages Act and Grain Cargoes Act
1884	Franchise Act (redistribution would follow in the new year). Begins his radical campaign
1885	the Radical Programme published; launches a political campaign of the same name. Gladstone government falls. General election in November produces deadlock. Hawarden Kite
1886	Gladstone returns to government with Chamberlain at the Board of Trade. Home Rule Bill introduced. Chamberlain resigns and recommends a federal alternative. Later votes against the Bill, alongside Hartington and Tories. Salisbury returns to government
1887	failure of Round Table Conference. Leaves for the USA to negotiate US–Canadian Fishing Treaty
1888	returns from USA with fiancée, Mary Endicott. Establishes Liberal Unionist association. Marries Mary, his third wife
1891	shares for the first time with Salisbury a platform in Birmingham. Takes over leadership of the Liberal Unionists in the Commons
1892	Smallholdings Act. Salisbury government defeated at the general election
1893	second Home Rule Bill introduced
1894	Rosebery replaces Gladstone as Prime Minister
1895	Liberal ministry falls. Victory for Unionists at subsequent general election. Salisbury forms first Unionist ministry, with Chamberlain entering the Colonial Office. Jameson Raid
1897	parliamentary inquiry into the Raid. Alfred Milner appointed British High Commissioner in South Africa. Colonial Conference
1898	Kitchener's victory against Mahdi at Omdurman
1899	Boers attack Natal and Bechuanaland, provoking Transvaal crisis. Black Week
1900	Transvaal annexed. Khaki election returns Unionists to power
1902	Peace of Vereeniging. Cab accident is used to replace the ailing Salisbury with his nephew Balfour. Sails for South Africa
1903	returns to Britain. Launches tariff reform campaign in Birmingham. Resigns from Cabinet to concentrate on tariff campaign
1905	Balfour resigns
1906	general election at which Unionists win just 156 seats. Valentine accord agreed between Balfour and Chamberlain. Chamberlain paralysed by a stroke
1910	Balfour pledges a referendum for tariffs
1912	Bonar Law removes pledge against party opinion
1913	Bonar Law forced to retract. Tariffs will now be decided by a Colonial Conference

1914   Chamberlain dies and is buried in Birmingham

Notes

1   J. L. Garvin, *The Life of Joseph Chamberlain, 1836–1885*, Vol. 1 (London, Macmillan, 1935) p. 122.
2   D. Bebbington, *Victorian Non-Conformity: Headstart History Papers* (Bangor, The Dorset Press, 1992), p. 5.
3   J. Parry, *Democracy and Religion: Gladstone and the Liberal Party, 1867–1874* (Cambridge, Cambridge University Press, 1986) p. 223.
4   Garvin, *Life of Chamberlain* p. 64.
5   P. Marsh, *Joseph Chamberlain: Entrepreneur in Politics* (New Haven, Yale University Press, 1994), p. 19.
6   R. Jay, *Joseph Chamberlain: A Political Study* (Oxford, Oxford University Press, 1981), p. 7.
7   Jay, *A Political Study*, p. 7.
8   Garvin, *Life of Chamberlain*, p. 85.
9   Garvin, *Life of Chamberlain*, p. 87.
10 M. Cowling, *1867: Disraeli, Gladstone and Revolution. The Passing of the Second Reform Bill* (Cambridge, Cambridge University Press, 1967), pp. 56–7.
11 Garvin, *Life of Chamberlain*, p. 69.
12 T. A. Jenkins, *The Liberal Ascendancy, 1830–1886* (London, Macmillan, 1994), p. 126.
13 Marsh, *Entrepreneur in Politics*, p. 58.
14 R. Quinault, 'Joseph Chamberlain: a reassessment', in T. Gourvish and A. O'Day, (eds), *Later Victorian Britain, 1867–1900* (London, Macmillan, 1988), p. 75.
15 J. Parry, *The Rise and Fall of Liberal Government in Victorian Britain* (London, Yale University Press, 1993), p. 239.
16 Parry, *Rise and Fall*, p. 274.
17 Jay, *A Political Study*, p. 39.
18 Garvin, *Life of Chamberlain*, p. 305.
19 Jay, *A Political Study*, p. 71.
20 Jay, *A Political Study*, p. 76.
21 Jay, *A Political Study*, p. 74.
22 J. Belchem, *Popular Radicalism in Nineteenth Century Britain* (London, Macmillan, 1996), p. 137.
23 B. Coleman, *Conservatism and the Conservative Party in the Nineteenth Century* (London, E. Arnold, 1988), pp. 171–2.
24 Jay, *A Political Study*, p. 77.
25 D. Judd, *Radical Joe* (London, Hamish Hamilton, 1976), p. 93.
26 Jenkins, *The Liberal Ascendancy*, pp. 169–72.
27 Jenkins, *The Liberal Ascendancy*, pp. 170–2; T. Jenkins 'Hartington, Chamberlain and the Unionist Alliance, 1886–1895', *Parliamentary History*, 11:1 (1992), 108–38.
28 B. Porter *The Lion's Share: A Short History of British Imperialism, 1850–1983* (London, Longman, 1975), p. 188.
29 Porter, *The Lion's Share*, p. 134.
30 A. L. Friedberg, *The Weary Titan: Britain and the Experience of Relative Decline*,

1895–1905 (Princeton, Princeton University Press, 1988), pp. 45–51.
31 Jay, *A Political Study*, p. 207.
32 Jay, *A Political Study*, p. 237.
33 J. Charmley, *A History of Conservative Politics, 1900–1996* (London, Macmillan, 1996), p. 17.
34 A. Sykes, *Tariff Reform in British Politics, 1903–1913* (Oxford, Oxford University Press, 1979), p. 6.
35 Jay, *A Political Study*, p. 317.
36 Jay, *A Political Study*, p. 321.
37 Jay, *A Political Study*, p. 324.
38 P. Clarke, *A Question of Leadership from Gladstone to Thatcher* (London, Penguin, 1991), pp. 61–81.
39 Charmley, *A History*, p. 12.
40 A. Gamble, 'An ideological party', in S. Ludlam and M. Smith (eds), *Contemporary British Conservatism* (London, Macmillan, 1996), p. 21.

Further reading

Chamberlain has attracted a great deal of interest from biographers. Few will move far into the field without drawing upon the research of J. L. Garvin and J. Amery, *The Life of Joseph Chamberlain, 1836–1914* (London, Macmillan, 1932–69), Vols I to VI, a superb and detailed account of his life. Of the shorter and more recent works, several deserve mention: D. Judd's *Radical Joe* (London, Hamish Hamilton, 1976), R. Jay's excellent high-political analysis, *Joseph Chamberlain: A Political Study* (Oxford, Clarendon Press, 1981), and P. Marsh's recent and more 'rounded' biography, *Joseph Chamberlain: Entrepreneur in Politics* (New Haven, Yale University Press, 1994). Two lively, and differing, overviews are provided by R. Quinault, 'Joseph Chamberlain: a reassessment', in T. Gourvish and A. O'Day, (eds), *Later Victorian Britain, 1867–1900* (London, Macmillan, 1988) and P. Clarke, 'Joseph Chamberlain: the first modern politician', in his *A Question of Leadership: From Gladstone to Thatcher* (London, Penguin, 1991). Chamberlain's role within Liberalism can be gleaned from T. A. Jenkins', *The Liberal Ascendancy, 1830–1886* (London, Macmillan, 1994) and J. Parry, *The Rise and Fall of Liberal Government in Victorian Britain* (London, Yale University Press, 1993), while his activities within the Unionist alliance are explored in R. Shannon, *The Age of Salisbury, 1881–1902* (London, Longman, 1995). A. Friedberg, *The Weary Titan: Britain and the Experience of Relative Decline* (Princeton, Princeton University Press, 1988) provides an excellent examination of Chamberlain and imperial matters. A. Sykes, *Tariff Reform in British Politics, 1903–1913* (Oxford, Oxford University Press, 1979) does the same for Chamberlain and tariff reform.

Arthur James Balfour

Jane Ridley

Background

Arthur James Balfour was born in 1848 at Whittingehame, East Lothian. He was the eldest son and third child of James Balfour, a wealthy Scottish landowner and coalowner whose father had made a fortune as a military contractor to the East India Company. James Balfour died of tuberculosis when Arthur was seven. Balfour and his three sisters and four brothers were brought up by their mother, Blanche, a sister of the Prime Minister, Lord Salisbury and a woman of strong religious beliefs and still stronger character. Balfour suffered from delicate health as a child, but he received a typical governing-class education, being sent first to Eton and then to Trinity College, Cambridge, where he received a second class degree in moral sciences in 1869. At the age of twenty-one he inherited the Whittingehame estate of 14,000 acres.

At Cambridge, Balfour came under the influence of the philosopher Henry Sidgwick, who later married Balfour's sister, Eleanor. Sidgwick was a moral philosopher who attempted to answer the question 'why should I be good?' in a world where Darwin's *Origin of Species* (1859) had undermined the religious certainties that underpinned traditional moral codes. 'He never did anything but wonder whether Christianity was true,' wrote J. M. Keynes, 'and prove that it wasn't and hope that it was.'[1] Sidgwick was a member of the Apostles, the elite society of dons and undergraduates which debated questions of metaphysics and philosophy. He recruited Balfour and, although only briefly an Apostle, Balfour left Cambridge with a life-long interest in philosophy.[2] His first book, *A Defence of Philosophic Doubt* (1879),[3] was an attempt to defend religious belief against the attacks of science by showing that the philosophic basis of science was flawed. It was abstrusely written, and its title invited people to think (quite wrongly) that it was a defence of religious doubt.

In politics, Balfour's philosophy was something of a liability. He was attacked for equivocating, for always seeing two sides to a question and for his apparent lack of firm convictions. Equally damaging was his interest in spiritualism, another concern which he shared with Sidgwick. Balfour was a member of the Society for Psychical Research, becoming President in 1892. Yet philosophy equipped Balfour with a mental training which historians have been slow to notice. His skill in dissecting arguments and exposing the inconsistencies of opponents was unrivalled; philosophy made Balfour one of the best debaters of his day. He was refreshingly open to new ideas, and his ability to see both sides of a question meant that he enjoyed resolving disputes by defining compromise solutions. As leader, he preferred to negotiate consensus rather than lead from the front.

A second early influence on Balfour was his uncle Robert, Lord Salisbury. After the death of Balfour's mother in 1872, Salisbury acted as guardian to the Balfour family and mentor to Arthur. Prompted by Salisbury, the twenty-six-year-old Balfour entered parliament. He was elected Conservative member for the Cecil family borough of Hertford in 1874. Salisbury's house, Hatfield, became a second home to the young Balfour, who at first owed everything in politics to his uncle.

The third background point to note about Balfour is that he was a bachelor. Of the statesmen collected in this book, Balfour was the only one who never married. He was briefly romantically involved with Gladstone's niece, May Lyttelton, but after her death from typhoid in 1875 he never came close to marrying anyone. At home at Whittingehame, Balfour was pampered and worshipped by adoring sisters and, later, by even more adoring nieces.

Through his friendship with May's brother, Alfred Lyttelton, Balfour became the leader of a social clique known as the 'Souls'. Other Souls included Margot Tennant (later Asquith), Lady Elcho, Lady Desborough and the politicians George Wyndham, George Curzon and St John Brodrick. Balfour later appointed Souls to office, but in the 1880s and 1890s the group's importance was more social than political. They excelled at conversation, games – tennis, golf – and flirtation, conducting affairs according to an elaborate stylised code. From 1885 Balfour engaged in a romantic friendship with Lady Elcho (who was safely married).[4] He was a dedicated golfer, and renowned for his social charm. Charm is a device not only for coaxing the best out of people, but also for persuading them to do what they don't really want to do; a political skill at which Balfour excelled.

Apprenticeship

Balfour took little part in politics during his first parliament, the Disraeli government of 1874–80. His intellectual energies he devoted to philosophy, and he was still uncertain whether to leave politics and devote himself to philosophy. He waited two years before making a maiden speech. In 1878, when Salisbury became Foreign Secretary, Balfour became his Parliamentary Private Secretary, and accompanied his uncle to the Congress of Berlin.

Balfour first attracted notice in Opposition after the 1880 election as a member of the Fourth Party. This was a group of four, led by Randolph Churchill, who sat below the gangway on the Opposition side of the House, taking a line independent of the Conservative front bench, whose leader was the dull Stafford Northcote, dubbed 'the Goat'. In 1881 Beaconsfield died, leaving Salisbury as the natural successor to the leadership. Salisbury was challenged by Randolph Churchill, who in 1883 emerged as heir to 'Elijah's Mantle' and leader of 'Tory Democracy' – the party in the constituencies as represented at the conferences of the National Union. Balfour acted as Salisbury's lieutenant, informing him of Churchill's every move and playing a key part in the defeat of Churchill's bid to democratise the party machine in 1884.

In 1885, when Salisbury formed his first government, Balfour was rewarded with the office of President of the Local Government Board (outside the Cabinet) which he held for the five month 'caretaker' administration. He mishandled the only issue he was required to deal with (a local government bill) but his ambition was now apparent. The borough of Hertford was abolished under the 1885 Redistribution Act and, on Salisbury's advice, Balfour strengthened his claims to office by obtaining election for Manchester East, a large working-class constituency.[5] After Gladstone's introduction of Home Rule in 1886, Balfour acted as Salisbury's intermediary in negotiating terms with the Liberal Unionists, especially Joseph Chamberlain. Home Rule was defeated, Gladstone lost the election and when Salisbury formed his second government in July 1886, Balfour was appointed Secretary for Scotland. His success in quashing the agitation of the Skye crofters led to his promotion to the Cabinet in November 1886. He saw himself as a counterpoise to Randolph Churchill, his chief rival; but Churchill destroyed himself by petulantly resigning as Chancellor of the Exchequer at Christmas 1886, leaving the way clear for Balfour's advance.

Chief Secretary for Ireland, 1887–91

Balfour's appointment as Irish Chief Secretary in March 1887 was greeted with disbelief. Still under forty, he had little over a year's experience of office and he was known, if at all, as a languidly effective debater ('Pretty Fanny'). Salisbury knew him to be a valued intermediary in high-level negotiations, but that hardly justified appointing him to Ireland, the toughest job in the government. Still smarting from the loss of Home Rule, the country was then in the grip of the Land War, the Land League campaign against landlords who unfairly evicted tenants, which was fuelled by rural poverty and crime. Yet the very survival of the Unionist government depended on its ability not only to govern Ireland but also to 'solve' the Irish Question.

Balfour's strategy was two-pronged.[6] First, he upheld coercion. He began by introducing a Crimes Bill (1887), giving special powers for the suppression of political crime for an unlimited period. This Bill Balfour pushed through the House almost single-handed, aided by the guillotine. He also introduced a Land Bill, protecting tenants against unfair eviction; at the same time the Land League was proclaimed as illegal. The test came at Mitchelstown in County Cork where police fired on rioters and killed two (September 1887). The affair was muddled, but Balfour resolutely backed the police. 'After that,' commented Carson, his law officer, 'there wasn't an official in Ireland who didn't worship the ground he walked on.'[7] Pretty Fanny had become Bloody Balfour; and the nationalists found that in the tactical game of cat-and-mouse they had at last met their equal.

Second, Balfour gave Ireland a development programme. A Light Railway Act (1889), serving the marginal agricultural land of the west known as the Congested Districts, was followed by the Congested Districts Act (1890). A pioneering piece of legislation drafted by Balfour himself, and 'a frank and striking departure from the Victorian tradition of laissez-faire', the Act established a board empowered to give grants for development schemes in the Congested Districts.[8] In 1891 Balfour introduced a Land Purchase Bill, providing government credit to enable peasants to purchase their holdings, a policy which led eventually to the liquidation of the Irish landlord class.

Balfour's four years in Ireland disproved the charge of political dilettantism, and demonstrated his capacity for constructive legislation. His weak point was the 'democracy'. Like Peel, another tough-minded and constructive administrator who also served his apprenticeship in Ireland, Balfour lacked an instinctive 'feel' for public opinion. Essentially a creature of high politics, he rarely read a newspaper, relying instead on Lord Salisbury's judgement, always uncannily accurate where public opinion was concerned.

Limelight

Leader of the House, 1891–1902

W. H. Smith, the Leader of the House of Commons, died in October 1891. Claiming that the party would accept no one else, Salisbury appointed Balfour to replace him. Balfour pretended, as was his habit, that he accepted reluctantly out of public duty; in fact he had told Salisbury as early as 1889 that he was the only acceptable candidate.[9] Officially titled First Lord of the Treasury, Balfour now acted as second-in-command to Salisbury, who combined the Foreign Office with the Premiership in the Lords. 'So Arthur Balfour is really leader,' wrote Randolph Churchill, 'and Tory Democracy, the genuine article, at an end!'[10]

In Opposition to Gladstone's fourth government, Balfour directed the campaign in the Commons against the Second Home Rule Bill. By pursuing obstructionist tactics, opposing the Bill almost word for word, Balfour forced the government to guillotine the debate, thus giving credibility to Salisbury's claim that the Bill had barely been discussed by the Commons and ought therefore to be rejected by the Lords – in spite of the fact that the Liberals claimed an electoral mandate for Home Rule.[11] It was a new kind of Opposition. The constructive energies which in office Balfour had devoted to drafting legislation, he chanelled into another book, the *Foundations of Belief* (1895),[12] once more defending religion against science.

During Salisbury's governments of 1895–1902 Balfour served again as First Lord of the Treasury. He had no formal departmental responsibilities. However, he was required to attend constantly when the House was sitting, much as Disraeli or Gladstone had done as Prime Minister; he wrote daily to the Queen and organised Commons business. He was more active in preparing and managing legislation then his Conservative predecessors, though this led to trouble in 1896, when he was forced to withdraw an Education Bill, transferring control of Church schools to county councils, owing to opposition on his own side.

At the Foreign Office Balfour acted as Salisbury's deputy. He directed the first, critical phase of the Boer War, in the winter of 1899–1900, when Salisbury's health was failing, coolly and decisively handling the crisis over the defeats of Black Week (December 1899) which led to the replacement of Buller by Roberts. He later admitted that Black Week gave him more anxiety than anything he had before experienced, even in Ireland. But the public speeches he made defending the conduct of the war were inept and ill-received, demonstrating once more his weak point as a politician – 'the uncertainty of his instinct for gauging the popular mind, or persuading it to follow his own'.[13] Military planning and strategic thinking interested him far more than 'selling' policies or defending the government's war record in parliament.

Prime Minister, 1902–05
In July 1902, shortly after the conclusion of peace with the Boer Republics, Lord Salisbury resigned and Balfour succeeded as Prime Minister. His succession was generally expected and created little surprise. Question-marks hung over him nevertheless. He had no experience of administering a first class department of state such as the Treasury or Foreign Office. By contrast with Joseph Chamberlain, the Liberal Unionist leader, he appeared timid, cautious and incapable of making up his mind. The first bachelor Prime Minister since the younger Pitt, he lacked the identity with family values which allowed the bearded, patriarchial Salisbury to appeal so effortlessly to the democracy. Nor was he an effective speaker on the public platform, Edwardian Britain's equivalent to today's television.

Balfour made little change to the composition of the Cabinet he inherited, signalling his support for Salisbury's views. Four members of the Cecil family sat in the Cabinet: Balfour himself, his brother Gerald (President of the Board of Trade), Salisbury's son-in-law, Selborne (First Lord of the Admiralty) and his son, Lord Cranborne (Lord Privy Seal, 1903). This exposed Balfour to the old charge of nepotism; critics complained that the country was governed by the Hotel Cecil. Joseph Chamberlain continued as Colonial Secretary, and this gave rise to an alternative view: namely that the government was dominated by a single overmighty minister, Radical Joe. The most significant change was forced on Balfour by the resignation of Sir Michael Hicks Beach as Chancellor of the Exchequer. Balfour replaced him with C. T. Ritchie, an outsider to the charmed circle whose appointment he soon had cause to regret.

Balfour's long experience as Salisbury's deputy gave him an unrivalled understanding of the working of the governmental machine. In 1902 he introduced new procedure rules, known as the parliamentary railway timetable, giving precedence to government business in the House of Commons and curbing the opportunities for private members. The Committee of Imperial Defence (CID), which Balfour formed in 1902, provided a forum for service chiefs and politicians; a characteristically innovative scheme for co-ordinating military and diplomatic strategy. The early papers which Balfour drafted for the CID provided a lucid analysis of the costs and implications of defending India against Russian invasion, assuming a war, not with Germany, but with France and Russia. In 1904 he contributed a cogent paper on home defence in the light of the Anglo-French entente. He also prompted a major reorganisation of the War Office.[14]

In domestic policy Balfour was equally constructive. He was the chief architect of the Education Act of 1902. Working closely with the civil servant Robert Morant, Balfour introduced a Bill designed to please his party by preserving Church schools and at the same time free education from the sectarian bickering of Church and Chapel. The Bill gave rate aid to voluntary (i.e. Church) schools, until now dependent on central government grants, thus placing them on an equal footing with Board (i.e. Nonconformist) schools. Control of schools was transferred from School Boards, which were abolished, to Educational Committees of County Councils. The Bill succeeded in annoying both the Nonconformists, who objected to the 'Church on the Rates', and the Church, which complained about the restrictions placed on religious teaching in schools. But it established a rational administrative framework for education which proved remarkably enduring. Another key measure was Wyndham's Irish Land Purchase Act (1903), providing credit for Irish tenants to buy their holdings. The 1904 Licensing Act, drafted by Balfour himself, also provided a lasting solution to a difficult problem.

Balfour's constructive achievements were eclipsed by the fiscal dispute, which originated in Chamberlain's proposal to initiate imperial preference by remitting the 1s duty on corn in favour of the colonies. This was agreed by the Cabinet in November 1902, but the 'free-trader' members of the Cabinet (and especially Chancellor of the Exchequer Ritchie) opposed it. In February 1903 Ritchie, by now under the influence of the free-trader officials at the Treasury, informed Balfour of his intention to abolish the corn duty in his budget, thus going back on what Balfour believed the Cabinet had decided the previous November. Chamberlain, who was in South Africa, was understandably aggrieved, yet when Ritchie threatened resignation, Balfour made no serious attempt to check him. For Chamberlain, who was already angered by the 1902 Education Act with its attack on School Boards, Ritchie's free-trade Budget was one provocation too many. He responded with his 'Birmingham speech' (15 May 1903), demanding the adoption of imperial preference or tariff reform. The speech was received with an enthusiasm which surprised even Chamberlain, confronting Balfour with a major Cabinet crisis.

Balfour rarely attempted to impose authority as Prime Minister, and his handling of the Cabinet may have made confusion worse. His understanding of the issues, however, was shrewd and realistic. Ever a pragmatist, he had long seen the limitations of Cobdenite free trade, recognising frankly the dangers of foreign competition. On the other hand, he recognised that Chamberlain's proposals were too crude and too extreme to be either workable or politically acceptable. He proposed a compromise policy, freedom of fiscal negotiation, giving the power to impose retaliatory tariffs, which he outlined in the summer of 1903 in his pamphlet, *Economic Notes on Insular Free Trade*.

At a Cabinet meeting in September 1903, Balfour dismissed two free trade ministers, Ritchie and Lord Balfour of Burleigh. To their fury, he failed to inform the meeting that Chamberlain had also resigned, a fact which in their view entirely altered the position, though Balfour was convinced there was no place for them in the government. A few weeks later, the free trader Duke of Devonshire resigned, in spite of Balfour's strenuous efforts to dissuade him. For Balfour the crisis was an elaborate game; the sheer difficulty of achieving a solution invigorated him.[15]

Balfour reconstructed his Cabinet, replacing the five outgoing ministers, but he failed to win the battle either for public opinion or for his party. His policy of retaliation was workable no doubt, far more so than Chamberlain's tariff reform, but it divorced fiscal reform from imperialist sentiment, handing the Liberals the election-winning issue of free trade. Balfour's Sheffield speech (October 1903), announcing retaliation, was received with dismay by tariff reformers and free traders alike, and in the sessions of 1904 and 1905 the party disintegrated in parliament. Chamberlain grew increasingly hostile, undermining free-trader MPs in the constituencies and attacking Balfour for vacillating over tariff reform.

Balfour has been accused of clinging to office. In truth he was himself indifferent towards tariff reform. He cared far more about the work he was doing in foreign policy and defence – matters which, in his view, were far too important to leave to a Liberal government. He resigned in December 1905.

Leader of the Unionist Opposition, 1906–11
Split, demoralised and exhausted by nearly twenty years in office, the Unionists were reduced to a mere 157 MPs at the 1906 election. Balfour him-

self was defeated at Manchester East. His lacklustre leadership was naturally blamed. If it is the job of the party leaders to win elections and unite their parties, Balfour certainly failed, but the magnitude of the 1906 defeat spurred him to renewed efforts in Opposition. Returned to the House of Commons as member for the City of London, he was snubbed by Campbell-Bannerman for equivocating on the fiscal issue – 'Enough of this foolery!'[16]

The majority of Unionist MPs supported tariff reform, but Joseph Chamberlain was incapacitated by a stroke in July 1906, and Balfour reunitied his party in a series of public speeches announcing a programme of moderate tariff reform. Prompted by Balfour, Lord Lansdowne, the leader of the Unionist peers, mobilised the Upper House to wreck the Liberal government's legislative programme. Plural Voting, Licensing, Education and Land Bills were destroyed; Old Age Pensions and Trades Disputes were allowed to pass. In 1909, inspired by Balfour, the Unionist peers rejected Lloyd George's Budget. Rejection was received enthusiastically by the Unionist party, but it triggered a crisis which eventually destroyed Balfour's leadership.

At first events went Balfour's way. In the January 1910 election which followed rejection, the number of Unionist MPs increased by 116 to 273, destroying the overall majority of the Liberals (275), who were reduced to dependence on the Irish. Balfour gambled on a Liberal–Irish split. In fact Asquith bought Irish support by agreeing to curb the veto powers of the House of Lords, the essential preliminary to Home Rule. When the Lords rejected the Parliament Bill, precipitating a second election in December 1910, Balfour failed to convert his minority into an overall majority. The number of Unionist MPs held steady at 271. One reason for the stagnation of the Unionists was Balfour's pledge to refer tariff reform to a referendum, a last-minute change intended to limit the electoral damage caused by tariff reform which had the unintended effect of exposing the Unionists to attack for constitutional innovation. To make matters worse for Balfour, Asquith succeeded in extracting conditional guarantees before the December election from the inexperienced George V, who agreed to create peers if the Liberals won and if the peers again rejected the Parliament Bill. The announcement of the guarantees in July 1911 provoked a major crisis in the Conservative Party. Lansdowne insisted that the Unionist peers should abstain and allow the Bill to pass; Balfour favoured a compromise course of resisting the Bill and provoking a small creation of peers, but he failed to make his policy clear or to impose it upon Lansdowne, and the die-hard Right of the party swung into open revolt, determined to die in the last ditch and provoke a mass creation. Amid a welter of bitterness and recrimination, the Parliament Bill passed in August 1911. Confessing that, 'politics have been to me quite unusually odious',[17] Balfour retreated to Bad Gastein. He resigned as leader in November 1911.

Return to office, 1915

Balfour took little active part in politics for the three years after 1911. He retained his seat in the Commons, devoting himself to philosophy (he delivered the Gifford Lectures in 1914); to his credit, he refrained from criticising or interfering with his successor, Bonar Law. With the outbreak of war in August 1914, however, Balfour's mastery of defence issues made his advice indispensable to the Liberal government. Asquith invited him to join the CID, and he became a member of the War Council. In May 1915 he was appointed First Lord of the Admiralty in the first Coalition in succession to Churchill. Here, 'behind characteristically indolent postures he brought to bear upon the issues ... so penetrating a judgement that ... at the Admiralty it was felt that if Balfour personally did not favour any particular action or policy, there was no need for further inquiry'.[18] He succeeded in repairing the damage done by the feud between Admiral Fisher and Winston Churchill, and in executing a smooth retreat from Gallipoli. However, his *communiqué* announcing the Battle of Jutland (May 1916) exaggerated the disasters, causing needless alarm – a typical Balfour gaffe.

Foreign Secretary, 1916–19

Balfour played no part in the intrigue leading to the removal of Asquith, but he supported Lloyd George as Prime Minister – in spite of the latter's earlier intrigue to remove him from the Admiralty. In December 1916 he was appointed Foreign Secretary by Lloyd George, passing, as Winston Churchill wrote, from one Cabinet to another, 'from the Prime Minister who was his champion to the Prime Minster who had been his most severe critic, like a powerful graceful cat walking delicately and unsoiled across a rather muddy street'.[19] However, he was no longer at the centre of the direction of the war. He was not a member of the War Council; the Foreign Office control of foreign policy was undermined by the 'Garden Suburb' of unofficial policy advisers which Lloyd George established at 10 Downing Street. Balfour's mission to America in April 1917 was important in securing America's entry into the war. But his diplomacy can be criticised for helping to realise the very dangers which he had so perceptively warned against in a Cabinet paper of October 1916: namely, the humiliation of Germany, the dissolution of the Austrian Empire and the encouragement of a pan-German state seeking to incorporate the Austrian Germans. Balfour is best known for the Balfour Declaration of 1917 inaugurating a Jewish homeland in Palestine. But Balfour's Zionist sympathies blinded him to the danger of Arab objections, and the ambiguous wording of the document evaded such key issues as Britain's relations with the new state. At Versailles, Balfour was largely detached from the peace negotiations. He claimed no responsibility for the treaty, which was Lloyd George's making not his.

Elder statesman, 1919–29
In October 1919, after the conclusion of the peace treaties, Balfour resigned as Foreign Secretary, remaining in the Cabinet as Lord President of the Council. He continued to work on foreign policy issues. In 1922 he was created Earl of Balfour. He remained loyal to the Lloyd George Coalition and held no office in the Bonar Law government. When Bonar Law died, Balfour advised the King on his successor. Returning from Sandringham, he was eagerly asked, 'and will dear George [Curzon] be chosen?'. 'No, dear George will not', was the reply. Baldwin became Prime Minister.

Balfour served as Lord President of the Council in the second Baldwin government of 1925–29. He died in 1930.

Legacy

The official biography of Balfour was written by his niece, Blanche Dugdale in two volumes (1936). Maintaining that if Balfour's career had ended in 1906 his reputation would have been nothing to what it later became, she devoted her entire second volume to his career after he ceased to be Prime Minister, from the age of fifty-eight until his death twenty-four years later. The achievements of the older statesman, in her view, overshadowed all that went before. Balfour's 'weak point', according to his niece, was public opinion: his inability to judge the popular mood together with his impatience of party ties.

The case against
Blanche Dugdale implicitly admitted that Balfour was a poor party leader and worse Prime Minister, and this has been the verdict of some subsequent historians. The copious documents from the Chamberlain archive, published by Julian Amery in his two volumes on *Joseph Chamberlain and the Tariff Reform Campaign* (1969),[20] reveal Balfour as vacillating, ineffective and subtly mendacious. A contemporary description of Balfour, 'shivering in philosophic doubt on the steps of a metaphysical bathing machine', aptly summarises the Chamberlainite critique.[21] Others have seen him as a Machiavellian plotter of massive cunning and minimal integrity. Alan Sykes accused Balfour of a 'negative' Conservatism, alleging that he was preoccupied with preserving the *status quo* in the interests of the propertied classes and opposed to collectivist social reform aimed at the working classes. By blocking Chamberlain's tariff reform from 1903–05, Balfour aborted the development of a Unionist programme of imperial unity and class co-operation. After Chamberlain's stroke, argued Sykes, Balfour captured tariff reform, diverting it from its radical imperialist origins into a domestic policy concerned with the defence of the propertied classes, and condemning his party to a permanent minority from which it was rescued only by the exceptional and unexpected events of the First World War.[22] John

Ramsden's study of party management concluded that 'the verdict on Balfour's leadership must be a harsh one'. As Opposition leader, Balfour was 'disastrous'. He was idle, often absent from his post and inaccessible to his followers, leaving too much party business in the hands of his private secretary, J. A. Sanders, a bald and rather sinister figure. According to Ramsden, Balfour 'equivocated too much and never grasped the effect of his equivocation on his party supporters'.[23] Bonar Law, by contrast, emerges as a leader who restored party unity, bringing a 'new style' of vigorous, hard-hitting leadership and professional business management methods.

To these charges must be added the matter of class. Critics see Balfour as a pampered aristocrat whose life was spent in a cocoon of family adoration and aristocratic country houses; a man who stayed in bed until lunchtime and devoted his considerable intellectual powers to such unproductive activities as playing games and puzzling over insoluble philosophical conundrums. Never did he earn his own living. His rise to power was due entirely to Uncle Robert (Salisbury); he was the creature of nepotism and he in turn surrounded himself with relations (the Hotel Cecil) and fellow members of the aristocratic coterie of Souls. 'His underlying sense of class superiority, [that] is the trouble with him,' said Lloyd George;[24] and it was Lloyd George who later remarked that Balfour's place in history was no more than the scent of perfume on a pocket handkerchief.[25] Balfour has become the whipping-boy for historians of aristocratic decline, excoriated by David Cannadine as 'the worst Tory leader of the twentieth [century]'.[26]

The revival of Balfour's reputation
Recently the pendulum has swung the other way, and Balfour's reputation has begun to recover. Historians hesitate before condemning him. No longer is he seen as a latter-day James I, a clever Scottish fool. Recent work has highlighted the scope and effectiveness of Balfour's constructive legislation, and the far-sightedness and cogency of his defence analysis. More interesting still is the new understanding which is only now beginning to emerge about Balfour's Premiership and his period as leader of the Opposition.

Defence policy
Ruddock Mackay's *Balfour. Intellectual Statesman* (1985) was the first study systematically to exploit the Balfour material in the Public Record Office (PRO). (Previous biographers had relied on the extensive Balfour papers in the British Library, supplemented by the material still remaining at Whittingehame.) The PRO material relates to Balfour's official work in government, and it includes the papers he wrote for the CID. This material reveals Balfour as a strategic and defence thinker of great stature. None of his colleagues could equal the cogency of Balfour's grasp of the problems of home defence. Balfour's penetrating appraisal of the costs of defending India against Russia and simultaneously resisting French invasion at home pre-

pared the ground for the appeasement of France and Russia and the making of the ententes. In 1908, when Balfour was invited to address the CID by the Liberal government, his mastery of the issues left the meeting dumbfounded. During the early years of the First World War, Balfour's understanding of the strategic realities of the Western Front was equally impressive.[27]

Prime Minister
Balfour's Premiership (1902–05) is coming to be seen in a more favourable light. The Chamberlain tariff reform perspective distorts the reality of Balfour's achievements. Balfour inherited the fag-end of an administration which was already weakened by the political backlash against the Boer War. It was his achievement to use this opportunity to push through a considerable programme of legislative reform of enduring value. His legislative achievement was equalled only by Gladstone's government of 1868–74; and it dealt with similar areas: education, army, licensing and Ireland.[28] None of these were popular measures. Yet it is hard not to sympathise with a politician who considered that buying votes was profoundly immoral, who in an age of jingoism preferred reasoned memoranda on the costs of imperial defence to rabble-rousing speeches on tariff reform. Nor was Balfour corrupt. If he surrounded himself with friends and relations in office (and what Prime Minister does not?) this was because they shared his priorities and spoke the same language, even calling each other by their Christian names in Cabinet. For Balfour Cabinet office was the highest honour to which a man could aspire; the dignity of high office was perhaps the closest he came to a political ideal. Cushioned by his private wealth (which declined dramatically at the end of his life as a result of misguided investment in converting peat into electricity), he devoted his long career to state service. He held Cabinet office for a total of twenty-seven years, longer than both Churchill (twenty-six years) and Gladstone (twenty-four years).[29]

The Balfour of 1902–05 was free of sleaze, but his Premiership nonetheless bears a striking resemblance to John Major's. Like Major, he succeeded a strong, charismatic leader and conviction politician (Salisbury) who, like Thatcher, had presided over a Conservative recovery which was past its peak when Balfour took office. The Conservative ascendancy of the late nineteenth century ended in internal splits over an economic issue – whether to proceed to imperial economic unity and protectionism – which parallel the wrangling of the 1990s Conservative Party over European monetary integration. Balfour was a trimmer, like Major; a leader committed to maintaining party unity by defining compromise solutions. The quiet success of his managerial skills was obscured by the shrill cries of ideologues on the Right of his party. But if Balfour's analytical powers were the greater, he lacked Major's election-winning skills (or luck).

Leader of the Opposition, 1906–11
The most controversial part of Balfour's career is his period as Opposition leader. If Balfour was so skilful a political manager, it is only reasonable to ask how he led his party to three successive election defeats, and was himself driven from office. How could so cool a strategist make the extraordinarily risky decision of rejecting the 1909 Budget?

The key issue is Balfour's handling of the House of Lords. In a letter to Lansdowne, the leader of the Unionist peers in 1906, Balfour advised that the party should fight very stiffly in the Commons and make the Lords the theatre of compromise. This did not happen. Instead the Lords effectively wrecked the Liberals' legislative programme. Historians have argued that this strategy was dictated by Unionist partisanship and/or aristocratic class interest, and that the House of Lords was 'Mr Balfour's Poodle'. Recent research shows a more complex picture. Ill-drafted Liberal measures barely discussed in the Commons were rejected or amended. But, in anticipation of the Salisbury convention of 1945, Bills for which government could claim a mandate, however faulty, were allowed to pass. One Bill for which the Liberals certainly could not claim a mandate was the 1909 Budget. The decision to reject was constitutionally proper, especially as the Bill was a clear case of tacking, containing matter extraneous to finance.[30] Balfour was under pressure from his party to reject; but he would never have authorised rejection – and thus forced an election – if he had not believed that his party would ultimately win, as it had in 1892–95.

Balfour's Opposition strategy was an attempt to apply the methods which had worked so well in Salisbury's day. It failed because the Liberal Party was far stronger in 1910 than in 1895. Balfour did nothing wrong, but times had changed and the old methods no longer worked. Rejection of the Budget sparked Lloyd George's 'peers versus people' campaign, raising the spectre of class politics, something for which Balfour was quite unprepared.[31]

Balfour's own party was changing too. 1906 was a watershed election. A generation of Conservative MPs retired or was defeated, but the full nature of the change was not apparent until 1910. The party's social composition changed very little, but a new type of Conservative MP emerged: the professional politician, dedicated to a parliamentary career. Known as the 'young men', these MPs made new demands on the party machine and on the leadership. It is to Balfour's credit that in 1910–11 he initiated a radical restructuring of the party in response to these pressures. Not only did he initiate a key reform of the organisation, establishing the important Unionist Organisation Committee (1911); he encouraged the formation of specialist committees of backbenchers, and he smiled on the semi-official Unionist Social Reform Committee, which endeavoured to write a social policy for the party.[32] Credit for these changes is usually given to Bonar Law; in fact it was Balfour who was the party's moderniser.

Finally, what kind of Conservative was Balfour? It is too simplistic to see him as a proto-Thatcherite, an exponent of the small state. Perhaps the closest parallel, though he would have hated it, is Peel. Balfour had none of the romanticism of Disraeli or Baldwin. He was every inch an official politician, committed to governmental solutions to political problems. Like Peel, he was a hard-working rationalist and, in an undemonstrative kind of way, a Christian Conservative.

Chronology

1848	born, Whittingehame, East Lothian
1856	death of father (James Balfour)
1869	graduates from Trinity College, Cambridge. Second class degree in Moral Sciences. Inherits Whittingehame estate
1872	death of mother (Blanche Balfour)
1874–85	Conservative MP for Hertford
1878	Parliamentary Private Secretary to uncle, Lord Salisbury
1879	publishes *A Defence of Philosophic Doubt*
1880	member of Fourth Party with Randolph Churchill
1885–86	President of Local Government Board
1886–1906	Conservative MP for Manchester East
1886	becomes Secretary for Scotland in July
1886	November, promotion to Cabinet
1887	March, appointed Irish Chief Secretary
1891–92	Leader of the House of Commons and First Lord of the Treasury. Deputy leader to Salisbury
1895	publishes *Foundations of Belief*
1895–1902	First Lord of the Treasury and Leader of the House under Salisbury
1902	succeeds Salisbury as Prime Minister in July
1902	Education Act
1902	November, Cabinet agrees to remit corn duty in favour of colonies
1903	May, Joseph Chamberlain's Birmingham speech. Cabinet splits over tariff reform
1903	Balfour dismisses free trade ministers and reconstructs Cabinet in September
1903	October, Balfour's Sheffield speech. Announces policy of retaliation
1904	Licensing Act
1905	Balfour resigns office in December
1906	January, Conservative election defeat. Defeated in Manchester East. Elected for City of London
1909	Unionist peers reject Lloyd George's Budget
1911	Conservative Party splits over Parliament Bill in July
1911	resigns as leader in November
1915	appointed First Lord of the Admiralty
1916	becomes Foreign Secretary in Lloyd George Coalition in December
1917	Balfour Declaration announcing Jewish Palestine
1919	resigns as Foreign Secretary in October. Remains Lord President of Council until 1922

1922	created Earl of Balfour
1925–29	Lord President of Council
1930	died in March at Whittingehame

Notes

1. Robert Skidelsky, *John Maynard Keynes* (London, Macmillan, 1992), Vol. I, Ch. 2, p. 34.
2. Richard Deacon, *The Cambridge Apostles* (New York, Farrar, Strauss and Giroux, 1986), pp. 46–7.
3. A. J. Balfour, *A Defence of Philosophic Doubt* (London, Hodder & Stoughton, 1879).
4. Jane Ridley and Clayre Percy (eds), *The Letters of Arthur Balfour and Lady Elcho* (London, Hamish Hamilton, 1992).
5. Robin Harcourt Williams (ed.), *Salisbury – Balfour Correspondence* (Hertford, Hertfordshire Record Society, 1988), p. 101.
6. The definitive account is L. P. Curtis, *Coercion and Conciliation in Ireland 1880–1892* (Princeton, Princeton University Press, 1963).
7. Blanche Dugdale, *Arthur James Balfour* (London, Hutchinson, 1936), Vol. I, p. 147.
8. Dugdale, *Balfour*, Vol. I, p. 175.
9. Balfour to Salisbury, 23 November 1888, in Robin Harcourt-Williams, *Salisbury–Balfour Correspondence*, pp. 260–2.
10. Lord Randolph Churchill to his wife, 23 November 1891, quoted in W. S. Churchill, *Lord Randolph Churchill*, 2 Vols (London, Macmillan, 1906), Vol. I, p. 452.
11. Corinne Comstock Weston, *The House of Lords and Ideological Politics* (Philadelphia, American Philosophical Society, 1995), Ch. 5.
12. A. J. Balfour, *The Foundations of Belief* (London, Longman, 1895).
13. Dugdale, *Balfour*, Vol. I, p. 303.
14. Ruddock F. Mackay, *Balfour. Intellectual Statesman* (Oxford, Oxford University Press, 1985), pp. 115–33.
15. Alfred Gollin, *Mr Balfour's Burden* (London, Blond, 1965).
16. Campbell-Bannerman, quoted in Dugdale, *Balfour*, Vol. II, p. 31.
17. Jane Ridley and Clayre Percy, *Letters of Arthur Balfour*, p. 269.
18. *Dictionary of National Biography* (Balfour), 2 Vols (Oxford, Oxford University Press, 1975), Vol. II, pp. 2497–8.
19. Cited in Mackay, *Balfour*, p. 303.
20. Julian Amery, *Joseph Chamberlain and the Tariff Reform Campaign*, 2 Vols (London, Macmillan, 1969).
21. Cited in Robert Blake, *The Conservative Party from Peel to Churchill* (London, Fontana, 1972), p. 169.
22. Alan Sykes, *Tariff Reform in British Politics* (Oxford, Clarendon Press, 1979), pp. 143–4.
23. John Ramsden, *The Age of Balfour and Baldwin* (London, Longman, 1978), p. 42.
24. Lord Riddell, *More Pages from My Diary*, (London, Country Life, 1934), p. 5.
25. David Cannadine, *Decline and Fall of the British Aristocracy* (Yale, Mass., Yale University Press, 1990), p. 226.

26 Cannadine, *Decline and Fall*, p. 226.
27 Mackay, *Balfour*, pp. vi, 172.
28 David Brooks, *The Age of Upheaval* (Manchester, Manchester University Press, 1995), Ch. 2.
29 Mackay, *Balfour*, p. 354.
30 Jane Ridley, 'The Unionist Opposition and the House of Lords, 1906–1910', *Parliamentary History*, 2 (1992), 235–53.
31 E. H. H. Green, *The Crisis of Conservatism* (London, Routledge, 1995), pp. 308–9.
32 Jane Ridley, 'The Unionist Social Reform Committee 1911–1914: Wets before the Deluge', *Historical Journal*, 30 (1987), 391–413.

Further reading

Balfour has had several biographers. None are definitive. The official biography is by his niece, Blanche Dugdale, *Arthur James Balfour* (2 vols, London, Hutchinson, 1936). See also Max Egremont, *Balfour* (London, Collins, 1980) and Jane Ridley and Clayre Percy (eds), *The Letters of Arthur Balfour and Lady Elcho* (London, Hamish Hamilton, 1992). Ruddock Mackay's *Balfour. Intellectual Statesman* (Oxford, Oxford University Press, 1985) stresses Balfour's work on defence issues.

Balfour's relationship with Salisbury can be traced in Robin Harcourt-Williams (ed), *The Salisbury–Balfour Correspondence 1869–1892* (Hertford, Hertforshire Record Office, 1988). L. P. Curtis' *Coercion and Conciliation in Ireland, 1880–1892* (Princeton, Princeton University Press, 1963) is a useful study of Balfour's Irish policy. Robert Skidelsky's *John Maynard Keynes* (vol. I, London, Macmillan, 1992) is valuable on the Cambridge intellectual background.

Balfour's handling of tariff reform has been exhaustively studied. See A. M. Gollin, *Mr Balfour's Burden* (London, Blond, 1965); R. A. Rempel, *Unionists Divided: Arthur Balfour, Joseph Chamberlain and the Unionist Free Traders* (Newton Abbot, David and Charles, 1972) and Alan Sykes, *Tariff Reform in British Politics* (Oxford, Clarendon Press, 1979). For a critical view of Balfour's leadership, see John Ramsden, *The Age of Balfour and Baldwin* (London, Longman, 1978). Balfour's Opposition strategy in the House of Lords is considered in Jane Ridley, 'The Unionist Opposition and the House of Lords, 1906–1910', *Parliamentary History*, 2 (1992). See also David Brooks, *The Age of Upheaval* (Manchester, Manchester University Press, 1995) and E. H. H. Green, *The Crisis of Conservatism* (London, Routledge, 1995).

Herbert Asquith

Harry Bennett

Background

Herbert Henry Asquith (1852–1928) was born in Morley, Yorkshire on 12 September 1852. His father, Joseph Asquith, a Nonconformist wool-spinner and weaver, died in 1860 leaving four children to be brought up by their mother, Emily.[1] Herbert was educated at a Moravian boarding school near Leeds before being sent in 1863 to live with relatives in London while attending the City of London School. He quickly established a reputation for himself as a pupil of outstanding academic promise and a natural orator. In 1870 Asquith won a scholarship to Balliol College at Oxford. In later life he would continue to regard this as his proudest moment.[2] He gained a first class degree from Balliol, seemingly as a matter of course. Like so many men of his political generation, he steadily accumulated the accolades that would mark him out for high office in the future: the Presidency of the Oxford Union, the Craven scholarship (1874) and election to a fellowship at Balliol College (1874). However, while Asquith's achievements were similar to those of several of his contemporaries, such as George Curzon, those contemporaries had come to Oxford from Eton rather than the less prestigious City of London School.

After Oxford Asquith embarked on a legal career. He entered Lincoln's Inn and was called to the Bar in 1876. Asquith was not an immediate success, however, and it was not until the early 1880s that his reputation in the legal field began to match his earlier academic achievements. In 1877 Asquith married Helen Melland, by whom he had five children.

Apprenticeship

While pursuing his legal career, Asquith devoted much of his leisure time to politics as a passionate Gladstonian Liberal. With his legal career firmly established, in 1886 he stood for parliament as the Liberal candidate for East Fife. After a week-long campaign he was elected. East Fife was to return him at every general election over the next thirty-two years. The oratorical ability which had won him the support of the East Fife electorate enabled Asquith to make an immediate and significant impact in a House of Commons where skill in debate was vital to the political fortunes of the young member. Asquith did not waste words: he did not bore his audience with overly long speeches. His sense of timing and command of audience were of the highest order. He was particularly active in denouncing the Conservative government's policy of coercion in Ireland. The Irish problem was to be one of the major themes in Asquith's career. In 1888 he was appointed junior counsel to Charles Stewart Parnell, the Irish leader who had been brought before a Parliamentary Commission accused of condoning political murder. His cross-examination of one of the witnesses enhanced both his political and legal reputation.

In 1891 Helen Asquith died of typhoid, leaving him a widower with five young children. Three years later Asquith married Margot Tennant – twelve years his junior and a well-known figure in polite London society.[3] Five more children resulted from this marriage, although three died in infancy.

Against the traumas of his personal life, Asquith's political career continued to progress. From 1892 to 1895 he served as Home Secretary under Gladstone. By the end of that period Asquith had emerged as one of the leading figures of his party. With a combination of luck and good judgement, he had been a success as Home Secretary, handling such difficult questions as the release of Irish dynamiters and riots at Featherstone in August 1893. Steering a Factory Bill through the House of Commons during 1894–95 sharpened his administrative and managerial abilities. His credentials as a possible future Prime Minister were by now well established with both party and public.

In the 1895 election, however, the Liberals were driven from office and Asquith was to remain on the Opposition benches until 1906. The Liberal Party found itself beset by internal difficulties, leading to the resignation of Lord Rosebery as leader in 1896. When Rosebery's successor, Sir William Harcourt, resigned in 1898, Asquith was widely tipped to become the next Liberal leader. Even so, Asquith was willing to defer to the seniority of Sir Henry Campbell-Bannerman. Influencing this decision were two important considerations: first, Asquith's legal services were in considerable demand and he dared not jeopardise the chance to establish the family finances; second, he was not yet ready to devote the whole of his time to politics. He was an indifferent attender at the House of Commons, and further party divisions over the outbreak of the Boer War in 1899 did little to increase his attachment to politics. Indeed, Asquith found himself in serious disagreement with the views of Campbell-Bannerman.

By nature Asquith was not a born politician in the modern sense. On his contemporaries he made a great impression as a brilliant speaker, parliamentarian and intellectual – but not as a politician.[4] Particular subjects such as Ireland might excite him, but the cut and thrust of party politics and political intrigue were not something to live or die for in Asquith's eyes. Instead he clung to some kind of early nineteenth-century notion that politics were the preserve of the amateur, the gentleman and the public spirited. One had to be seen to have a vibrant social life and interests outside politics. Such a view might be typified as aristocratic, and it probably reflected Asquith's acute awareness that he had come from fairly humble beginnings to academic, legal and ultimately political prominence.[5] His aristocratic pretensions were in sharp contrast to the changing political and social structure of Britain at the turn of the century.

Limelight

After the ending of the Boer War in 1902 Asquith quickly re-established his influence within the Liberal Party. He became a vehement defender of free trade while the Conservative government was busy destroying itself over the question of tariff reform. In December 1905 the Balfour government resigned and the Liberals were returned to office with Campbell-Bannerman as Prime Minister. Asquith was appointed Chancellor of the Exchequer and, to all intents and purposes, heir apparent. In the two years before February 1908, when Campbell-Bannerman fell seriously ill, Asquith proved himself to be an able, orthodox if unspectacular Chancellor. He also proved himself to be the best debater on the government benches, as the Conservative-dominated House of Lords emasculated government bill after government bill. Tensions between the Conservative and Liberal Parties were played out in a battle between the Lords and Commons. In the political rhetoric of the day, this battle increasingly appeared as the democratically elected Lower Chamber versus the unelected, aristocratic and autocratic Upper Chamber. The Liberals had come to power with what the Conservatives regarded as a radical agenda, especially over Ireland. The Conservatives were determined to prevent the implementation of that agenda, and the constitutional right of the House of Lords to reject or amend new legislation offered the means to do exactly that.

In April 1908 Asquith was appointed Prime Minister as the dying Campbell-Bannerman resigned. Rarely was such an appointment so inevitable. Asquith's rise to the highest office appeared serene, unhurried and untroubled. However, the political situation in 1908 was particularly difficult. The Lords were holding up the passage of key Liberal legislation and the Cabinet was divided over whether it should support spending on social services rather than fund increased naval building to keep pace with that of Germany. The issue threatened to divide the party with the result that, in the Budget of 1909, money had to be found for both social services and naval building. Increased taxation to the tune of £14,000,000 did nothing to endear the Budget to the Lords, who subsequently rejected it.

This raised a vitally important constitutional issue.[6] For more than two centuries it had been regarded as a convention that the Lords would not hold up the passage of government money Bills. For it to have that power would mean that the Lords could bring down governments by depriving them of the finance necessary to run the country. In Asquith's eyes, the Lords' challenge to the Commons represented a challenge to the established order and to the idea of British democracy.

Convinced of the constitutional necessity of settling this point, but concerned about the implications for the Liberal Party, Asquith appealed to the country.[7] In the election of January 1910 the Liberals secured a mandate, gaining 275 seats as compared with 273 for the Conservatives. Henceforth, the Liberals would have to depend for an overall majority on the votes of the 82 Irish and 40 Labour MPs. Although Asquith refused to make deals with the Irish nationalists, the Budget was eventually carried in the Commons once again. On 28 April the Lords accepted the Budget without a division.

Asquith was determined, however, to turn this tactical success into strategic victory. The supremacy of Commons over Lords had to be established once and for all. Thus Asquith, after considerable debate within the Cabinet, had prepared a Parliament Bill limiting the power of the House of Lords.[8] It proposed that if any Bill were to be passed by the Commons in three successive sessions, over at least a two year minimum period, that Bill would automatically become law despite the objections of the House of Lords. The power of veto would be removed from the Lords. Now they would only be able to delay the passage of legislation. Faced with such an assault on the privileges of their House, the Lords made it quite clear that they would not pass the Parliament Bill. Only if the King flooded the Lords by the creation of a vast number of new Liberal peers could the Bill be got through. Edward VII had seen that this difficulty might arise before the January 1910 election, and had made it clear that he considered that in such an eventuality the Liberal government would have to seek a fresh mandate from the people. Only then could such a sweeping constitutional change be carried through. The death of Edward VII in May 1910 took some of the steam out of the issue and Asquith endeavoured to reach a settlement through a constitutional conference. It proved impossible to settle the issue through the conference and, after gaining an understanding with the new King George V – that he would be willing to create sufficient peers if that was the will of the people – Asquith plunged the country into another general election in December 1910.

That election merely confirmed the result of the January poll, with the

Liberals and Conservatives each gaining 272 seats. With the support of the Irish and Labour members, the Parliament Bill was passed by the Commons and sent to the Lords. However, it was not until August 1911 that the Lords reluctantly passed the Parliament Bill by a majority of seventeen votes. The Bill was allowed to pass by a group of peers who had second thoughts about carrying their opposition into the last ditch and risking the end of Conservative dominance in the Upper Chamber. The amount of bitterness that had by now developed between Lords and Commons, Liberal and Conservative is difficult to comprehend. However, the antagonisms generated by the Parliament Bill crisis were only a foretaste of what was to come.

Amid the recurrent crises, the Liberal government had managed to bring in social reforms of real significance. The Old-Age Pensions Act of 1908 and the National Insurance Act of 1911 (designed to help the sick and the unemployed) are usually associated with the name of Lloyd George, the Chancellor of the Exchequer, but as Prime Minister, Asquith deserves a share of the credit for these compassionate measures establishing the foundations of the welfare state.

In 1912 Asquith introduced a Home Rule Bill which would give Ireland control over the majority of its affairs. Party tensions immediately reached new levels. By the end of 1912 Ulster Protestants were drilling and training for war with the encouragement of figures in the Conservative Party such as F. E. Smith. In the face of such provocation, the Asquith government did well not to resort to coercion or inflammatory gestures. With the removal of the House of Lords' veto, the Ulstermen claimed that force would be the only means available to save themselves from political domination by the Catholic majority. In 1913 Andrew Bonar Law, the Conservative leader, proclaimed: 'If the Government attempt to force ... [Home Rule] upon Ulster ... and if Ulster resists, we will support them in their resistance to the utmost of our power'.[9] The tensions over the Home Rule Bill had now been channelled to produce the threat of civil war in Ireland. Indeed, George Dangerfield has argued that such was the extent of tensions over Ireland and other matters that it was only the outbreak of war in 1914 that saved Britain from exactly such a conflagration.[10] The Curragh mutiny in March 1914, in which a group of army officers indicated that they would rather resign from service than coerce the Ulstermen, served as the high point of tensions over Home Rule. Eventually, the controversy narrowed down to arguments about the area of Ulster to be excluded from Home Rule. Overshadowed by the outbreak of war in August 1914, and paralleled by a controversy over the disestablishment of the Anglican Church of Wales, the Home Rule Bill was carried into law in September 1914, with a further Act suspending its operation for the duration of hostilities.

While relations between the political parties were scarcely harmonious, the country was beset by other causes of rising discontent. Labour relations were one area of particular concern, as was the campaign for women's votes.

Asquith was a particular target for the suffragists as he was opposed to granting women the vote.[11] On one occasion a suffragette threw a scythe in his direction.[12] While regarding women as equal in intellect to men, he feared for their physical and mental robustness. He had a view of women which placed them in the domestic bliss of the home rather than in the hurly burly of politics. Even so, Asquith was to be won over by the part played by women in the expansion of Britain's industrial production during the First World War. He was to support the Enfranchisement Act of 1918 and the passage of legislation making possible the entry of women into parliament in the following year.

Asquith was unfortunate in having to face quite the range and extent of domestic crises that he did. He was then doubly unfortunate in having to contend with a number of international crises, one of which would lead to the First World War. In handling these crises Sir Edward Grey, the Foreign Secretary, was accorded a considerable degree of latitude. Indeed, foreign affairs remained the preserve of an inner circle of Grey, Haldane and Asquith. The influence of the Cabinet as a whole on foreign affairs was rarely felt. From the Agadir crisis of 1911 Asquith and Grey drew the conclusion that Germany was the most serious threat to peace, and they worked steadily to strengthen the *entente cordiale* with France. Detailed staff discussions with the French about naval and military dispositions in a future emergency certainly encouraged France in the belief that Britain was an ally in all but name. In the July crisis of 1914, Grey perhaps reacted too slowly to the course of events and the government was left to face the agonising decision about whether to go to war or not. Asquith was convinced that Britain could not allow German domination of the Continent, although he did delay Britain's entry into the war until the German attack on Belgium convinced public opinion and most Cabinet ministers that British neutrality would not be possible.[13] Asquith made it plain to the country on 6 August that they had made 'every effort any government could possibly make for peace', while asserting that the maintenance of British honour and the adoption of neutrality in the conflict were quite incompatible.[14]

The war did not go the way Asquith, or virtually anyone else in Europe, expected, as a war of movement turned into the attritional slaughterhouse of the Western Front. The Conservative Opposition grew increasingly uneasy with its 'patriotic' policy of not criticising the government, and in May 1915 Asquith formed a Coalition Government.[15] However, continued attrition on the Western Front, coupled with accusations about shortages of shells and the failure of the Dardanelles expedition, all served to increase pressure on the government.

For Asquith 1915 was a bad year, but 1916 was to prove even worse. The Easter rising in Dublin and the failure of the Somme campaign shook the government. Although conscription was belatedly introduced there was a widespread feeling that the government was not prosecuting the war with sufficient vigour. Press criticism grew.

In December 1916 Asquith resigned as Prime Minister. The process by which this happened is still a matter for debate among historians, and the precise course of events may never be established.[16] By November discontent with Asquith's leadership had reached serious proportions. On 20 November Lloyd George met Bonar Law to see whether the Conservative leader would transfer his support from Asquith to Lloyd George. Law was willing and by 30 November a plan had been hatched to turn Asquith into a figurehead Prime Minister while Lloyd George conducted the business of the war as Chairman of a war executive committee. By early December Lloyd George had proposed exactly such a plan to Asquith. Aware that his position was under threat, Asquith tried to conciliate Lloyd George. However, Lloyd George made it plain that he would resign unless Asquith accepted the proposed change in roles. On 3 December Asquith appeared to cave in to most of Lloyd George's demands. Unfortunately, news of what had transpired between the two appeared in the press the following morning. On 5 December, completely outmanoeuvred and seeing that he would be regarded as a powerless figurehead, Asquith resigned as Prime Minister leaving the field to Lloyd George.

Asquith was bitter at his treatment at the hands of Lloyd George. Exhaustion, a little self-pity and patriotism meant that Asquith refrained from political activity for a time. In 1918, however, Asquith re-emerged on to the political scene when it was alleged that Lloyd George had misinformed the nation about troop strength during the German spring offensives. By accident or design, in the Maurice debate of May 1918 Asquith's unsuccessful attempt to have the allegations investigated by a House of Commons Select Committee was supported by ninety-eight Liberal MPs.[17] This marked a watershed in the history of the Liberal Party. From this point on Asquith, who had never resigned leadership of the party, found himself leading a section of it considered as Opposition by the government of that other great Liberal, Lloyd George. In the controversial 'coupon' election of 1918, Asquith and his 106 Liberals would not receive the government seal of approval by award of the coupon.

That election was to be the nadir of Asquith's political fortunes. Overestimating the loyalty of the East Fife electorate, Asquith neglected the constituency to campaign for the Liberal cause elsewhere.[18] At the polls East Fife rejected Asquith, leaving the Asquithian Liberal Party without its leader in the House of Commons. Asquith might well have taken this as his cue to retire gracefully from politics, but in 1920 he fought and won a by-election at Paisley. His campaign was one of his finest, as the injustices of the peace treaties and renewed conflagration in Ireland reanimated him. Although his contemporaries commonly testify to a marked diminution of Asquith's powers, on return to parliament his speeches on Irish and foreign affairs showed renewed vigour.[19] Asquith led the Liberal Party through some of the darkest periods of its history. In the autumn of 1923 the

Asquithian and Lloyd Georgian wings of the Liberal Party were reunited by Baldwin's drive for protection. However, the cosmetic reunion hid continuing antagonisms on all sides.

In January 1924 Asquith faced the choice of whether to support a Labour or Conservative minority government. He chose the Labour Party on the grounds that Labour should be given a chance to govern, especially in the precarious circumstances of a minority government. In addition, he was aware of the class dangers of giving the impression of the Liberal and Conservative Parties conspiring to keep Labour out of office. Moreover, he was not about to make a pact with the party that had tried to slay the sacred Liberal cow of free trade. The Labour government came to an end in October 1924, and in the ensuing election Asquith was defeated in Paisley. He was immediately offered a peerage by the King, and in 1925 he returned to parliament as Earl of Oxford and Asquith.

Again Asquith might have gracefully retired from politics, but instead he continued to lead the Liberal Party until October 1926. His decision to continue undoubtedly owed much to his animosity towards Lloyd George, which reached a head during the course of the General Strike. After resigning the party leadership Asquith settled down to write and enjoy social life. On 15 February 1928, he died at home in Sutton Courtney, Berkshire.

Legacy

Perhaps surprisingly for a man who occupied the Premiership for eight years during one of the most turbulent periods in British history, there are only two modern biographies of Asquith (R. Jenkins, *Asquith*, London, Collins, 1964 and S. Koss, *Asquith*, London, Allen Lane, 1976). With the exception of relatively short or limited aspects of his life, such as the rather confused passage of events in December 1916, Asquith is an enigmatic historical figure rather than one giving rise to vibrant debate among historians. This may in part be explained by the nature of primary sources available to historians. Asquith's papers in the Bodleian Library reflect the fact that he was less than meticulous in preserving his correspondence. Asquith's government was the last which operated without the benefit of Cabinet minutes, and for the most part one has to rely on Asquith's published works and the private papers of his contemporaries to gain an insight into his world.[20]

In terms of personal achievement, Asquith was a remarkable success. He had risen from humble origins to academic, legal, political and social heights. The rise in his social status in particular was signified by the award of the Earldom of Oxford and Asquith in 1925.

As a Member of Parliament, Asquith was similarly successful. To represent East Fife from 1886 until 1918 was noteworthy. To then return to parliament in the autumn of his career by winning at Paisley in 1920 was a personal triumph.

As a minister Asquith showed a sound grip. His periods as Home Secretary and Chancellor of the Exchequer revealed a capacity for efficient administration, together with a cautious, limited approach to problems. If he was unspectacular then he was also safe.

In terms of party leadership, Asquith had a mixed record. He was for the most part quite a successful party manager. Maintenance of Liberal unity from 1908 to 1916 owed much to his conciliatory, consensus approach to politics. During 1917, Asquith did not seek to worsen the split in the Liberal Party. When the Maurice debate proved a watershed in the party's history in 1918, it was on an issue of national security, and it was Lloyd George not Asquith who used the vote to establish the loyalties of members of the parliamentary Liberal Party. Asquith's role in keeping independent Liberalism afloat from 1919 to 1922 should not be underestimated, nor should his role in reuniting the party in 1923.

While Asquith was a good party manager, he was not a source of inspiration. Asquith was by nature conservative in his views on most problems.[21] Reform was always to be limited and usually based on precedent. Asquith had been inspired by Gladstone and the issues which excited him. When Asquith took over in 1908 he did so at a critical time.[22] The drive for social reform had been largely blocked and the party needed a new purpose. Asquith had the sense to realise that in the constitutional issue the Conservative Party had offered up a new mission for his administration which could form a rallying point for the disparate elements within the Liberal Party. The battles to force through the People's Budget and the Parliament Act may well have been inspired by Asquith's democratic sentiments and respect for the conventions of parliament, but he also embraced the struggles for party political reasons. The fight to secure the passage of the Parliament Act was just as important to Asquith as the repercussions of it receiving the Royal Assent.

While the Liberals had portrayed the issue as one of life or death, the Act itself represented only a moderate curb on the power of the House of Lords. Even with the veto removed they still retained considerable power. Wholesale democratic reform of the Upper Chamber was not undertaken. Asquith fully recognised that the Parliament Act represented less than a complete triumph for the principles of democratic government. He freely admitted in the House of Commons in 1913: 'We are ... under the Parliament Act handicapped seriously in carrying out our legislation as compared with the party opposite'.[23] Asquith never intended to democratise the workings of the British political system, but he was only too well aware that the fight against the Lords provided a useful means to rally the party behind him. Combined with Gladstonian issues such as the defence of free trade and Home Rule for Ireland, constitutional reform provided the means to inflict satisfying defeats on the Conservatives in the general elections of 1910.

After the First World War the Liberal Party badly needed a fresh programme. Gladstonian Liberalism had run its course with the end of the

Edwardian age. Asquith never entirely came to grips with this, and he did not seek to develop a new Liberalism.[24] Thus in terms of party programmes, Asquith's leadership of the party was essentially sterile. In government after 1908, perhaps this did not matter very much. Even so, with the values of Edwardian British society being pulled apart by social, economic and political changes, a gradual reshaping of Liberal ideology would have been useful. After the war it was absolutely essential to redefine Liberalism for a new and growing electorate. With party politics emerging along the lines of Socialism versus anti-Socialism, just where did the Liberals fit in? What alternative did Liberalism offer? Asquith failed to rise to this challenge. Although the party would begin to redefine itself during Asquith's period of leadership, it would be in spite of Asquith rather than because of him. Lloyd George, not Asquith, would be the driving force behind this process.

As a political tactician, Asquith's record was again mixed. Circumstances and the views of Edward VII and George V forced Asquith into two elections in 1910. The Liberals gained majorities in both contests and support for Home Rule was sufficient to largely neutralise the dangers of the Irish nationalists voting with the Conservatives, especially while led by 'Bloody' Balfour.

It is rather more difficult to interpret Asquith's decision to support Labour in 1924 as a success. Asquith may well have believed in allowing Labour to govern in the circumstances of a minority government, and may not have wanted to give the impression of a Conservative/Liberal anti-Socialist block.[25] He may even have believed that Socialism would prove unworkable in government, leading to splits within the Labour Party. Unfortunately, the experiment was to establish Labour's credentials as a party of government, leading to further decline in support for the Liberal Party and the defection of some of the most able men within it. In the course of fifteen years after 1908, the Liberal Party under Asquith went from party of government to minority third force in British politics. The decline was cataclysmic.

The outbreak of war in 1914 marks a watershed in any appreciation of Asquith's Premiership. The war was to transform Asquith's reputation as Prime Minister. In peace Asquith had proved quite a successful leader. Indeed, Churchill was to rate him as one of the best peacetime Prime Ministers in Britain's history.[26] Constitutional reform was undertaken and old-age pensions established. In securing passage of a Home Rule Bill, Asquith succeeded where Gladstone had failed. The preparations for war by the government after 1908 were sufficient to ensure a swift military response to the German invasion of Belgium in July 1914 and to meet the growing German naval menace.

As leader of a Cabinet of brilliant men such as Haldane, Lloyd George, Grey, Morley and Churchill, Asquith's style of leadership was particularly well suited.[27] Under Asquith their talents flowered. He genuinely regarded himself as a first among equals, rather than as a forceful authoritarian initiator of policy. His instinct was to seek consensus among his ministers and to conciliate those whose views did not impress the Cabinet. That strength in peace became perhaps his greatest handicap in war, when decisions needed to be quick and decisive. Liberal and Conservative alike became concerned at what they saw as paralysis and indecision.[28] In war, his powers of judgement and personality were found to be lacking.

Asquith too slowly perceived the nature of the war in which Britain was now engaged. It would not be over by Christmas and to be victorious Britain would ultimately have to field a large land army in Europe while maintaining her large navy. The war would not be fought by the pre-war professional armies of Europe – it would have to be fought by the peoples of Europe in a total war. The division between home front and frontline would become increasingly blurred. War of movement would give way to war of attrition, in which human losses would be horrendous and the industrial infrastructure of nations would be pitted against each other in the search for ever more potent means of destruction.

Asquith failed to perceive the changing nature of war. He failed to see that a *levée en mass* would be essential. He failed to see that the job of winning the war could not be left in the hands of the generals. He failed to see that the old, tried and trusted methods of government that had served Britain for so long simply had to change. He failed to see that public morale needed the impression of dynamic government, and that a close relationship with the press might be beneficial to party, government and country.[29] He failed to detect the coup of December 1916 or to handle it skilfully when it broke.

Asquith's record as wartime Prime Minister appears dogged by failure. However, as George Cassar has recently argued, historians may well have been too critical in the attack on Asquith's war leadership.[30] If Asquith did misjudge the nature of a changing war, then he was in the overwhelming majority. The mistakes he is perceived to have made would have been made by virtually all his contemporaries. He was a prisoner of extraordinary circumstance, and by December 1916 he was both tired and depressed by the death of his eldest son, Raymond.

Perhaps Asquith's most important legacy originated from the direction of British foreign policy in the period 1908–14. Asquith's role in shaping British policy towards Germany is difficult to establish. He certainly accorded Lord Grey, the Foreign Secretary, a considerable amount of latitude in the conduct of Britain's external relations, and he was only too well aware of the elements in his party that were happy to embrace the idea of Anglo-German naval rivalry. Either by action or default, Asquith played a vital role in the development of European tensions which would spill over into war in 1914. When the Sarajevo crisis broken in June–July 1914, both Asquith and Grey fatally underestimated its importance. In any case, Asquith was more concerned with the prospects for party and Cabinet unity than with the enunciation of a clear line of policy that might have led to a reconsideration of the decisions for war being taken across Europe. That war would lead to the downfall of Asquith and the Liberals, incalculable damage to Britain's economy, and would touch the lives of every man, woman and child in Britain. The memorials to the 'glorious dead' of the First World War, which can be found in even the smallest village, mark the passing not only of a generation, but also of Asquith's party and an era in which Britain was the pre-eminent force in world affairs. They are the most lasting reminder of Asquith's ultimate failure.

Chronology

1852	born, Morley, Yorkshire
1864	enters City of London School
1869	wins scholarship to Balliol
1870	enters Balliol
1872	gains first class in classical moderations
1874	gains first class in *literae humaniores*
1875	leaves Balliol
1876	called to the bar
1877	marries Helen Melland
1886	returned as MP for East Fife
1887	makes maiden speech in House of Commons
1888	acts as junior counsel in the Parnell case
1891	Helen Asquith dies of typhoid fever
1892	appointed Home Secretary
1894	marries Margot Tennant
1895	resigns as Home Secretary with the downfall of the Liberal government
1905	appointed Chancellor of the Exchequer
1908	becomes Prime Minister
1909	People's Budget passed by Commons but rejected by Lords. Asquith denounces the Lords and dissolves parliament
1910	January general election takes place (Liberals 275, Conservatives 273, Irish Nationalists 82, Labour 40). Death of Edward VII, Accession of George V. Asquith dissolves parliament. December general election (Liberals 272, Conservatives 272, Irish Nationalists 84, Labour 42)
1912	introduces Home Rule for Ireland Bill
1914	Curragh mutiny. Britain declares war on the Central Powers. Home Rule Bill receives Royal Assent
1915	Anglo-French forces land at Gallipoli. Forms coalition government
1916	opening of the Battle of the Somme. Asquith resigns as Prime Minister
1918	Coupon election. Asquith loses his seat
1920	wins by-election at Paisley
1925	created Earl of Oxford and Asquith
1926	resigns leadership of the party
1928	dies at Sutton Courtney, Berkshire

Notes

1. On Asquith's Nonconformity see C. Binfield, 'Asquith: the formation of a Prime Minister', *United Reformed Church History Society Journal*, 2 (1981), 204–42.
2. Earl of Oxford and Asquith, *Memories and Reflections 1852–1927*, Vol. I (London, Cassell, 1928), p.13.
3. D. Bennett, *Margot: A Life of the Countess of Oxford and Asquith* (London, Gollancz, 1984).
4. See tributes by Baldwin, MacDonald and Lloyd George, 16 February 1928, *Parliamentary Debates [Commons]*, fifth series, 213 (London, HMSO, 1928), cols. 1075–1079. R. Kircher, *Powers & Pillars: Intimate Portraits of British Personalities* (London, Collins, 1928), pp. 13–19.
5. S. Koss, *Asquith* (London, Penguin, 1976), p. 9.
6. For a useful survey see E. Green, 'Neutering Mr. Balfour's poodle: Parliamentary crisis 1910–11', *Modern History Review*, 7 (1996), 24–6. See also R. Jenkins, *Mr. Balfour's Poodle* (London, Heinemann, 1954).
7. For the concerns surrounding an election in January 1910, see C. Hazlehurst and C. Woodland, *A Liberal Chronicle: Journals and Papers of J. A. Pease, 1st Lord Gainford* (London, The Historians Press, 1994), 129ff.
8. P. Rowland, *The Last Liberal Governments: The Promised Land 1905–1910* (London, Barrie and Rockliff, 1968), 282ff.
9. Bonar Law, 7 July 1913, *Parliamentary Debates [Commons]*, fifth series, LV, (London, HMSO, 1913), col. 80.
10. G. Dangerfield, *The Strange Death of Liberal England* (London, MacGibbon and Kee, 1966).
11. See diary entries for 2 October 1909 and 23 November 1910, W. S. Blunt, *My Diaries*, Vol. II (New York, Octagon Books, 1980), pp. 275, 332.
12. J. Spender and C. Asquith, *Life of Herbert Henry Asquith, Lord Oxford and Asquith*, Vol. II (London, Hutchinson, 1932), p. 19.
13. For the divisions within the Cabinet see E. David (ed.), *Inside Asquith's Cabinet: From the Diaries of Charles Hobhouse* (London, John Murray, 1977), pp. 179–81.
14. Asquith, 6 August 1914, *Parliamentary Debates [Commons]*, fifth series, 65 (London, HMSO, 1914), col. 2078.
15. D. Pugh, 'Asquith, Bonar Law and the first coalition', *Historical Journal*, 17 (1974), 813–86.
16. See, for example, J. Jones, 'Lloyd George, Asquith and the conspiracy myth: some new evidence', *National Library of Wales Journal*, 28, (1993), 219–27; R. Murphy, 'Walter Long, the Unionist Ministers, and the formation of Lloyd George's Government in December 1916', *Historical Journal*, 29 (1986), 733–45; J. McEwan, 'The press and the fall of Asquith', *Historical Journal*, 21 (1978), 863–83; D. Price, 'The fall of Asquith: a matter of opinion', *Contemporary Review*, 230 (1977), 143–7; Lord Beaverbrook, *Politicians and the War 1914–1916* (London, Thornton Butterworth, 1928), 206ff.
17. G. Martin, 'Asquith, the Maurice debate, and the historians', *Australian Journal of Politics and History*, 31 (1983), 435–44. See also T. Wilson, *The Downfall of the Liberal Party 1914–1935* (London, Collins, 1966), pp. 109–12.
18. Earl of Oxford and Asquith, *Memories and Reflections 1852–1927*, Vol. II: (London, Cassell, 1928), pp. 171–2. See also S. Ball, 'Asquith's decline and the

general election of 1918', *Scottish Historical Review*, 61 (1982), 44–61.
19 On Asquith's decline see, for example, Cyril Asquith's chapter on his father in J. Spender and C. Asquith, *Life of Herbert Henry Asquith*, Vol. I (London, Hutchinson, 1932), p. 209.
20 Instead of Cabinet minutes one finds terse post-Cabinet letters to the King, Asquith MSS 5–8.
21 For an overall summary, see R. Quinault, 'Asquith's Liberalism', *History*, 77 (1992), 33–49.
22 B. Murrary, *The People's Budget 1909/10* (Oxford, Oxford University Press, 1980), p. 51.
23 Asquith, 7 July 1913, *Parliamentary Debates [Commons]*, fifth series, LV, (London, HMSO, 1913), col. 85.
24 Earl of Birkenhead, *Contemporary Personalities* (London, Cassell & Co., 1924), pp. 31–2.
25 M. Cowling, *The Impact of Labour 1920–1924* (Cambridge, Cambridge University Press, 1971), pp. 350–1. See also T. Wilson (ed.) *The Political Diaries of C. P. Scott* (London, Collins, 1970), 449ff.
26 W. Churchill, *Great Contemporaries* (London, The Reprint Society, 1941), p. 125.
27 See C. Hazlehurst, 'Asquith as Prime Minister, 1908–1916', *English Historical Review*, 88 (1970), 502–31.
28 See, for example, Chamberlain to Chelmsford, 8 December 1916, in A. Chamberlain, *Down the Years* (London, Cassell, 1935), p.116; and Churchill to Scott, 10 April 1916, in M. Gilbert, *Winston S. Churchill*, Vol. III companion 2 (London, Heinemann, 1971), p. 1487.
29 See J. Simon, *Retrospect* (London, Hutchinson, 1952), p. 271.
30 G. Cassar, *Asquith as War Leader* (London, Hambledon, 1994).

Further reading

Roy Jenkins' *Asquith* (London, Collins, 1964) and Stephen Koss', *Asquith* (London, Allen Lane, 1976) remain the starting point for those students wishing to read in more depth about Asquith. These modern biographies supplement the older two-volume study by Spender and Asquith, *Life of Herbert Henry Asquith* (London, Hutchinson, 1932). Of the more specialised works, Cameron Hazlehurst's, 'Asquith as Prime Minister, 1908–1916', *English Historical Review* (Vol. 88, 1970, 502–31) provides real insight into the Asquith Premiership, and George Cassar's, *Asquith as War Leader* (London, Hambledon, 1994) offers refreshingly new ideas about Asquith's conduct of the war.

David Lloyd George

Robin Barlow

Background

Despite being born in Manchester and living for most of his life in London and Surrey, Lloyd George will always be remembered as a Welshman. He was brought up, from the age of one, in a small village, Llanystumdwy, in southern Caernarfonshire. All Lloyd George's formal education was at the village school, his formative political experiences occurred in this part of north-west Wales, and he represented his home constituency of Caernarfon Boroughs for fifty-five years.

The George family had arrived at Llanystumdwy through financial necessity. Lloyd George's father, William George, had died in 1864, leaving a pregnant wife and two children. Elizabeth George had turned to her brother, Richard Lloyd, a highly respected local shoe-maker, for help. Not only did Richard Lloyd provide stability and security for the family, but his deeply held religious and political views were to have an important influence on his young nephew. Hence David George, in acknowledgement of his debt, took his uncle's name also, and was to be known as David Lloyd George. Despite the claims that Lloyd George and many of his early biographers often made, his upbringing was not impecunious, and certainly not by the standards of nineteenth-century rural Wales.[1] Clearly his background was not privileged compared with many of his later parliamentary colleagues, but it was in comparison to most of those in Llanystumdwy.

After leaving the village school in 1879, Lloyd George became articled to a solicitor in Porthmadog, having rejected the other careers open to an upwardly mobile Welshman: the Church, medicine and teaching. In 1884 he passed his law exams, opened his own offices, and was soon earning a reputation as a forthright and eloquent lawyer. The legal practice in Criccieth, in partnership with his younger brother William, was to provide Lloyd George with the financial security to allow him to pursue his political career.

Lloyd George grew up at an exciting time in Welsh history, a time of revival for Welsh culture and political identity. Three major influences from this period were to have an important impact on Lloyd George's later life. First, the Welsh language. Lloyd George was brought up in a Welsh household and Welsh was always his first and most familiar medium of communication; he learnt English at school as his second language. Second, Nonconformity.[2] Lloyd George grew up in an intensely religious environment; Richard Lloyd was an unpaid Pastor of a Baptist sect, the Disciples of Christ, and the whole family would walk the four miles to Chapel three times on a Sunday. Closely bound up with Nonconformity were issues such as the disestablishment of the Welsh Church, the extension of undenominational schools, the abolition of tithes and temperance – all of which Lloyd George was to involve himself with in later years. The religious influences of his boyhood 'stayed with Lloyd George throughout his life, and moulded his political enthusiasms'.[3] Third, nationalism. Lloyd George believed fervently in Wales' right to internal, devolved self-government, although there is no clear evidence that he ever intended that Wales should completely sever its links with the United Kingdom.

Despite being one of the great political mavericks, Lloyd George was the product of his time and place. John Grigg maintains that of all twentieth-century Prime Ministers, none has 'had a more clearly defined ethnic and cultural provenance, or has seemed more rooted, politically, in his home soil'.[4] Kenneth Morgan has led the way among historians in stressing that Lloyd George was an 'outsider' in British politics, though to many he was also to become a virtual 'outsider' in Wales.[5]

Apprenticeship

Lloyd George was caught up in politics from a young age, and as a newly qualified solicitor he soon became active in Liberal politics. He was a frequent public speaker on such diverse topics as temperance, disestablishment and equal burial rights in churchyards. In 1889, aged twenty-six, he was elected to the first Caernarfonshire County Council, and became known as the 'Boy Alderman'. In 1890, despite lacking the advantage of either financial backing or social position, Lloyd George was elected Member of Parliament for Caernarfon Boroughs, a marginal constituency held by the Conservatives since 1886. The electorate of 4,500 was dominated by businessmen and the professional middle class, and Lloyd George scraped home by eighteen votes after a recount. It was not until 1906 that this was regarded as a safe seat for the Liberals and, for much of the 1890s, holding his parliamentary seat was a major political consideration for Lloyd George.

In his early years in parliament, Lloyd George was a conscientious and hard-working House of Commons man, who concentrated mainly on Welsh issues such as disestablishment of the Anglican Church. He did so for two reasons: first, because he fervently believed in the justice of such causes and, second, because he realised that if he gained prominence in Wales, this would give him a springboard to make an impact on the British political scene. From 1896 onwards, when he had undoubtedly made a name for himself in parliament, Lloyd George began to take a more prominent part in national and international affairs. This change of tack was also born out of frustration to achieve his goals of disestablishment, and the failure of his attempt to unite the North and South Wales Liberal Federations – to become, as some claimed, the 'Welsh Parnell'.

Lloyd George came to the forefront of national attention after the outbreak of the Boer War in October 1899. Most Liberals supported the imperial cause on patriotic grounds, and there was certainly widespread popular rejoicing at such events as the relief of Mafeking. Lloyd George, from the outset of the war, was a strong opponent on the grounds that it was both unnecessary and unjustifiable. He was not a pacifist, nor a Little-Englander, nor in general an anti-imperialist; he did nevertheless consistently condemn war on principle. As with the First World War, he maintained that any war had to be waged only as a last resort, and in a just cause. For Lloyd George, there was no justice whatsoever in the British case. He was accused of being a traitor and a pro-Boer, and his opposition to the war was both courageous and unpopular. In December 1901 he addressed a meeting in Birmingham, when a crowd of 30,000 tried to storm the building. A policeman and a demonstrator died, and Lloyd George only escaped by being smuggled out disguised as a policeman. Closer to home, he was shouted down and had to flee from a meeting in Bangor, in his own constituency. In 1900, he only narrowly scraped home in the 'khaki' election (fought to legitimise the government's policies in the Boer War), but by 1902, at the end of the war, he was a nationally known figure, a symbol of the new radicalism, with a reputation for courage and principle.

Balfour's Education Bill of 1902 initially provided Lloyd George with another opportunity to extend his national profile. Although he had some sympathy with the Bill's educational purposes, his main objection was that the 14,000 voluntary schools, mainly controlled by the Church of England, would receive public funding, yet retain much independence. Nonconformist opposition centred on Wales, where a numerical majority allowed democratically elected Liberal councils (illegally) to frustrate the implementation of the law. This was an important crossroads for Lloyd George. On the one hand, he saw himself being caught up in what might become a purely Welsh issue again, whereas he was seeking national prominence. On the other hand, he could not afford to lose his power base, which had helped to promote his growing influence as a radical Liberal. He shrewdly steered a middle path, whereby he emerged as not only a key figure in Welsh politics, but as someone who had gone from being a 'promising figure for a ministerial post into a near-certainty for Cabinet office'.[6]

The issue of free trade was more straightforward. In 1903 Joseph Chamberlain had resigned from the government to launch a crusade for tariff reform, which had the unintended effect of uniting the Liberal Party, which had been beset by division. Lloyd George threw himself into opposing Chamberalain's policies, realising fully that tariff reform was an integral part of a wider programme of social reform, which could then be financed without the need for new taxation.

In December 1905, Balfour suddenly resigned as Prime Minister and the Liberal Campbell-Bannerman was asked to form a new government. In the ensuing general election in January 1906, the Liberals gained a landslide victory. It was generally expected that Lloyd George would be given government office, and he had been regularly writing to his wife with predictions of his certain inclusion in the next Liberal Cabinet. It was rumoured in the newspapers that he was to get the Home Office but, with perhaps a hint of disappointment, he was appointed President of the Board of Trade. It was nevertheless to be a key post, because it involved the defence of free trade, while also bringing the new minister into the field of labour and industrial relations. Lloyd George had realised that the Board of Trade had much 'latent power', and he certainly intended to grasp the opportunity to make his mark: 'He who had always been a wrecker, had now to become a builder'.[7]

President of the Board of Trade

The twenty-eight months Lloyd George spent at the Board of Trade were the beginning of the most constructive period of his life and, for a number of reasons, highly significant in the development of many of his ideas and methods of government. First, he learnt how to secure the passage of legislation, showing industry and patience in becoming the master of complicated and often unglamorous Bills. He never had a reputation for being an avid reader of parliamentary papers, or departmental briefs, but he was always able to grasp the essentials of an issue after an oral briefing or discussion. Although his tendency to leap from one subject to another earned him the soubriquet of 'the Goat', the method proved effective. Second, Lloyd George became adept at bringing together all the interested parties concerned with any Bill, and thrashing out differences before the legislation reached the House of Commons. This brought Lloyd George into contact with leading businessmen and entrepreneurs, and this was later to prove of great importance during the First World War. Third, he became involved with labour matters for the first time, and built up links with trade unions which lasted profitably until 1916. He successfully solved a national railway strike in 1907. Fourth, Lloyd George's political priorities changed in this period, as he turned increasingly towards the necessity of social reform. This was reinforced by the death of his eldest daughter, Mair, aged eighteen, in November 1907. He wrote to his wife of 'the multitudes whom God has sent me to give a helping hand out of misery and worry a myriad worse than ours'.[8]

The legislative output of the Board of Trade under Lloyd George's tenure was notable: the Merchant Shipping Act (1906), Patents and Design Act (1907) and the Port of London Authority Act (1908) all pay testimony to his legislative skills. Perhaps more importantly, however, he derived from his legislation, and equally from his administrative experiences, 'a vivid appreciation of the potential power of the State'.[9]

Chancellor of the Exchequer
In April 1908, after the resignation of Campbell-Bannerman as Prime Minister and the succession of Asquith, the subsequent reshuffle elevated Lloyd George to the Chancellorship of the Exchequer. He was to become the most inventive Chancellor of the twentieth century; he saw the Treasury as a vehicle for social reform extending its range of activities way beyond the merely financial. He now firmly believed that the role of the state was to try to overcome the worst problems of sickness, unemployment, poor housing and old age; Lloyd George wanted to implement a great programme of reform, a revolution of policy. As Chancellor, he had to provide the financial basis for all this, and disprove the claim of the tariff reformers that import duties were the surest way to pay for the welfare system. Lloyd George was sufficiently pragmatic also to realise that the proposed reforms would steal the thunder of the emerging Labour Party.

In 1908 the original scheme for old-age pensions was introduced and, although Lloyd George gained much of the credit, the planning and genesis were the work of Asquith. However, the credit for the 1909 'People's Budget' must go to Lloyd George. He devised a comprehensive social strategy which aimed to tackle the ills of poverty, unemployment and sickness, and indeed Lloyd George referred to it as a 'war budget'. It was 'an exercise in social engineering, taxing the rich principally for the benefit of the poor'.[10] In Lloyd George's famous remark, he also had to 'rob somebody's hen roost', because of the likelihood of a financial deficit in 1909–10 due to increased naval expenditure, an extra one million people qualifying for pensions, and a trade depression. The Budget changed the whole emphasis of British public finance, with a shift from indirect to direct taxation. Graduated income tax, a supertax, petrol taxes and a motor licence are all too familiar to the modern taxpayer. Perhaps the most controversial provisions concerned the new taxes on land, especially those taxes on the increased values of urban land following development.

The Chancellor presented his Budget on 29 April 1909, in a four-and-a-half hour speech, which through necessity he read. A fellow Liberal MP, Hilaire Belloc, thought Lloyd George spoke like 'a man in the last stages of physical and mental decay'.[11] In November 1909, the House of Lords rejected the Budget, precipitating a power struggle between the democratically elected Liberal government and the Upper Chamber. After a general election in January 1910, which was effectively a referendum on the Budget, the Liberal majority was reduced, leaving them reliant on the support of Irish and Labour members. After a further general election in December, the powers of the House of Lords were markedly reduced by the Parliament Act of 1911, and it was the 'People's Budget', passed in May 1910, which set the whole process in motion.

Throughout 1910–11, Lloyd George was also deeply involved in developing his plans for health and unemployment insurance, which were embodied in the National Insurance Act of 1911. He had become particularly attached to the idea of insurance, because it obviated the need for tax-raising measures to pay for it and steered well away from the Chamberlain tariff route. However, Lloyd George also realised that a state insurance scheme rattled the cages of many powerful vested interests, such as the Friendly Societies, the trade unions and the British Medical Association. It was greatly to the Chancellor's credit that he managed to win round the opposition with a mixture of concession, coercion, negotiation and charm. From January 1913, a significant proportion of the population was guaranteed sickness, disability and maternity benefits, and free access to, and treatment by, a doctor. In addition, two-and-a-quarter million workers in cyclical trades were insured against unemployment for up to fifteen weeks per year.

After 1911, it can be argued that the creative and innovative phase of Lloyd George's parliamentary career was largely behind him. Indeed, the years 1912–14 were ones of failure and near disaster, both for Lloyd George and the Liberal Party. The Marconi scandal of 1912 threatened to end his career, after he had bought £1,000 of shares in the company which was to benefit from government contracts. No actual corruption was ever proven, but as Chancellor of the Exchequer he acted foolishly at best, disingenuously at worst. It was only the loyal support of Asquith which saved Lloyd George's bacon.

At this point also, he began an affair (which was to culminate in marriage in 1943) with Frances Stevenson. His marriage to Margaret, which had taken place in 1888, although unconventional, remained solid. She stayed in Criccieth, brought up their children, attended to constituency business, and did her husband's washing which arrived by post from London. Frances Stevenson became Lloyd George's constant companion in London and Surrey, and later his Personal Secretary, bringing some order to the chaos of his personal life. Indeed, by the time of the Paris Peace Conference of 1919, they were treated as man and wife. Paradoxically, this relationship 'produced an unusual stability and domesticity into Lloyd George's personal life'.[12]

By 1914, the Liberal government was on the ropes, beset by problems with Irish Home Rule, female suffrage and worsening labour relations. Lloyd George's land campaign, begun in 1912, had foundered, while a Welsh Disestablishment Bill, introduced in 1912, had been delayed by the House of

Lords. Lloyd George's attempts to introduce a women's suffrage Bill in 1913 had also failed. However, despite these setbacks he was still determined to push forward with reforms, because Lloyd George saw this as the best way to challenge his opponents and revive Liberal fortunes. The outbreak of war was to ruin such plans.

Limelight

The First World War
Although Lloyd George claimed in his Memoirs that he was not heavily involved in the formulation of Foreign Policy between 1908 and 1914, this is clearly not the full picture. He did concentrate on domestic rather than foreign affairs, but he had gradually distanced himself from the pacifist reputation he had acquired during the Boer War. At the time of the Moroccan Crisis in 1911, Lloyd George publicly exhibited his change of attitude with clear support for a robust response to Germany. When a peaceful solution seemed imminent, he declared that it was a pity war had been avoided on this occasion.[13]

In July and August 1914, Lloyd George underwent agonies of conscience. He still held firm to his Nonconformist belief that all war was evil, yet he increasingly felt that Germany's policies were unwarranted and overtly aggressive. The event which decisively pushed Lloyd George into wholehearted support for war was the violation of Belgian neutrality. Once he had crossed this personal Rubicon, he was unshaking in his belief that war had to be waged until a complete victory was won, whatever the cost or physical sacrifice. A rousing speech at the Queen's Hall, London, in September 1914, not only showed his commitment to the war, but also illustrated the qualities of leadership and inspiration that were lacking in many of his Liberal colleagues. He referred to Germany as the 'road hog of Europe', which was trying to crush the 'little five-foot-five nations' such as Belgium (or, indeed, Wales). He called on the nation to scale the forgotten great peaks of 'Honour, Duty, Patriotism and the great pinnacle of a Sacrifice pointing like a rugged finger to Heaven'. It was a 'Prime Ministerial speech',[14] though perhaps not consciously so. As Chancellor, Lloyd George had astutely helped to ride out the financial crisis caused by the declaration of the war. The Treasury had issued £1 and 10s notes (known as Bradburys, after the Under-Secretary of State, Sir John Bradbury), a war loan was set up, and income tax and supertax were raised to help pay for the war.

Having established financial stability, the Chancellor now turned his attentions and energies to the wider issues affecting the war, such as manpower and munitions. He soon realised that the demands of a total war necessitated using every resource available, and this required central organisation, direction and co-ordination. The relationship between the individual and the state was to change irrevocably during the war, and this was frequently at the prompting of Lloyd George.

In the early months of 1915, Lloyd George became increasingly critical of the running of the war. He blamed Asquith for his slow and uncertain handling of policies, and he blamed Kitchener, the Secretary of State for War, for not keeping the Army supplied with the shells it needed. In May 1915, a Coalition Government was formed, Lloyd George becoming Minister for Munitions and now able to involve himself much more directly in the running of the war. The Coalition had emerged at the instigation of Bonar Law, yet later critics maintained that Lloyd George had engineered it to create the favourable conditions for his rise to the Premiership.

Ministry of Munitions, 1915–16
In simple statistical terms, there is no doubt about Lloyd George's success at the newly formed Ministry. Monthly output of shells rose from 70,000 in May 1915 to over one million by July 1916, while machine gun production quintupled. Lloyd George achieved such success for three main reasons. First, he clearly realised the goal he had to reach and was therefore prepared to change radically the method of supply. The private sector was never going to be able to satisfy the Army's needs, and so Lloyd George built state munititions factories (sixty by the end of 1915) under central control and direction. Second, he brought into the government men of 'push and go' from business, such as Eric Geddes from the North Eastern Railway Company. Third, he was prepared to cut a swathe through administrative red tape, if it meant he would achieve his objective and victory would ultimately be achieved. Lloyd George's realistic assessment of the demands of a total war, logically led him along an illiberal road to be an advocate of conscription. He realised that both the Army and industry needed manpower, and the only way to maximise this reserve was by state control. Vital industries had to maintain their workforce, while the remainder would be conscripted into the armed forces.

Secretary of State for War, 1916
In June 1916, following Lord Kitchener's death, Lloyd George found himself in a 'gilded cage' – a post which he did not want, despite his frequent criticism of the Military High Command. His forced acceptance of this change was an indication of the relatively weak position in which he now found himself. He had alienated himself from many Liberals over conscription; he had lost support from previous collaborators, such as Masterman and Churchill; his relationship with Asquith was becoming increasingly strained; and, while Conservatives were willing to work with him over specific issues, they were still distrustful and would certainly not grant him wider support.

Lloyd George's tenure of the War Office was marked by his efforts to outmanoeuvre the Generals (whom, he said, always spoke in generalities) and instigate a more decisive and dynamic decision-making process. To facilitate this, he proposed a new three-man War Council with executive powers which would exclude the Prime Minister. This was a perfectly reasonable proposal intended as a way of controlling the war effort, and hopefully the General Staff. It was to precipitate the fall of Asquith, and the accession of Lloyd George.

Prime Minister in War, 1916–18

In November 1916, Frances Stevenson wrote in her diary that 'the running of the War needed more ingenuity, imagination, inventiveness and originality'.[15] Lloyd George was to bring these in abundance. When he became Prime Minister, his position was certainly not secure: he relied on support from both the Conservative and Labour Parties, yet neither group really trusted him, and the Asquithian Liberals were understandably hostile. Against this background, Lloyd George gradually came to exercise powers greater than any previous Premier. As Cabinet government gave way to Prime Ministerial rule, and the state entered into every individual's life as never before, many claimed that Lloyd George was little more than a dictator.

Lloyd George has been frequently described as 'the man who won the war', and while this owes more to hyperbole than historical evidence, certain key factors can be identified. The new Prime Minister created a more decisive and efficient structure of government. A War Cabinet was set up, with its members free from departmental responsibilities, able to concentrate totally on the war. New Ministries of Food, Labour, Pensions, Shipping, National Service and Reconstruction were formed, and a new Prime Ministerial office and secretariat (originally housed in the gardens of Downing Street and thus known as the 'Garden Suburb') brought greater administrative efficiency.

Lloyd George was prepared to fight a battle with the Generals over the strategic direction of the war. This is not to say that he was always correct (as with the Nivelle offensive), but he was prepared to challenge military orthodoxy and, more importantly, ensure that the Generals were made accountable to elected politicians for their actions.

Lloyd George and his government ensured that Britain, though reliant on imported foodstuffs, was kept adequately fed. In the autumn of 1916, the shipping losses were so great that Jellicoe, the Commander-in-Chief of the Grand Fleet, had thought Britain would be forced into accepting peace. The Admiralty was not in favour of convoys, and although it is apocryphal that Lloyd George physically stormed into the building and demanded the policy be initiated, he certainly ensured that the convoy system was given a fair trial in April 1917. It proved highly successful, and Trevor Wilson has said that this ranks high among the 'decisive events' of the war.[16] Lloyd George also instigated a more interventionist food policy at home, increasing production and reducing the need for imported goods.

Finally, the Prime Minister gave the country leadership, and by and large maintained the confidence of the British people. His public persona inspired confidence and, although he did not lead a party, he led the nation.

Prime Minister in Peace, 1918–22
At the end of the war, in November 1918, Lloyd George's position was not impregnable. He owed his Premiership to a particular wartime situation which no longer existed. He was a politician without a party, and certain policies he had initiated and supported during the war (for example, conscription) had alienated him from his pre-war allies and supporters. Furthermore, the revulsion many felt for the experiences of war was inextricably linked with the man who was responsible for British policy.

Lloyd George decided that a Coalition Government was the best option to deal with the post-war international and domestic situation, freed from the distraction of party political wrangling. The Conservatives, mindful of not having won a general election since 1900, and fearful of the Labour Party and a new and unknown electorate, decided to continue the marriage of convenience with Lloyd George and the Liberals. Dubbed the 'coupon' election – after Asquith's pejorative reference to the letter signed by Bonar Law and Lloyd George endorsing Coalition candidates – the government won an emphatic victory. Bonar Law commented: 'Lloyd George can be Prime Minister for life if he wants'.[17]

At the end of the war, Lloyd George had begun a programme of reform with such measures as the Representation of the People Act (1918) and the Education Act (1918). The mood of the electorate in 1918, however, had been less concerned with social and political reform than with a strident desire to see Germany pay for the war. Lloyd George had pandered to this at election time, but was soon back-tracking at the Peace Conference in Paris in 1919. He held firm that there should be a moderate territorial settlement, deploring the creation of any new Alsace-Lorraine or the fostering of Bolshevism within the defeated nations. As far as reparations were concerned, Lloyd George was prepared to accept a figure which would satisfy public opinion, and the Right of the Conservative Party in the House of Commons, while personally favouring a moderate burden. Chris Wrigley summarised Lloyd George's performance as being a blend of 'opportunity and idealism'.[18]

Lloyd George had vowed that he would build a 'fit country for heroes to live in',[19] and certainly in 1919–20 there were notable legislative achievements. The Housing Act (1919) saw 170,000 new homes built by local authorities with Treasury subsidy, old-age pensions all but doubled, and the Unemployment Insurance Act (1920) made unemployment insurance virtually universal for manual workers. In matters of industrial relations, Lloyd George's ability to talk a tough game, yet to make concessions where necessary, saw successful settlement of the railway workers' strike in 1919 and the dockers' strike in 1920.

Seemingly at the height of his powers in 1920, Lloyd George was to find himself out of office by 1922 after seventeen years in government. The causes of the decline in his position were economic, political and social.

Government foreign policies were not producing a noticeably more stable Europe, and Lloyd George's hopes for an international diplomatic success at the Genoa Conference in 1922 were undermined by the Rapallo Agreement between Germany and Russia. Industrial relations had deteriorated markedly: working days lost through strikes peaked at eighty-six million in 1921, and union members no longer trusted the Prime Minister. Severe economic depression had made the continuance of a radical reform programme all but impossible. Indeed, many of Lloyd George's cherished programmes for housing and education went into reverse under the financial cuts of the 'Geddes Axe' (named after Eric Geddes, whose Committee recommended various economies). Although Lloyd George had succeeded in negotiating the agreement which created the Irish Free State in 1921, he had been criticised by the political Right for negotiating with so-called murderers, and by those of a more Liberal persuasion for the actions of the infamous 'Black and Tans'. (These were auxiliary soldiers, often unemployed ex-servicemen, employed to retaliate against the IRA; they used violent tactics in which the civilian population frequently suffered.) Lloyd George's support for Greece against Turkey, resulting in the Chanak crisis, brought Britain close to a war with which few sympathised. Finally, the Conservative Party (on the evidence of by-elections) came increasingly to realise that Lloyd George was no longer the electoral asset he had once been, and that their chances of success at the polls would be greater as an independent party. Distrust and dislike of the 'Welsh wizard' were further heightened by the honours scandal, when Lloyd George was accused of instigating a formal tariff for honours, open to all-comers with sufficient cash.

To some historians, such as Chris Wrigley, the surprise of the years 1920–22 was not that Lloyd George was ousted in October 1922, but rather that he stayed at the top of the greasy pole for so long.[20] In Harold Macmillan's phrase, Lloyd George had been a 'prisoner of the Tories'. He had dominated policy in a semi-dictatorial way, yet no Prime Minister in a parliamentary system, without a party majority in the legislature, can hope to remain in power for long. The Conservative Party acted as a brake on Lloyd George's vehicle of ambition, slowing him down as it saw fit; a meeting of Parliamentary Party at the Carlton Club in October 1922 pulled him abruptly to a halt.

Out of office
Although Lloyd George never regained political office after 1922, he remained a key figure in the future of the Liberal Party. The general election of 1922 proved that only a united party had an electoral future, when they secured 29 per cent of the vote and 117 seats, trailing behind the Labour Party with 142 and the Conservatives with 344 seats. The Liberal MPs were split between 60 Asquithians and 57 Lloyd George Coalitionists. Despite the clear necessity for unity, it was to be Baldwin's proposals for tariff reform

which finally brought about reunion in November 1923, immediately prior to the general election. It was something of a triumph which saw the Party winning 30 per cent of the vote and 158 seats. However, in the election of the following year, the support fell away dramatically to 18 per cent of the vote and only 42 seats. Lloyd George now realised that his own political future was inextricably bound up with that of the Liberal Party.

In 1926 Lloyd George was formally elected as leader of the Liberal Party and he set about reorganising and restructuring the party machine to give it a realistic chance of mounting an electoral challenge in the new three-party system. More importantly, he needed to determine clearly a distinct party platform based on non-Socialist but radical policies. It was to be based on a revival of his New Liberal ideals of the pre-war period. A series of reports and papers, known collectively as the 'coloured books' because of their covers, re-established Lloyd George's reputation as a man of ideas. He envisaged an enhanced role for the state, both in directing labour, organising private companies and property, and also in guaranteeing minimum wages and broadening welfare provisions. He also suggested a cure for unemployment, with a programme of investment in housing, roads and other public works. It was said that Lloyd George was a Keynesian economist before Keynes himself.

In the 1929 general election, the Liberal Party and Lloyd George made all the running, with a carefully prepared radical manifesto. The party's organisation was in good shape, and 513 candidates were put up – the largest number since 1910. In spite of winning 23 per cent of the vote, they won only 59 seats. The Liberal Party was never again to occupy the centre stage of British political life, while Lloyd George became only an important 'voice off'.

In May 1940, at the age of seventy-seven, Lloyd George played a part in removing Chamberlain from office and was later offered government office by Churchill and then the Ambassadorship in Washington. He declined both but, to the incredulity of many of his supporters, he accepted a life peerage in 1945.

Legacy

Over one hundred biographical works have been produced on Lloyd George, together with thousands of other monographs and studies. However, historians are no nearer 'painting the chameleon' or 'tethering the broomstick' than they were in 1919 when J. M. Keynes wrote his famous biographical essay on Lloyd George.[21] His personality, character and career are full of contradictions and paradoxes, which makes consistent analysis fraught with difficulty: the voice of Nonconformist conscience whose personal morality was frequently held up to question; the liberal who advocated conscription; the leader who waged total war, who became the foremost peacemonger of the 1920s; the humble Welshman who preferred to live in Surrey and to play golf; the arch-critic of the aristocracy and the House of Lords, who accepted a peerage; the man who was always worried about money, yet who left £139,855 in his will. And so the list could go on.

Lloyd George's list of achievements is impressive, however. First, and most importantly, he was one of the greatest constructive statesmen of this century, to which his legislative achievements bear testimony. He passionately believed that government could and should change society for the better and also try to put right the injustices suffered by ordinary people. The legislative programme of the period 1908–12 has shaped the welfare system throughout the twentieth century, and his Budgets changed the basis of British public finance. The two, of course, are inextricably linked. The intention was to redistribute income from the rich to the poor via social welfare schemes.

Second, Lloyd George was important not only for what he did, but for what he was. He symbolised the rise of the 'cottage-bred man' to the highest political office, epitomising the late Victorian and Edwardian democratic revolution on political life. Furthermore, he was important to Wales, helping to give it the self-respect and sense of national identity that comes from seeing a Welsh-speaker from Llanystumdwy in Downing Street.

Third, Lloyd George gave the machinery of government a new vitality and direction. His willingness to bring businessmen, entrepreneurs and experts into government – men such as H. A. L. Fisher at Education – was effective and novel. He was highly skilled at seeking opinion from all interests likely to be affected by a measure and for smoothing off any points of friction. This process of extra-parliamentary negotiation became a Lloyd George trademark and reached its maturity in the passage of the National Insurance Act in 1911.

Fourth, Lloyd George was the indispensable leader of the nation when it successfully repelled the aggression of the German Empire. His achievements at the Ministry of Munitions have been described as the 'most conspicuous single triumph by any politician throughout the War'.[22] Indeed, it can be argued that Lloyd George laid the basis for victory in the Second World War, when policies on rationing, manpower and munitions were rapidly adopted, and when Churchill ensured that defence strategy was firmly under political rather than military control. Lloyd George also saw the war as a great opportunity to effect social change, speed up the process of domestic welfare and promote democratic advance.

Finally, Lloyd George had many redeeming characteristics: he had charm, a lively sense of humour, rarely bore a grudge and was always approachable. He was one of the few politicians, it was said, who did not change when he reached high office; he despised pomposity. He was undoubtedly one of the finest political orators of the twentieth century, and also the master of debate in the House of Commons.

After Lloyd George's fall from power in 1922, and certainly after his death in 1945, historians and commentators were highly critical: he became a convenient 'whipping boy for all the ills from which Britain in the inter-war period was ailing'.[23] His reputation has undoubtedly been salvaged by historians such as Kenneth Murray, John Grigg, Chris Wrigley and Michael Fry. However, they are still able to add a considerable weight of evidence to the debit column of Lloyd George's career.

First, Lloyd George has been accused of hastening, and by some historians of causing, the demise of the Liberal Party. With the benefit of hindsight, the wisest policy of Lloyd George, and certainly the party, in 1918 would have been to dismantle the Coalition and attempt to reunite the party, fighting the general election on a clear platform of international and domestic reconstruction. In 1922, Asquith was probably more culpable in defeat than Lloyd George, and in 1923 the party lacked a realistic manifesto to appeal to its traditional voters. By 1924, the horse had bolted. The decline of the Liberal Party had many deep-seated socio-economic causes, ranging from the decline of Nonconformity to the weakening of rural communities and agrarian radicalism. Indeed, it can be argued that, in the period before 1916, Lloyd George rescued Liberalism from 'the show suffocation that awaits a political party which has outlived its mission'.[24]

Second, and closely allied to the first criticism, is the claim that Lloyd George actively sought to push Asquith out of office in 1916 for reasons of personal ambition, and that this trait also dominated his actions in the period 1922–24. Bradley Gilbert maintains that Lloyd George's ascent to the Premiership was as much a story of Asquith's decline in vigour and leadership as it was the thrust of Lloyd George's ambition. Martin Pugh argues that Lloyd George did not actively promote the fall of Asquith, merely that he wished to ensure that he was in a favourable position when the fall occurred.[25] Early in his career, Lloyd George had written to his wife warning her of his 'juggernaut of ambition', but this is hardly an unusual characteristic for a politician.

Third, Lloyd George is accused of inconsistency in his views and a failure to remain loyal to Liberalism. As Lord Beaverbrook commented, Lloyd George always wanted the driver's seat, and he did not care too much in which direction the vehicle was heading.[26] Lloyd George was a pragmatic politician who was prepared to dilute his ideological purity to achieve his goals, whether of social reform, winning the war or securing peace. Perhaps he was not a true Liberal in that he was never committed, for example, to defending the freedom of the individual or constitutional reform, but he did not waver greatly over the issues of free trade, social reform or Imperialism. J. M. Keynes' comment that Lloyd George was 'rooted in nothing' is easier to refute when one remembers that Lloyd George's career spanned sixteen years as a backbencher, followed by seventeen years in office, followed by twenty-two years in Opposition. Inconsistencies are inevitable in a career of this length, especially one which has been picked over by historians in such detail.

Finally, there has always been the lurking suspicion that Lloyd George did not quite play the game by the rules; John Campbell has observed that 'his rivals regarded him in rather the same way that amateur cricketers used to regard their professional colleagues. In the sporting sense, as in the social, Lloyd George was not a gentleman'.[27] If the word 'sleaze' had been in the political lexicon in the early part of the twentieth century, it would have stuck to Lloyd George like glue. Today's press would have destroyed Lloyd George. The whiff of financial and social scandal was never far from him after the Marconi affair and the start of his relationship with Frances Stevenson. He was never to leave this fully behind.

Lloyd George's legacy surrounds us today: in Britain we can point to old-age pensions, national insurance for sickness and unemployment, and the taxation system. His legacy abroad is evident still in Russia, Ireland, Palestine and the Middle East. Lloyd George never wanted power for power's sake; he wanted to find solutions to the problems of society and the international order. Above all, he wanted to make a difference, and in this he undoubtedly succeeded.

Chronology

1863	born January, in Manchester
1864	death of father. Moves to Llanystumdwy
1878	articled clerk in Porthmadog
1884	begins to practise as a solicitor
1888	marries Margaret Owen
1889	elected Alderman, Caernarfonshire County Council
1890	wins Caernarfon Boroughs by-election
1896	fails to unite Welsh Liberal Party
1899	Boer War. Begins opposition to the war
1900	'khaki' election. Conservative government
1902	begins campaign against Education Act
1905	appointed President of the Board of Trade in new Liberal government
1906	Liberals win general election
1907	daughter, Mair, dies
1909	People's Budget which is later rejected by House of Lords
1911	Parliament Act. National Insurance Act
1912	Marconi scandal
1913	launches Land Campaign
1914	supports British declaration of war
1915	Minister of Munitions in Coalition Government
1916	Secretary of State for War, later Prime Minister of Coalition Government
1918	'coupon' election. Coalition Government continues: Education Act. Representation of the People Act
1919	Paris Peace Conference. Housing Act
1920	Unemployment Insurance Act
1921	Irish treaty
1922	National Liberal Party formed. Chanak crisis. Carlton Club Meeting. Lloyd George resigns. General election, Conservative government formed
1923	united Liberals lose general election

1924	Labour minority government. General election, Conservative government formed
1926	becomes leader of the Liberal Party in succession to Asquith
1931	National Government formed
1940	denounces Neville Chamberlain in Norwegian Campaign debate
1941	death of Margaret
1943	marries Frances Stevenson
1944	moves to Llanystumdwy
1945	accepts title of Earl Lloyd George of Dwyfor. Dies 26 March and is buried in Llanystumdwy

Notes

1 See, for example F. Owen, *Tempestuous Journey* (London, Hutchinson, 1954).
2 G. I. T. Machin, 'Lloyd George and Nonconformity', in J. Loades (ed.) *The Life and Times of David Lloyd George* (Bangor, Headstart History, 1991), pp. 33–47.
3 Machin, *Life and Times of Lloyd George*, p. 35.
4 J. Grigg, *Lloyd George and Wales* (Aberystwyth, The National Library of Wales, 1988), p. 2.
5 K. O. Morgan, 'Lloyd George and Welsh Liberalism', *The Life and Times of Lloyd George*, p. 4.
6 C. Wrigley, *Lloyd George* (Oxford, Blackwell, 1992), p. 34.
7 B. B. Gilbert, *David Lloyd George, the Architect of Change, 1863–1912* (London, Batsford, 1987), p. 284.
8 Machin, *Life and Times of Lloyd George*, p. 45.
9 M. Pugh, *Lloyd George* (London, Longman, 1988), p. 32.
10 S. Constantine, *Lloyd George* (London, Routledge, 1992), p. 36.
11 P. Rowland, *Lloyd George* (London, Barrie and Jenkins, 1975) p. 216.
12 Constantine, *Lloyd George*, p. 42.
13 F. W. Wiemann, 'Lloyd George and the struggle for the Navy estimates of 1914', in A. J. P. Taylor (ed.), *Lloyd George: Twelve Essays* (London, Hamish Hamilton, 1971), pp. 71–91.
14 Pugh, *Lloyd George*, p. 79.
15 A. J. P. Taylor (ed.), *Lloyd George: A Diary by Frances Stevenson* (London, Hutchinson, 1971), p. 128.
16 T. Wilson, *The Myriad Faces of War* (Cambridge, Polity Press, 1986), p. 436.
17 Pugh, *Lloyd George*, p. 128.
18 Wrigley, *Lloyd George*, p. 96.
19 This phrase was first used by Lloyd George in a speech at Wolverhampton, 23 November 1918. Quoted in Constantine, *Lloyd George*, p. 100.
20 Wrigley, *Lloyd George*, p. 113.
21 J. M. Keynes, *Essays in Biography* (London, Macmillan, 1933), pp. 36–7.
22 Pugh, *Lloyd George*, p. 87.
23 K. O. Morgan. *Lloyd George* (London, Weidenfeld and Nicolson, 1974), p. 17.
24 B. B. Gilbert. *Lloyd George, the Organizer of Victory, 1912–16* (London, Batsford, 1992), p. 17.
25 Wrigley, *Lloyd George*, p. 80.

26 K. O. Morgan, *David Lloyd George 1863–1945* (Cardiff, University of Wales Press, 1981) p. 83.
27 J. Campbell, *Lloyd George: The Goat in the Wilderness 1922–31* (London, Jonathan Cape, 1977), p. 6.

Further reading

Historians do not have difficulty in finding either primary or secondary material on Lloyd George. The best concise biographies are by M. Pugh, *Lloyd George* (London, Longman, 1988); S. Constantine, *Lloyd George* (London, Routledge, 1992); C. Wrigley, *Lloyd George* (Oxford, Blackwell, 1992); and K. O. Morgan, *Lloyd George* (London, Weidenfeld and Nicolson, 1974).

J. Grigg's multi-volume work is readable and penetrating: *The Young Lloyd George* (London, Eyre Methuen, 1973); *Lloyd George: The People's Champion, 1902–11* (London, Methuen, 1978); and *Lloyd George: From Peace to War, 1912–16* (London, Methuen, 1985). B. Gilbert has completed two volumes of a political biography, which is highly detailed but lacks the sparkle of Grigg's work: *David Lloyd George, the Architect of Change, 1863–1912* (London, Batsford, 1987); and *David Lloyd George, the Organizer of Victory, 1912–16* (London, Batsford, 1992).

Much useful information and background material can be found in various collections of letters and diaries: A. J. P. Taylor (ed.), *Lloyd George, a Diary by Frances Stevenson* (London, Hutchinson, 1971); C. Cross (ed.), *Life with Lloyd George, the Diary of A. J. Sylvester, 1931–45* (London, Macmillan, 1975); and A. J. P. Taylor (ed.) *My Darling Pussy: The Letters of Lloyd George and Frances Stevenson* (London, Hutchinson, 1971).

Two collections of essays concentrate on important single issues: A. J. P. Taylor (ed.), *Lloyd George: Twelve Essays* (London, Hamish Hamilton, 1971) and, more recently, J. Loades (ed.), *The Life and Times of David Lloyd George* (Bangor, Headstart History, 1991). An outstanding single-volume general work on the war years is T. Wilson, *The Myriad Faces of War* (Cambridge, Polity Press, 1986).

James Ramsay MacDonald

Robert Garner

James Ramsay MacDonald's political career spanned over four decades, from his arrival in London in the late 1880s until his resignation from the Cabinet in 1937. The importance of his role in the emergence and evolution of the Labour Party cannot be exaggerated and, since Labour itself became in this period one of the two main parties, MacDonald, as leader of the party and then Prime Minister, had a profound influence upon the direction of the country itself. Yet MacDonald's career is also marked by controversy and tragedy. His name, for many, is synonymous with betrayal. Thus his adoption of a moderate parliamentary reformism was seen as an obstacle to genuine Socialist advance which was, it is alleged, a real possibility between 1918 and 1931. Linked to this ideological and strategic critique is a personal attack. Here, it is often claimed, is the classic example of a working-class leader beginning his political life as an anti-war Socialist, but being deradicalised by the trappings of office and the eager courting of the Establishment. This chapter will consider MacDonald's life and career in order to throw some light on this controversy. It will be suggested that the 'betrayal' thesis represents at best exaggeration and at worst a fundamental misunderstanding of MacDonald himself and also the political environment within which he had to operate.

Background

James Ramsay MacDonald was born on 12 October 1866 in Lossiemouth, a small port in the north-east of Scotland. He is the only Prime Minister to have been born illegitimately and, as the son of a manual worker and a domestic servant, he also had, with the possible exception of John Major, the lowest social origins of any person who has occupied the highest governmental position. MacDonald spent the first nineteen years of his life in his native Scotland and, while politically active, he did not become a Socialist until moving to Bristol in 1885. A few months later, in the early part of the following year, he moved to London where he joined the Fabian Society. MacDonald's first employment of a political nature did not occur until 1888 when he was taken on as a Private Secretary by the Liberal and Radical politician, Thomas Lough.[1]

Apprenticeship

MacDonald and the emergence of the Labour Party, 1866–1906
Like many others who were later to gravitate towards independent Labour politics, MacDonald immersed himself in late nineteenth-century progressivism which sought to formulate a new left-wing Liberalism more sympathetic to the representation of the working man. Initially, MacDonald, again like many of his Socialist contemporaries, was unconvinced that the achievement of Socialism was dependent upon the creation of a separate Labour Party. His confidence in the Liberal Party was shaken, however, by the unwillingness of the local Liberal Association in Southampton to adopt him as a parliamentary candidate in 1892, and a similar attitude towards another potential working-class candidate in the Attercliffe district of Sheffield.[2] As a consequence, in 1894 MacDonald joined the Independent Labour Party (ILP), a Socialist society which had been created a year earlier in Bradford. Very quickly, MacDonald, along with Philip Snowden and Keir Hardie, became a leading member of the ILP and he unsuccessfully fought Southampton in 1895 as an ILP candidate. In the meantime, MacDonald's personal life was taking shape. In 1896 he married fellow Socialist, Margaret Gladstone, and between 1898 and 1910 they had six children.

MacDonald's experience of local Liberal hostility to organised labour was far from unique. Indeed, by the end of the nineteenth century, many trade unions were convinced of the need for separate independent labour representation and, with this end in mind, representatives from some unions and the Socialist societies (the Fabians, the ILP and the Social Democratic Federation) met, at the end of February 1900, to create the Labour Representation Committee (LRC). MacDonald became the first Secretary, and for some time the LRC's headquarters were at his first-floor flat at 3 Lincoln's Inn Fields. Here, MacDonald and his assistant, James Middleton, worked together on desks situated alongside the beds of the MacDonald's two eldest children, Alastair and Malcolm. At the 1900 election, the LRC endorsed fifteen candidates and two of these – Richard Bell at Derby and Keir Hardie at Merthyr – were elected. MacDonald stood in Leicester but was defeated in a two-member constituency where the Liberals won both seats.

The next five years saw the continuing growth of the LRC as more unions joined, not least because of their growing recognition that the Liberals were unable and unwilling to support political redress, a need that was intensified after the House of Lords' Taff Vale judgement in 1901 which threatened union funds during strike action. The Liberals, in turn, felt threatened by the LRC and they sought an electoral pact, which was agreed to after discussions between MacDonald and the Liberal Chief-Whip, Herbert Gladstone in 1903. This agreement gave some LRC candidates a free run against Conservatives, and in the 1906 election the LRC's growing strength was confirmed when the party won thirty of the fifty seats fought. This time MacDonald was returned in Leicester, and at the age of thirty-nine he arrived at Westminster where he was elected Secretary of the newly renamed Labour Party.

MacDonald and the evolution of the Labour Party, 1906–22
MacDonald realised that if Labour was going to be transformed into an effective political party, rather than a mere parliamentary pressure group for the trade unions, it would need a wider set of principles upon which to base a coherent policy programme. This set of principles was established by MacDonald in a series of books written between 1906 and the early 1920s.[3] It is instructive to examine the ideas MacDonald puts forward in these, since they not only provide a guide to his own political actions as leader of the party but also represent the dominant ideological strand within the Labour Party during its formative years.

For Barker, MacDonald's books 'represent a coherent, systematic and sustained attempt to formulate a theory of Socialism that would work in England'.[4] Despite this assessment, it should be said that MacDonald's political writings were not particularly sophisticated or original, deriving in large part from the work of such luminaries as Sidney Webb, the major exponent of Fabian Socialism, and R. H. Tawney.[5] Nevertheless, MacDonald did more than anyone else to popularise a set of basic principles which may be described as Labour Socialism.

This ideology had four major elements. In the first place, MacDonald expressed an unyielding faith in the utility of parliamentary action. This stress on parliament as the only viable and acceptable vehicle of change derived its importance from two additional articles of faith, namely the autonomy of the state and a denial of the class struggle. Thus, for MacDonald: 'Socialism marks the growth of society, not the uprising of a class. The consciousness which it seeks to quicken is not one of economic class solidarity, but one of ... growth towards organic wholeness'.[6]

His commitment to constitutional procedures itself determined that change must be gradual. In addition, MacDonald's acceptance of Darwinian biology led him to develop a (not too original) theory of social evolution whereby higher forms of life slowly emerge out of lower forms. Socialism, then, was no less inevitable than any strict deterministic Marxist account. Socialism was, he wrote, 'the stage which follows liberalism, retains everything of value in liberalism by virtue of its being the hereditary heir of liberalism'.[7]

A characteristic element of MacDonald's thought, and, indeed, of British Socialism in general, was its ethical strand.[8] Thus he denounced capitalism for its competitive, materialistic and self-seeking nature which, it was argued, should be replaced by the Socialist values of mutual aid, co-operation and public service. A Socialism which was a frame of mind rather than a fixed creed was unlikely to have much idea of the detailed programme of change which would be necessary for Socialists working through a parliamentary system. Not surprisingly, this was the case. What practical proposals MacDonald did advocate centred around the simplistic notion of public ownership replacing private ownership. It was not until the 1930s that Labour developed, through the public corporation model, a more precise set of plans detailing how this transformation was to occur.

The brand of Socialism which MacDonald helped to shape and promote can be contrasted with three other currents of thought prominent within the Labour Party at the time. In the first place, Labour Socialism was clearly opposed to the Marxist emphasis on extra-parliamentary action and the reality of the class struggle. Less obviously, it was also at odds with the labourist ideology of trade unions and the more radical brand of Socialism characteristic of the ILP in the 1920s. In the former case, traditional trade unionism was based on working-class self-identification and the desire for limited benefits in terms of, for example, higher wages, better working conditions and the maintenance of trade union rights. This labourist ideology was clearly contrary to Labour Socialism's emphasis on governing in the interests of all members of the community and in its vision of a new social order based upon collective ownership and the creation of a new ethic governing the relationship between members of society.[9] In the latter case, the James Maxton brand of Socialism which characterised the ILP in the 1920s sought rapid strides towards the achievement of Socialism, a strategy which was contrary to Labour Socialism's assertion that a Socialist party could only go as far as public opinion would allow, even if this meant that the achievement of the Socialist commonwealth was to be an extremely slow and gradual process.

Up until 1914, Labour's progress was frustratingly slow. The party was able to persuade the Liberal government to introduce the Trade Disputes Act in 1906 which nullified the Taff Vale judgement, but little else was achieved. The Parliamentary Labour Party (PLP) was small, had little finance and was very inexperienced. Even after the 1910 elections, with the minority Liberal government now dependent upon the support of Irish and Labour members, Labour was not able to take advantage because the last thing it wanted was another election. This was partly because the Osborne Judgement of 1909 severely affected the party's ability to raise election finance and partly because a Liberal government was preferable to a Conservative one.

For MacDonald, this was a period of highs and painful lows. After the second election in 1910, he was elected unopposed as leader of the PLP. At the age of forty-four he had become the leader of a significant parliamentary party. During this period, however, his private world fell apart. In the space of barely more than a week in 1910, his youngest son and his mother died. Worse was to follow in 1911, when his wife died suddenly of blood poisoning. It is clear that MacDonald never really recovered from his wife's death.[10] It was, as one of his biographers has said, 'with a numbed inner self that he led the Labour Party'.[11]

Edwardian politics was to come to a grinding halt with the First World War. It also represented a turning point for MacDonald and his party. Initially, the PLP had strong reservations about supporting British intervention. As public opinion became increasingly jingoistic and Germany's aggression became more intense, however, a shift occurred and on 5 August 1914 the PLP decided, by a majority, that it would support the war. MacDonald immediately resigned as leader and was replaced by Arthur Henderson. MacDonald's decision to resign and oppose the war was consistent with his oft-stated anti-Imperialism, his hostility to the Russian autocracy and his support of German social democracy. His were not pacifist objections, however, and he was inclined to ignore the war rather than actively oppose it, although he did participate in the Union of Democratic Control, an organisation set up to campaign for a democratic foreign policy.

That Labour did not split was due partly to the fact that very few senior Labour figures inside and outside parliament opposed the war and partly due to Henderson's reluctance to force the issue and purge the anti-war elements. Unity was secured by the creation, on the outbreak of war, of the so-called War Emergency Workers National Committee, a committee of trade union and Socialist organisations designed to defend the immediate interests of the working class during the crisis and later to play an important role in the development of Labour's strategy for the reconstruction of post-war Britain.[12] MacDonald's participation in this organisation kept him at the centre of Labour politics.

Not surprisingly, MacDonald was overwhelmingly rejected by Leicester voters at the 1918 election. In a 'khaki' election, with Lloyd George promising to make Germany pay 'until the pips squeak' and to build a 'land fit for heroes', MacDonald's anti-war stance was a fatal handicap. Indeed, he was the target for a great deal of personal abuse at this time, the press discovering, and making considerable capital out of, MacDonald's illegitimacy.[13] With the continuation of the wartime Coalition, Labour candidates in general were faced with a united opposition (of Conservatives and Lloyd George Liberals) and returned only fifty-seven candidates. As well as MacDonald, other pre-war leaders such as Henderson and Philip Snowden were also defeated. In retrospect, of course, the real significance of the election was the underlying strength of the Labour vote and the severe divisions within the

Liberal Party. Benefiting, for the first time, from the newly enfranchised working-class voters the party secured over 2 million votes, compared with barely 500,000 in 1910. The Asquithian Liberals fought separately from the Coalition candidates and returned only twenty-eight seats.

Equally important was that Labour during the war was able to occupy the enviable role of exercising power without responsibility. Thus Labour MPs occupied ministerial positions and trade union co-operation for the war effort was essential, but it was the Liberals, under Asquith and then Lloyd George, who had central responsibility for the organisation of the war effort. This created enormous personal and ideological problems for the Liberal Party. A key development was Arthur Henderson's resignation from Lloyd George's Coalition in August 1917 which gave him the time to set about transforming Labour's organisation. As a result, by 1918 the Labour Party had a new Constitution, allowing individual membership in newly created constituency parties, and a statement of aims (*Labour and the New Social Order*)[14] written by Sidney Webb and based upon the ideas popularised by MacDonald. By contrast, the Liberals were divided, demoralised and lacking a coherent purpose.[15] In this context, MacDonald was content to bide his time.

Limelight

To Downing Street and back, 1922–29
Most of Labour's parliamentarians elected in 1918 were inexperienced, politically untalented trade unionists. They were led first by the Scottish miner, William Adamson and then by J. R. Clynes, another man with deep trade union roots. It was no surprise, therefore, when upon his return to the Commons as the member for Aberavon in 1922, MacDonald successfully challenged Clynes for the leadership. As David Howell points out, for the next nine years MacDonald 'exercised an awesome domination over his party'.[16] In the 1922 election, Labour almost tripled its number of seats from 57 to 142 and, for the first time, looked like a potential party of government. By contrast, the Liberals were still divided (Lloyd George fighting the election as leader of the National Liberal Party). Consequently, as the second largest party in the Commons, Labour became the official Opposition.

After securing the leadership, MacDonald's aim was to ensure that Labour presented itself immediately as an alternative government. He had been critical of the limitations of the trade union-dominated parliamentary leadership between 1918 and 1922, and he was equally hostile to the raucous behaviour of some of the left-wing Clydeside MPs, seeing their obstructionist behaviour as both futile and inimical to the task of building Labour as a party fit to govern. 'A party with the reputation of an old London vestry,' he wrote, 'will never be allowed to form a Government in this country.'[17]

This apparent pragmatism did not mean the absence of ideology. That the parliamentary Labour Party was concerned with using power as a means to further the party's ideological ends came out clearly in a Commons debate in 1923 on the 'Failure of the Capitalist System'. The debate, on a private member's motion, reflected how widely Labour Socialism had been accepted within the parliamentary party. A succession of Labour speakers sought to defend the motion, which included the key passage that 'legislative effort should be directed to the gradual supplanting of the capitalist system by an industrial and social order based on public ownership and democratic control of the instruments of production and distribution', against opponents who sought to extol the virtues of capitalism. MacDonald was clear in his own mind about the significance of the debate. That it had taken place, he argued: 'May mark progress and announce to the world that there is a body of men in the British House of Commons who believe in Socialism and are ready to challenge opponents upon it'.[18]

A further illustration of the importance of Labour Socialism as a guide to the activities of the party during this period was the Communist issue. Numerous times during the 1920s the newly formed Communist Party of Great Britain sought affiliation with Labour. Time after time it was turned down, by successive party conferences, on the grounds that Communism was ideologically inconsistent with Labour Party membership. Not only this. Many individual members of the Communist Party were also Labour members. Gradually, they were weeded out on the grounds that one could not be members of two such diametrically opposed parties.

Labour entered government for the first time in 1924 after an election in which they increased their share of the seats to 191 and their share of the vote to 4.4 million (30.5 per cent). The newly united Liberal Party was only able to pick up 159 seats, thus confirming Labour as the second largest party in a parliament where no one party had an overall majority. MacDonald's commitment to parliamentary politics seemed justified. As he wrote in his diary: 'At noon there was a Privy Council at Buck. Pal.; the seals were handed to us – and there we were Ministers of State. At 4 we held our first Cabinet. A wonderful country'.[19] MacDonald was equally impressed with the attitude of the Monarch to the arrival to high political office of the illegitimate son of a domestic servant. Royalty, he wrote, had been 'considerate, cordially correct, human and friendly'.[20]

Dependent upon the Liberals for support in the Commons, it was clear from the outset that the new Prime Minister had limited aims. Since he had doubts about the government's long-term survival prospects, MacDonald was determined that Labour should use this opportunity to demonstrate that the party was fit to govern. The strategy of respectability was clearly behind the composition of MacDonald's first Cabinet, which contained four ex-Liberals and two life-long Conservatives. In policy terms, to describe the first Labour government as a Socialist administration is to pay scant regard to the facts.[21] Nationalisation, the long-standing means by which a Socialist society was to be created, was promised for the mines and the railways but the government failed to achieve either. Indeed, it did not attempt to achieve these objectives, although support was given for a private member's bill seeking to nationalise the mines. In its defence there is no doubt that, had the government introduced nationalisation bills, it would have been defeated.

Two other aspects of the first Labour government's record need to be noted. The first is the Budget introduced by the Chancellor of the Exchequer, Philip Snowden. This was a typical exercise in Liberal finance. Direct taxes were cut by £14.5 million and indirect taxes by £29 million. One should not, however, equate this with reneging on Socialist policy since, in an era where deficit financing was frowned upon even by Socialists, such financial prudence was not seen as inconsistent with social reform.

The second aspect of policy worth commenting upon is the Labour government's attitude towards industrial disputes.[22] The trade unions, not surprisingly, expected the government to show a certain amount of favouritism towards the organised working class. That this was not to be could have been predicted given that the government was led by a man who did not regard this as the function of a Labour administration. The conflict came to a head in February 1924 when the dockers came out on strike after a pay demand was rejected by the port employers. The government refused to take sides in the dispute, only insisting upon ensuring that essential supplies would be maintained. To this end, MacDonald was even prepared to consider using the Emergency Powers Act, although this did not prove necessary as the strike was settled. A similar pattern of events occurred during a London transport strike in March, which again was settled before the government could intervene. The consequence was that the traditional labourist practices of trade unions had isolated the Labour government from the institutions of the organised working class. This was inevitable given the Labour Socialist ideology which placed considerable stress on the need for a Labour government to govern in the national interest. This conflict was to emerge again during the General Strike of 1926.

Not surprisingly, the first Labour government did not survive the year. Defeated on a vote of confidence, MacDonald settled for another spell in Opposition confident that his limited ambitions had been met. This was confirmed by Labour's defeat in the subsequent general election and the arrival of Stanley Baldwin in Downing Street. The period between 1924 and 1929 consolidated MacDonald's position as leader and further enshrined Labour Socialism as the party's official ideology. MacDonald faced two challenges, one from the Left of his own party and one from the trade unions. In the former case, the ILP, now led by the fiery Clydeside MP James Maxton, was disturbed by what it perceived as the minimum progress made by the Labour government and therefore sought a future Labour administration to move swiftly to the achievement of Socialist objectives. To this end, the ILP campaigned on the 'Socialism in Our Time' platform. With the help of the trade union block vote, MacDonald ensured this was defeated at successive party conferences in the late 1920s.[23] As an alternative, at the 1928 Conference, the party adopted *Labour and the Nation*,[24] a programme largely written by Tawney which confirmed Labour's ultimate Socialist goal but also, as with *Labour and the New Social Order*, reaffirmed the gradualism by which this would be achieved.

The General Strike of 1926 further illustrated the gap between the labourism of the trade unions and Labour Socialism. MacDonald was generally uneasy about the industrial ferment and he and his colleagues gave only guarded support to the objectives of the unions. As he wrote after the strike was over: 'I thought the decision to have a general strike was wrong and that the best thing to do was to cry it off without delay'.[25] In the run-up to the 1929 election, the conflict between Labourism and Labour Socialism had declined. With high unemployment and legislative restrictions, the industrial muscle of the labour movement had been severely weakened and political redress was the only option left. As a result, MacDonald was able to demand loyalty in return for the election of a Labour government. Those who thought this would improve the prospects of organised labour were to be severely disappointed.

Downing Street and beyond, 1929–37
Labour was returned to office in June 1929, again without an overall majority, although this time the party was the largest in the Commons. What happened during the subsequent two years has been documented in detail by a number of historians.[26] It was dominated by two related issues. First, the government was overwhelmed by an economic crisis and, second, as a result of this, it ended in disarray as MacDonald, in 1931, agreed to form a National Government, splitting the Cabinet in the process.

As in 1924, MacDonald's government failed to fulfil, despite *Labour and the Nation* and the manifesto, its Socialist promise. No nationalisation schemes were attempted or apparently even considered. Moreover, the Trade Disputes and Trade Union Act, passed in 1927 by the Conservative government in the aftermath of the General Strike, was not repealed. It was clear from the outset that unemployment was the biggest problem facing the Labour government. Indeed, the 1929 election had been largely fought on the issue, the electorate overwhelmingly rejecting Lloyd George's ambitious schemes to get people back to work. About 1.5 million people were registered as unemployed when Labour took office and the numbers gradually increased, to 2 million in July 1930, 2.5 million in December and 2.7 million by June 1931.

MacDonald set up an Unemployment Committee upon returning to Downing Street but, despite suggesting a number of public works schemes, little was achieved because the committee had no executive authority and it continually came up against the financial orthodoxy of Snowden. Realising its failure, MacDonald abandoned it, early in 1930, in favour of an Economic Advisory Council which met monthly under his Chairmanship. Despite the membership of economic radicals such as G. D. H. Cole and John Maynard Keynes, and the range of ideas available, such as the underconsumptionist analysis enshrined in the ILP's Living Wage proposals, the government stuck to its orthodox economic policy. Snowden was fiercely opposed to any radical experiments and MacDonald lacked both the intellectual ability and the strength of character to change Snowden's mind or remove him from the Treasury. This victory for the orthodoxy was confirmed when the memorandum circulated by the maverick Labour MP Oswald Mosley in 1930, advocating massive government intervention in the economy to deal with the problems, was rejected by the Cabinet, the parliamentary Labour Party and the Labour Conference.

There was now little viable challenge to the view that deflation was the answer to Britain's economic problems. The government appointed a Committee on National Expenditure presided over by Sir George May to recommend economies in government spending. When it reported, in August 1931, its pessimistic predictions of future government deficits precipitated a financial crisis. In order to forestall a run on the pound, the Bank of England urged the government to restore foreign confidence by balancing the budget. On 23 August, MacDonald appealed to the Cabinet to accept economies of £78 million, which included a 10 per cent cut in unemployment benefit. The Cabinet was split, eleven in favour, including MacDonald, Snowden, Webb and Herbert Morrison, and nine against, including Henderson, Addison and Clynes. As a consequence, MacDonald asked his colleagues for their resignations, and went to Buckingham Palace to inform the King. The following day, much to the shock and anger of his colleagues and the party in the country, MacDonald announced to the Cabinet that he had accepted the Monarch's offer to become Prime Minister of a National Government. He attempted to persuade some of his colleagues to agree to serve in the new administration but, with the exception of three (Thomas, Sankey and Snowden) they refused.

The party was in a deep state of shock. James Middleton wrote to MacDonald that he witnessed his stand 'with the awe the heroic is bound to command, mingled with almost the deepest sadness I have ever known'.[27] For others in the party any sadness experienced was quickly replaced by anger and bitterness. This was reinforced when MacDonald called a snap election and fought a campaign against his former colleagues. In the subsequent general election, Labour's parliamentary representation was reduced to a paltry fifty-two (although this disguises the fact that the party's share of the vote fell much less, from 37.1 per cent in 1929 to almost 31 per cent in 1931) and the party was not to regain power until the landslide victory of 1945.

Even though MacDonald remained in power, the long-term consequences for him were severe. His National Government became in all but name a Conservative administration. The immediate economic crisis was relieved as the pound was removed from the Gold Standard and protectionist measures introduced. However, with no party of his own, having been expelled from the Labour Party, MacDonald had committed political suicide. He continued as Prime Minsiter until 1935, when Baldwin replaced him. At the insistence of the King, MacDonald stayed on in the Cabinet as Lord President of the Council and he remained in this post despite losing his seat at Seaham in the 1935 election, returning as the MP for the Scottish Universities the following year.

MacDonald resigned from the government on 28 May 1937, the same day as Baldwin. By now in his seventy-first year, he was mentally and physically exhausted, although his faculties had begun to decline in the early 1930s. On his way to South America for an extended holiday with his daughter Sheila, MacDonald collapsed. On 9 November 1937, on board the ship taking them there, he died, a lonely man bitterly detested by the party he had done so much to build.

Legacy

For a generation after 1931 Ramsay MacDonald was a hate figure within the labour movement in Britain, and outside of it he was regarded more with pity than respect. The legacy of betrayal continues to this day. In assessing MacDonald's career in general, and the accusation of betrayal in particular, it is necessary to ask two related but distinct questions. In the first place, how far was MacDonald's behaviour throughout his political career consistent? It is necessary to ask this because many of the attacks on him have been of a personal nature. He was, it is argued, the victim of the 'aristocratic embrace', a man seduced by the Establishment to the extent that his radical convictions were softened.[28] As one German Socialist observed, the Labour leadership seemed, 'so dazzled by the glamour of society, so fascinated by the luxurious atmosphere of "swell" dinners and the fragrance of real Corona-Coronas that without either wishing or knowing it they became conservative to the marrow of their bones.'[29]

The second, and more fundamental question, is to ask how far the ideology and strategy MacDonald exemplified damaged the Labour Party and its Socialist project. This is distinct from the first question because we can accept that MacDonald did behave consistently, but also argue that his political project had negative consequences. In this context, it has been argued by left-wing historians such as Miliband and Coates that the moderate reformism adopted by Labour's leadership and its particular failure to support and advance working-class discontent had the effect of integrating the working class within the existing social order, thereby managing discontent and keeping it within safe bounds.[30]

In answer to the first question, there is no doubt that MacDonald, and other members of the Labour leadership, were aloof from the Labour movement and did conform to the age-old traditions of the British Establishment.

MacDonald's fondness for court dress and aristocratic society is well known. Nevertheless, it would be wrong to suggest that his experience of high political office de-radicalised him. While his objectives may have been radical, the means by which these were to be achieved – the gradual creation of a societal consensus for Socialism through exclusively parliamentary means – were already moderate and anyone reading his earlier published work would quickly realise this.

In the case of the first Labour government, for instance, MacDonald's insistence upon caution and respectability and his reluctance to give support to trade union disputes were quite consistent with the Labour Socialism he had helped to shape. This ideology, as we saw, went beyond the labourism of the trade unions, and if the party was to achieve its ends gradually through parliamentary means it had to attract the broadest measure of support in the country and, in addition, come to terms with the parliamentary machinery. These same considerations were evident in 1929. As a minority government, there was no mandate to carry out a radical Socialist programme and the effect of doing so would have been defeat in the Commons and probably at any subsequent general election.

Of course, MacDonald's widespread notoriety within the labour movement derives from his decision to enter into a Coalition Government rather than from his government's economic failures. None other than Clement Attlee could comment, for instance, that MacDonald's decision was 'the greatest betrayal in the political history of this country'.[31] In assessing MacDonald's actions in those fateful days, it should be noted first that it was not so much his decision to form a National Government which produced widespread condemnation but the way in which it was made, without consultation with his colleagues in the Cabinet and parliament and the party in the country. Had he consulted widely, it is just possible that he might have got his party's backing. As it was (although MacDonald himself did not see it in these terms), his desertion breached the underlying ethos of loyalty central to the British labour movement and for this he could not be forgiven.[32] On the other hand, had he battled on as Labour leader it is probable that his reputation would have been largely maintained. For MacDonald, however, this option was equally unacceptable because he would then have been forced to attack the very economy measures which he thought were in the national interest.

MacDonald paid a heavy price for the decision he made and, in retrospect, it was probably a price not worth paying. To have behaved differently, though, would have betrayed his whole approach to politics. It is true to say that he was flattered by the King's appeal. But couched as it was in terms of duty and the national interest, this appeal also coincided with MacDonald's own long-standing political beliefs and, although politically inept perhaps, the decision was nonetheless consistent. There is little evidence to suggest that MacDonald planned in advance to form a National Government, but he was certainly not averse to thinking along those lines. Crucially, such an idea was quite consistent with his long-standing rejection of class politics, and it was the prospect of serving the national interest that, above all, persuaded MacDonald to stay on. As he said during his broadcast to the nation on the crisis on 25 August 1931

> I have given my life to the building up of a political party. I was present at its birth; I was its nurse when it emerged from its infancy, and when it attained to adult years. At this moment I have changed none of my beliefs and none of my ideals ... My credentials are those of national duty as I conceive it and I obey them irrespective of consequences.[33]

The second question, relating to the viability of MacDonald's political project, is more difficult to answer, particularly in the limited space available here. It is appropriate to concentrate on three themes: the economic crisis of the 1929–31 Labour government; the relationship between the Labour leadership and the labour movement as a whole; and, finally, the relationship between the Labour leadership and the wider electorate.

For the Left, then and since, the second Labour government's failure represented the final proof of Labour Socialism's poverty. At the very least, a Labour government should have moved much more quickly in a Socialist direction, nationalising the commanding heights of the economy and protecting the working class against the economic blizzard. Some, in the early 1930s, even concluded that there was no realistic parliamentary route to significant social change.[34] In reality, the real tragedy of the second Labour government was not MacDonald's ultimate and fateful decision to form a National Government nor his government's moderation. Rather, it was the complete absence of a viable economic policy to deal with the here and now. For this, MacDonald was not exclusively to blame, since this was a general weakness of Labour Socialist ideology for which the party paid dear.

Labour Socialism was rooted in an ethical critique of the injustices of capitalism and a desire for a new form of society based around vague concepts such as fellowship and co-operation. Little thought had gone into the way in which the transition was going to be effected. More significantly, even less thought had gone into how a Labour government was going to manage capitalism.[35] If MacDonald was at fault it was his failure to take on board some of the proposals suggested by Mosley, J. A. Hobson and others – or at least persuade Snowden to consider them as alternatives to orthodox financial policy. But this was not MacDonald's failure alone. Rather, it was the failure of a whole political tradition. After 1945, armed with the fully worked out Keynesian model of demand management, Labour and Conservative governments would not make the same mistakes.

For left-wing historians, MacDonald's political strategy was flawed, above all, by its failure to support and mobilise its working-class constituency outside of parliament. The key problem with this critique is the assumption that there was a working-class constituency sufficiently or potentially radical for Labour to exploit. The accuracy of this assumption, however, is extremely dubious. There is evidence to suggest, for instance, that local Labour parties had absorbed the major elements of Labour Socialism. This can be seen, for instance, in their pride at Labour's arrival as a national party of government. This desire to be accepted into the existing political structure was also reflected in the effort local Labour parties expended to have their nominees chosen as Mayor of their respective locality, in addition to the recognition on the part of many local activists that Communist Party membership was incompatible with Labour Party membership.[36]

It is accurate to say that the early inter-war years was a period of considerable industrial ferment. It seems likely, however, that much of this involved trade union action of a limited labourist kind rather than regime-challenging action with wider political objectives. Some workers more than others, and some areas more than others, were doubtless more amenable to radical politics, but it seems safe to assume that Labour would have lost more support than it gained had it been prepared to support and encourage industrial militancy and advocate speedy and radical measures in parliament.

This brings us, finally, to the electoral dimension. The radical critique of the Labour leadership becomes even more untenable when it is realised that Labour did not succeed in attracting a majority of the working-class electorate in the inter-war period. It is faintly ludicrous to suggest that what was needed was more radicalism to attract these working-class voters given that they needed to be prised away from parties to the Right of Labour. Labour's replacement of the Liberals as one of the two major parties has long fascinated historians. One school of thought has it that this historical development was somehow inevitable, a product of the emergence of class as the key determinant of political affiliation.[37] The assumption here is that, from the 1920s onwards, Labour's electoral growth was guaranteed. Such a deterministic view, however, must be rejected. It did matter very much how Labour presented itself in the 1920s, and it was particularly vulnerable to Opposition smear campaigns seeking to label the party as extremist. MacDonald's concern to present Labour as a party of moderation and respectability denied the Liberal Party the opportunity to adapt to the new realities of post-1918 Britain. By 1924, despite the fact that Asquith and Lloyd George had ironed out their differences, the Liberal Party had become an electoral irrelevance. MacDonald deserves more credit than he has usually been given for this fundamental political realignment.

In the mid 1980s, striking miners held aloft placards bearing the name 'Ramsay MacKinnock'. Associating Neil Kinnock's name with MacDonald in order to attack his lack of support for their cause demonstrates that the legacy of the latter's 'betrayal' still runs deep within the labour movement. More significant, however, are the similarities in the political environment faced by MacDonald and recent Labour leaders. Then, as now, Labour was faced with the difficult task of earning the electorate's trust. Then, as now, respectability and moderation, coupled with an ethic of decency and fairness, were the hallmarks of the party's arrival as an electable party of government. Above all, modern Labour leaders have recognised that Labour cannot do anything unless it wins power, and for that to happen it has to have widespread support. MacDonald's recognition of this seventy or so years earlier ensured that Labour replaced the Liberals as the main opponents of the Conservative Party, and by so doing laid the groundwork for the party's election victory in 1945 and the creation of a more humane and just society.

Chronology

1866	born Lossiemouth, 12 October
1885	joins Fabian Society
1888	becomes Thomas Lough's Private Secretary
1894	joins the ILP
1896	marries Margaret Gladstone
1900	appointed Secretary of LRC
1903	negotiates Gladstone–MacDonald pact
1906	elected MP for Leicester
1906	becomes Secretary of PLP
1910	elected Chairman of PLP
1910	death of youngest son and mother
1911	death of Margaret MacDonald
1914	resigned from PLP leadership on outbreak of war
1918	defeated at Leicester
1922	elected MP for Aberavon
1922	elected leader of PLP
1924	forms first Labour government
1929	forms Second Labour government
1931	accepts King's offer to head National Government
1935	steps down as Prime Minister
1937	resigns from Cabinet
1937	dies (9 November) aboard ship on the way to South America

Notes

1 D. Marquand, *Ramsay MacDonald* (London, Jonathan Cape, 1977), pp. 23–5.
2 Marquand, *MacDonald*, pp. 34–6.
3 See B. Barker (ed.), *Ramsey MacDonald's Political Writings* (London, Allen Lane, 1972).
4 Barker, *Writings*, p. 12.
5 G. Foote, *The Labour Party's Political Thought: A History* (London, Croom Helm, 1985), Part Two.
6 Barker, *Writings*, p. 93.
7 Marquand, *MacDonald*, pp. 89–91.
8 A. Wright (ed.), *British Socialism* (London, Longman, 1983), pp. 1–4.

9   R. Garner, *The Ideological Impact of the Trade Unions on the Labour Party 1918–31* (Manchester, Manchester Papers in Politics, 2/89).
10 Marquand, *MacDonald*, ch. 7.
11 A. Morgan, *J. Ramsay MacDonald* (Manchester, Manchester University Press, 1987), p. 53.
12 J. M. Winter, *Socialism and the Challenge of War* (London, Routledge and Kegan Paul, 1974), ch. 7.
13 Morgan, *MacDonald*, p. 64.
14 Sidney Webb, *Labour and the New Social Order* (London, Labour Party, 1918).
15 T. Wilson, *The Downfall of the Liberal Party 1914–35* (London, Collins, 1966).
16 D. Howell, *British Social Democracy* (London, Croom Helm, 1976), p. 18.
17 *Socialist Review*, January 1923.
18 For the complete debate see *Hansard*, Vol. 161 H.C. Deb. cols. 2472–2512; *Socialist Review*, January 1923.
19 Marquand, *MacDonald*, p. 305.
20 Marquand, *MacDonald*, p. 314.
21 R. W. Lyman, *The First Labour Government 1924* (London, Chapman and Hall, 1957).
22 V. L. Allen, *Trade Unions and the Government* (London, Collins, 1960).
23 R. E. Dowse, *Left in the Centre* (London, Longman, 1966).
24 R. H. Tawney, *Labour and the Nation* (London, Labour Party, 1928).
25 *J.R.M. to Leo Strachey* 14 May 1926, James Ramsay MacDonald Papers, Public Record Office, 30/69/1007.
26 See, in particular, R. Skidelsky, *Politicians and the Slump* (London, Macmillan, 1967); C. L. Mowat, *Britain Between the Wars 1918–40* (London, Methuen, 1968), pp. 353–412; and Marquand, *MacDonald*, pp. 489–670.
27 *J.S.M. to Ramsay MacDonald*, 27 August 1931, Middleton Papers, Ruskin College Library, MID 27/28.
28 For the classic account see M. Weir, *The Tragedy of Ramsay MacDonald: A Political Biography* (London, Secker and Warburg, 1938).
29 E. Wertheimer, *Portrait of the Labour Party* (London, Macmillan, 1929).
30 R. Miliband, *Parliamentary Socialism* (London, Merlin Press, 1972); D. Coates, *The Labour Party and the Struggle for Socialism* (Cambridge, Cambridge University Press, 1975).
31 C. R. Attlee, *As it Happened* (London, Heinemann, 1954), p. 74.
32 H. M. Drucker, *Doctrine and Ethos in the Labour Party* (London, Allen and Unwin, 1979).
33 Reported in *The Times*, 26 August 1931.
34 See Foote, *Labour Party*, pp. 149–60.
35 See Skidelsky, *The Slump*.
36 R. Garner, *Ideology and Electoral Politics in Labour's Rise to Major Party Status 1918–31*, PhD thesis, University of Manchester, 1988, particularly pp. 263–70.
37 See R. McKibbin, *The Evolution of the Labour Party 1910–24*. (Oxford, Clarendon Press, 1974).

Further reading

Numerous biographies have been written about MacDonald. MacNeill Weir, his former Private Secretary, wrote a polemic on his 'betrayal', *The Tragedy of Ramsay MacDonald: A Political Biography* (London, Secker and Warburg, 1938), while Godfrey Elton published a much more sympathetic *Life of James Ramsay MacDonald* (London, Collins, 1939). By far the more thorough account is David Marquand's official biography, *Ramsay MacDonald* (London, Jonathan Cape, 1977). Ten years later, Morgan produced a more critical, and brief, account, *J. Ramsay MacDonald* (Manchester, Manchester University Press, 1987), which draws heavily upon Marquand's sources. MacDonald's writings are edited and commented upon by Bernard Barker, *Ramsay MacDonald's Political Writings* (London, Allen Lane, 1972), and Foote provides a workmanlike analysis of Labour's political thought in general in *The Labour Party's Political Thought: A History* (London, Croom Helm, 1985).

The emergence and evolution of the Labour Party has been a well-covered area of contemporary history. Paul Adelman's short book *The Rise of the Labour Party* (Harlow, Longman, 1972) is very accessible, as is Henry Pelling's standard *A Short History of the Labour Party* which has run to many editions (London, Macmillan 1961–96, 11 editions). McKibbin's work (1974) remains the most thorough account of the early years, although his emphasis on the importance of limited trade union objectives is flawed. Miliband (1972) and Coates (1975) provide very readable, albeit over-simplistic, left-wing critiques of the Labour Party.

Stanley Baldwin

Stuart Ball

Background

Three elements shaped Stanley Baldwin's character and outlook. His family owned an established manufacturing firm on a modest scale, from which he drew his experience of industrial relations. It was situated in the rural surroundings of the Severn Valley, and from his early years Baldwin developed an abiding love of the English countryside. Finally, he inherited from his parents a nervous and imaginative intelligence which was concealed by an outwardly stolid manner.

The Baldwins had been tenant farmers in Shropshire since Norman times, but in the eighteenth century a branch of the family moved south to Worcestershire where they began a range of small industrial concerns. The main business, a medium-sized iron foundry, did well in the early nineteenth century but declined to near collapse shortly before Stanley's birth in 1867, after which it recovered during the 1870s and 1880s due to the efforts of his father, Alfred. Stanley was brought up in an upper-middle-class household, solidly prosperous rather than rich. His father moved away from Liberalism in the 1880s and later sat as Conservative MP for the Bewdley division of Worcestershire from 1892 until his death in 1908; this was a safe seat, and the only time he faced an opponent was in 1906. However, Alfred played little part in national politics, as his time was devoted to the family firm and a business career which culminated in the Chairmanships of the Great Western Railway and the Metropolitan Bank. He was an introspective and intensely religious man, devoted to his wife. Stanley's mother, Louisa MacDonald, the daughter of a Wesleyan minister, came from a very different Highland Scottish background which was mixed with Irish and Welsh ancestry. She and her three sisters were lively and engaging personalities, educated and artistically gifted. Louisa published several novels, poetry and children's stories; two of her sisters married leading artists and the third was the mother of Rudyard Kipling. Baldwin often attributed the intuitive and emotional side of his character to his mother's Celtic background, although his personality and mannerisms had many similarities with his father's temperament.

As an only child, Baldwin developed his two life-long recreations of long country walks and reading, particularly history and literature. The pattern of his education at both Harrow and Trinity College, Cambridge, was of a promising start followed by loss of motivation, apparent laziness and poor results. After taking a third class degree in 1888, disappointing his father's expectations, he thought of becoming a priest but instead took the easiest course of returning to work for the family firm. He developed a capacity for hard work and became proficient in the business, but he never found it congenial or fulfilling. As well as gaining practical experience of industry, during these years Baldwin grew familiar with agriculture and became involved in local public life as a magistrate and county councillor. Always a shy figure, in 1892 he married the more extrovert Lucy Ridsdale. It was a happy and successful partnership, and Baldwin was to rely upon her for encouragement and emotional support. They had five children, although his relations with his eldest son, Oliver, were often difficult, and publicly so when the latter became a Labour MP.

Baldwin's political vision was formed during his early adult life in rural Worcestershire. It was not quite the bucolic idyll that he later depicted in his most famous speeches, but the day-to-day conduct of a small provincial firm was a world away from the huge factories and seething masses of the great industrial cities. The stronger local roots, the framework of stability and tradition, and the greater role for paternalistic responsibility and philanthropy struck a deep chord in Baldwin. The communal feeling between employer and worker in the family business was the inspiration and example upon which he drew when later he sought to extend this spirit to the nation; it gave substance as well as passion to his oratory. Equally important was his deep religious feeling, which took the outward form of a sense of obligation and vocation. It reinforced his emphasis upon following an open and honest course – articulated by simple rural images or cricketing metaphors, such as 'playing a straight bat'. By natural evolution Baldwin became sincerely convinced of the virtues of 'Englishness': fairness, moderation, civility and common sense. As a friend observed, 'he felt things deeply, and his conscience was more active than his intellect'.[1]

Apprenticeship

Baldwin first stood for parliament as Conservative candidate for the nearby borough of Kidderminster in the general election of 1906, but without success.

Two years later the death of his father created a vacancy at Bewdley, and Baldwin was returned unopposed in February 1908; he was by then aged forty, a comparatively late start for this period. He made little impact during his first eight years in the Commons, speaking rarely though quite well, and confining himself to industrial relations and his personal experience. Apart from a very minor role in the Unionist Social Reform Committee, an unofficial ideas group which was not factional or disruptive, Baldwin's career up to 1914 was one of inconspicuous loyalty. During these years he built a reputation as a modest, dependable figure, solidly in the Conservative mainstream. In 1914 Baldwin would not have been on anyone's list of possible future leaders of the Conservative Party or Prime Ministers – least of all his own.

The First World War was the first of two events which cleared the way for Baldwin's rapid and unexpected advancement – the other being the fall of the Coalition in 1922. In 1914 Baldwin was too old to fight, but many younger MPs did so; this became significant when the Conservative Party joined a restructured Coalition under Lloyd George in December 1916, and a larger share of posts had to be filled from the depleted Conservative ranks. Andrew Bonar Law, the leader of the Conservative Party since 1911, became Chancellor of the Exchequer and invited Baldwin to serve as his Parliamentary Private Secretary; the choice appears to have been made because Baldwin was thought steady and discreet. This work led naturally to a further step forward: in June 1917 Baldwin was appointed Financial Secretary to the Treasury (held jointly until May 1919, but his colleague was a businessman co-ordinating government purchases in the USA). This was the most prominent of all of the junior ministerships; in prestige it was equalled by the Under-Secretary at the Foreign Office, but the responsibilities of the Treasury were wider and involved more work in the House. In addition, Law's roles as the second figure in the government and a member of the five-man War Cabinet meant that Baldwin's responsibilities were much greater than normal. However, there was a tendency to assume that the younger men of promise would resume their rightful places when peace came. The result was that Baldwin's competent handling of the post enhanced his reputation without marking him out as a rising star. His standing, and the extent to which he knew the House and its Members, was reflected when he was considered as a possible Speaker in 1921.

Instead, in the reshuffle which followed Law's retirement due to ill-health in April of that year, Baldwin entered the Cabinet as President of the Board of Trade. This was one of the less prestigious posts; he was not expected to go further and had been chosen as a steadying presence who would reassure the Conservative backbenches after Law's departure. However, the failures and unpopularity of the government led to the steady erosion of Conservative support. During 1921 and 1922, the party below Cabinet level, in parliament and in the constituencies, became increasingly hostile to the idea of continuing under Lloyd George for another term. Within the Cabinet, Baldwin grew disenchanted with the cynicism and egotism of its leading figures. He formed a deep and lasting loathing of Lloyd George as a corrupting influence upon British public life, and determined to make a stand against him. When the crisis erupted in the autumn of 1922, Baldwin was the most important of the two Cabinet ministers who publicly opposed continuing the Coalition. The weight of Conservative authority and experience in the Cabinet was against them, and Baldwin expected his defiance to bring about the end of his political career. In fact the Coalitionists had overestimated their strength, and proved to be chiefs without indians. Law's successor as party leader, Austen Chamberlain, called a meeting of Conservative MPs at the Carlton Club on 19 October 1922 to isolate and expose the rebels, but instead they carried the day. A final blow was dealt by Law's decision to come out of retirement and oppose the Coalition, giving the rebels a credible alternative Prime Minister. Baldwin made a short but effective speech at the meeting, and was also one of those close to Law who overcame his reluctance to intervene.

Lloyd George immediately resigned, and Law became Prime Minister. The defeated Conservative leaders went into the wilderness and Baldwin, now one of the most senior and experienced figures among the anti-Coalitionists, became Chancellor of the Exchequer. In the following general election the Conservatives scored an unexpected overall majority. The only notable event during Baldwin's short tenure of the Exchequer was the crisis over the American debt payments in January 1923, in which Law's hostility to the terms which Baldwin had negotiated nearly broke up the government. In May 1923 the final collapse of Law's health forced his retirement, but the former Coalitionists had refused his offers to rejoin and were therefore out of the running. A new Prime Minister had to be found from within the present Cabinet, and the two possible choices were Lord Curzon, the vastly experienced but pompous Foreign Secretary, and Baldwin, the novice Chancellor of the Exchequer. Baldwin was chosen for several reasons: he had the support of key figures in the Cabinet, and was thought more likely to be able to reunite the party. Above all, the King considered that it would be a provocative gesture of class antagonism to have a Prime Minister in the House of Lords where the Labour Party – now the official Opposition – was almost unrepresented. Baldwin's emerging reputation as a moderate conciliator, suited to the age of the democratic franchise introduced in 1918, brought him by these unexpected twists to the Premiership on 22 May 1923. Having taken office as Prime Minister, he also succeeded Law as Conservative leader, being elected without opposition a few days later.

Limelight

Picking up the pieces, 1923–24
At first sight it might seem that Baldwin had assumed an ideal inheritance. The Conservatives were in office in their own right for the first time since

1905, with four and a half years of the parliament still to run. In fact, the situation was much less favourable. The Conservative share of the poll in 1922 had been only 38.5 per cent, and victory owed much to Liberal disarray and the number of three-cornered contests. Unemployment was rising and the Labour Party advancing, but the government seemed to lack direction. The Conservative Party was still disunited, and its morale was slipping. However, Baldwin's attempt to break out of this downward spiral was to end in confusion, crisis and an apparently unnecessary defeat; his first Premiership was to be one of the shortest on record, lasting barely eight months, and it could easily have been his last.

Soon after becoming Prime Minister, Baldwin concluded that a fundamental change in economic policy was necessary. Like most Conservatives, he blamed Britain's difficulties upon the maintenance of free trade and favoured Joseph Chamberlain's programme of tariff reform. However, due to a pledge given by Law in 1922, a fresh mandate would be required. The tariff policy was also an electoral liability, for many working-class voters feared that it would raise the cost of living. Once Baldwin revealed his intentions in October 1923, the situation slid rapidly out of control and an immediate election in December became unavoidable. The Conservatives were unprepared and their proposals were vague and contradictory; it was not surprising that they lost their majority, although they remained the largest single party in the House of Commons. When parliament met after the Christmas recess the Conservative ministry was ousted by combined Liberal and Labour votes, and the first Labour government took office in January 1924. Baldwin survived as leader because the alternative was capitulation to the former Coalitionists, and most of the party disliked that prospect even more. After a period of fruitless intrigue during the recess, the Conservative ex-Coalitionists came to realise this themselves. The outcome was the reunion of the party under Baldwin's continued leadership, confirmed by a party meeting in February 1924. The recovery of unity was welcome, but it was not the motive for Baldwin's misguided tariff venture; there had been no hidden plan, and certainly no expectation of defeat.

Baldwin and the Conservatives made good use of the period in Opposition during 1924, both to reorganise the party and to win wider support. The tariff policy was dropped, and in its place Baldwin promoted a moderate and attractive outlook which became known as the 'New Conservatism'. This was strongly identified with his own personality, which even in 1923 had been acknowledged to be one of the party's greatest assets. This pragmatic approach paid off, and in the election which followed the fall of the Labour government in November 1924, Baldwin's strategy was rewarded with a landslide victory. An important element in this had been the absence of Liberal candidates in many seats, but it was largely due to Baldwin's image and the tone which he set that many Liberal voters transferred their support to the Conservative candidate.

In search of stability, 1924–29
Baldwin was at the height of his powers during his second Premiership, presiding with confidence over a stable government which was to remain in office for four and a half years. He completed the reunion of the party by giving Cabinet posts to former Coalitionists such as Austen Chamberlain, who became Foreign Secretary, and Winston Churchill, who in a surprise move was appointed Chancellor of the Exchequer. In March 1925 Baldwin finally established an unquestioned authority over his Cabinet and party, with a speech asking his followers not to support a Bill on trade union law which had been introduced by a 'diehard' backbencher, F. A. Macquisten. This appeal for 'peace and goodwill in industry' was Baldwin's most famous oration: delivered with passionate sincerity in simple and moving language, it made a profound impact upon both the House and the public. Baldwin's foremost concerns during these years were the related problems of educating the new democratic electorate, the challenge from the Labour Party, industrial strife and unemployment. To the dismay of many in his own party, in 1925 he granted a subsidy to the troubled coal industry in the hope that this would enable a settlement to be found. Although this failed, when the coal dispute culminated in the General Strike of May 1926 Baldwin's combination of firmness but fairness ensured that the government retained public support, not least due to his two effective radio broadcasts. Baldwin's reputation and standing reached a peak with his handling of the strike, while its generally peaceful nature vindicated his approach. The only failure was in the coal industry itself, where the strike dragged on through the winter of 1926–27 in increasing bitterness and hardship. The disappointing outcome was not due to lack of effort: Baldwin spent much energy on attempts to broker a settlement, but was unable to apply effective pressure to either side. The result of these months of stress was physical and mental exhaustion, and while Baldwin was unwell in early 1927 the government drifted into the doldrums.

The main successes of Baldwin's second term were concentrated in the first two years, including the Locarno agreements and pensions for widows and orphans in 1925, and the second half of the government appeared to be a long ebb tide. The 1927 Trade Disputes Act was not harsh enough for many Conservatives, but aroused great Labour and trade union opposition. Conservative supporters were alienated by the granting of the vote to women at the age of twenty-one, by the failure to tackle the problems of agriculture, by the abandonment of proposals to strengthen the position of the House of Lords, and by the refusal to extend the protection of 'safeguarding duties' to the iron and steel industry: this was such a major sector of the economy that it would have been too close to introducing a general tariff, thereby breaching Baldwin's pledge of 1924. Baldwin set his face against this, for reasons of electoral pragmatism and in order to preserve his public reputation for being honest. In 1928 he publicly ruled out any protectionist commitment in the next manifesto, to the relief of MPs representing industrial marginals but giving further offence to MPs on the Right and the rank and file in the party's strongholds. There were no catastrophes or crises during the second half of the government, but an increasing impression of a lack of drive and inspiration. There were frustrations in foreign policy, especially over attempts to secure further international disarmament, and friction with the United States over limitations on the number of cruisers. On the home front, the ministry seemed to be doing no more than plodding dutifully onwards, in the hope that better times would turn up. This was more a matter of presentation than of policies: there was plenty of legislation, including local government and Poor Law reform, and finally in 1928 the de-rating policy – an attempt to regain the initiative which came too late and was difficult to get across to the public. In May 1929 Baldwin led a united, if rather tired, Cabinet into the election on a moderate platform which drew together all these themes, but the Conservatives lost many seats and the second minority Labour government took office. The most famous Conservative slogan from this campaign, 'Safety First', was afterwards taken by his critics to sum up Baldwin's political style and philosophy.

Troubles in Opposition, 1929–31
The Conservative defeat of 1929 was followed by two years of internal crisis which were to take Baldwin to the brink of resignation. He came under great pressure to adopt a protectionist programme including duties on food and raw materials imported from outside the British Empire. Baldwin resisted this because if the Conservatives were to return to power they would have to recover seats in the industrial Midlands and north, and he did not wish to be saddled with an unpopular policy when the precarious position of the minority Labour government could precipitate a general election at any moment. However, this pragmatic approach led to a crisis within the party which grew from the end of 1929 to the autumn of 1930. The dissatisfaction of the Conservative strongholds in the south was channelled through the 'Empire Crusade', a campaign against Baldwin mounted by his long-standing enemies, the press barons, Beaverbrook and Rothermere. Baldwin replied by accusing them of seeking to dictate through their newspapers, a tactic which rallied support and enabled him to win votes of confidence at party meetings summoned in June and October 1930. The crisis peaked in the late summer but was resolved in October 1930, when Baldwin appeased most protectionists by adopting a 'free hand' on tariffs; this was now a safer move as the world depression was eroding public support for free trade. The press lords continued their attacks with little effect until their final defeat in the Westminster St George's by-election of March 1931, the occasion of Baldwin's famous denunciation of their desire for 'power without responsibility – the prerogative of the harlot through the ages'.[2]

Baldwin did not shine in Opposition; he found it uncongenial, and his caution led to missed opportunities and infuriated some of his colleagues, who took it for laziness. The surprise was perhaps that he kept their support for as long as he did, although ironically his position was bolstered by the attacks of the press lords as these forced his colleagues to support him. There was a brief rupture in March 1931 which brought Baldwin close to resignation, but a spirited recovery on his part, together with the lack of any clear or more popular successor, saved his position. From the spring of 1931 Conservative morale rapidly improved, helped by the growing unpopularity of the tottering Labour government. After by-election successes in June, the Conservatives were looking forward to an election in the autumn and a victory on the scale of 1924. Instead, the sudden and unexpected financial crisis of August 1931 swept the party into the National Government.

Linchpin of the National Government, 1931–37
In the August crisis Baldwin agreed to serve under Ramsay MacDonald in a temporary cross-party team, and then found himself involved in a permanent Coalition in which the Conservatives were again by far the biggest party. Baldwin had not sought this outcome, but he found the arrangement to be politically and personally agreeable. He did not have the formal responsibility of the Premiership but was the essential figure in the National Government, enjoying an amicable relationship with MacDonald and the trust of the ministers from other parties; the government might not have been possible, and certainly would not have lasted, if there had been a different personality at the head of the Conservative Party. Baldwin took the prestigious but non-departmental post of Lord President of the Council, and concentrated his attention upon two areas. The first was keeping the Coalition together, and especially co-ordinating its parliamentary work; the second was India. Baldwin's determination to follow the bipartisan line on India established by his endorsement of the Irwin Declaration of November 1929 led during 1933–35 to a revolt by the Conservative right wing, led by Churchill. The 1935 India Act, placed on the statute books after a long struggle, was in many ways Baldwin's personal achievement.

After changing positions with MacDonald and becoming Prime Minister for the third time in June 1935, Baldwin won a comfortable victory in the general election in November. His final Premiership was dominated by two concerns: the conduct of the Fascist dictators abroad and of the new monarch at home. The hostile public reaction to the Hoare–Laval Pact in December 1935 shook the government and the fiasco reflected badly on Baldwin. In early 1936 he suffered a form of nervous breakdown, and the government drifted uneasily for several months. He recovered later in the year and skilfully handled the crisis over the marriage plans of Edward VIII which led to the monarch's abdication in December 1936. Baldwin's sense of duty and concern for the constitution made him take a steady line, but it was tempered by human sympathy and the need for tact and patience. Baldwin's explanations of the position in the Commons when the crisis became public were masterly in the sureness of their touch; the whole affair did much to restore his reputation, and enabled him to retire in a glow of public approval after the coronation of the new King, George VI, in May 1937. Rarely for a Prime Minister, he went more or less at the moment of his own choosing, although age and health played their part in this. He was made a Knight of the Garter and created Earl Baldwin of Bewdley. During the following few years he managed to keep to his stated intention of leaving the field clear for his successor, although he did not approve of everything Chamberlain did, and was privately supportive of Anthony Eden after the latter's resignation as Foreign Secretary in 1938. Baldwin's health declined in his final years, and he died in December 1947.

Character and methods
According to one of his ministers, Baldwin was 'a disconnectedly divided personality', one part of which was 'emotional, impulsive, secretive, and intensely personal in its likes, dislikes, and moral judgements'.[3] Baldwin was sometimes awkward in personal relations with his colleagues, but managed his Cabinets in a relaxed style. He sought consensus, and was proud of the fact that during 1924–29 only one relatively minor figure had resigned from the Cabinet because of disagreement on policy. That Cabinet was also notable for the continuity of its members in the same posts: Baldwin disliked making changes, even though by 1928 several ministers were running out of steam or suffering from ill-health. Baldwin was always more concerned with the general 'atmosphere' than with the details of policy, and considered that without trustworthiness no political endeavour would be effective. This fuelled the strongest emotion of his career: a loathing of Lloyd George and a determination that he should never return to power. Baldwin could charm, but there were also times when he seemed self-absorbed and unappreciative of the efforts of others on his behalf. He had a number of distracting nervous mannerisms, and was prone to lapsing into periods of exhaustion and inertia. However, once his habitual reluctance to take a step had been overcome, he was capable of swift and decisive action.

Baldwin spent many hours on the benches of the House of Commons and developed a sureness of touch in dealing with its moods. A member of his first Cabinet described his style as 'not in the least oratorical, but intensely human', with a delivery that was 'slow, steady, uneloquent but convincing'.[4] More important still was his rapport with the public, which resulted not from any great skill as a public speaker but from his personality and message. His speeches were published as pamphlets and books, and sold thousands of copies. He exploited the cinema newsreels and was the most accomplished politician of his age in the use of the new medium of radio, employing a conversational style as if addressing each listener individually. His public image of the pipe-smoking rural Englishman, honest but not clever, was both reassuring and popular. He became a trusted figure, familiar to the public at large in a way in which no previous Prime Minister had ever been. His religious faith and his gift of language – his cousin Kipling described him as the true poet in the family – enabled him to overcome his nerves and put his finger upon the national pulse.

The vision of a common rural heritage which Baldwin offered has been criticised as complacent and inappropriate to the problems of an urban and industrial society.[5] There is some justice in this, but it misses the essential point: Baldwin used such metaphors as the means, and not as the ends in themselves. Like any craftsman, the politician has to work with the materials which are available. Baldwin's aim was the restoration of industrial peace and political probity in a society greatly changed and disturbed by the strains of the First World War and the dislocations which followed. A focus upon the connections which bind society together and link the present with the past enabled Baldwin to reach a mass audience. A common touchstone was needed and, like Gladstone before him, Baldwin was effective because the message which he delivered sprang from the heart. It made a powerful appeal to the public mood of inter-war Britain, crossing class and party boundaries. Baldwin's sincerity and goodwill earned the respect of many of his opponents. The sacrifice of the war deepened Baldwin's sense of duty and obligation, a feeling shared by many of his generation. Baldwin gave practical effect to this by giving a substantial part of his wealth for the cancellation of war debt in 1919; the donation was made anonymously but in the hope that others would follow his example. After he became Prime Minister the story became known, further adding to his reputation for integrity and modesty.

Legacy

In his own time and since, Baldwin has seemed to be the defining figure of the inter-war years. The precise contribution of a Prime Minister is often difficult to determine: although he or she is the head of the government and bears ultimate responsibility for its successes and failures, particular measures are often associated with individual ministers. This was particularly the case with Baldwin, for he was not an interventionist: 'he never moves of his own motion', observed Austen Chamberlain.[6] He preferred to trust his chosen colleagues to tackle the problems in their domains, with difficult decisions or inter-departmental frictions being aired in the Cabinet under his adjudicatory Chairmanship. This could give the appearance – certainly to the impatiently active mind of one such as Neville Chamberlain – that Baldwin lacked a clear agenda and that he tended to drift, following opinion rather than leading it. There was some truth in this, and Baldwin could not have achieved such a record of electoral success without being adaptable and sensitive to the currents of public opinion. However, the problem with this view is that it concentrates upon the foreground at the expense of the wider picture. Baldwin's political role was that of a mediator and co-ordinator; his aim was the creation of an atmosphere which would bring together in a harmonious working relationship the various parts, whether they be his Cabinet team, the Conservative Party as a whole or the classes in the nation. Baldwin's effectiveness and his legacy need to be judged in this light, rather than by any specific legislation or programme.

The saviour of Conservatism
The survival and continued success of the Conservative Party since 1918 has been such a marked feature of modern British politics that it can easily be taken for granted. However, the decline of the Liberal Party between the wars and the fragmentation and rivalries of European movements of the Right, from Weimar Germany to Gaullist France, suggest that this was a far from certain outcome. In this respect Baldwin's simplest and most profound legacy was the preservation of the security, unity and confidence of the conservative elements in British society. Baldwin's achievement was to preside with deceptive smoothness over the adjustment of the Conservative Party, and more broadly of the upper and middle classes upon which it was based, to the coming of democracy with a full adult citizenship franchise. The direction in which Baldwin led the Conservative Party secured its position at a time of great uncertainty. The revolt against the Lloyd George Coalition in 1922, and the refusal to countenance any further such alliance, enabled the Conservatives to recover their independence and establish a separate identity. The Conservative split of 1922 was never permitted to become as deep or damaging as the splits in the Liberal Party during the First World War or the Labour rifts of 1931, the 1950s or the early 1980s. Although Baldwin's first attempts in 1923 were mishandled, reunion was achieved in the following year – around the new consensus which Baldwin and the anti-Coalitionists had shaped.

During this period the Conservative Party escaped from the blind alleys of the Edwardian era, and found itself once again at the centre of gravity of popular and patriotic feeling. Baldwin stood here not by calculation but by instinct, evoking simple images which interlocked with the values and traditions of British political culture: the rural past, the Christian virtues of charity and patience, tolerance based upon mutual respect, a generosity of spirit which accepted an element of merit in other points of view, an appeal to co-operation based upon goodwill, a desire to seek common ground. Baldwin wanted a stable capitalist system with a human heart, economic freedom with social responsibility. His skilfully worded appeals echoed these themes, emphasising getting along, pulling together and avoiding entrenched positions. His purpose could be summed up in the word 'tranquillity' – the quest for social and economic calm in which to recover from the strains of the Great War. It says much for Baldwin's success that fears of social upheaval faded during the 1920s. Baldwin's most distinctive contribution was the 'New Conservatism' of 1924–26, which emphasised social harmony, industrial partnership, co-operation rather than confrontation, and trust in the good sense of the people. It was principled, distinctive, moderate and unprovocative, and formed the context for the reformist social programme carried out by his second administration of 1924–29. Typical was the decision in 1928 to equalise the franchise for both sexes at the age of 21; many Conservatives disliked this and would have preferred a higher age (such as 25), but his course was accepted without great controversy as inevitable and in tune with the spirit of the age. A different personality as Conservative leader might well have sounded a harsher or more defensive note, much less resonant with the masses, and would have been unlikely to have matched Baldwin's ability to project 'a breadth of outlook, a tolerance and a warm humanity' while still guarding the social and economic interests of the middle and upper classes.[7] The tone set by Baldwin in the 1920s enabled the Conservatives to adjust to life within the National Government of the 1930s with remarkably little friction, unlike the previous experience of Coalition under Lloyd George. The reason was only partly electoral expediency; although collaboration was welcome in the crisis mood of 1931, the Conservatives no longer feared that they could not win elections in their own right. The stability of the National Government owed much to its better internal management, and to the fact that most Conservatives felt themselves to be comfortable working with men of goodwill from across the spectrum in a cautiously reformist ministry.

'Baldwinism' was an essential factor in the electoral success which the Conservative Party enjoyed between the wars. The decline of the Liberal Party led to a realignment of the electorate which benefited the Conservatives as much as it did Labour. Baldwin played a vital part in making this possible: he enjoyed widespread popularity with uncommitted, Liberal and even Labour voters. His simple Christian ethic exerted a strong pull on the 'Nonconformist conscience' which still moved many Liberals, especially in the middle class. For these reasons Baldwin was acknowledged to be the Conservatives' greatest electoral asset, although neither his appeal nor the party's organisational strength guaranteed certain victory. Baldwin fought five general elections as Conservative leader and lost two; both were occasions when the Liberal Party was at its most united and energetic, and able to draw back many of its former supporters. Even so, the defeats of 1923 and 1929 were setbacks rather than disasters, with the Conservatives retaining around 260 seats on both occasions. Taken as a whole, the inter-war era was one of Conservative electoral dominance; they were the largest party in the House of Commons throughout, apart from the short period of the second Labour government of 1929–31.

The architect of stability
Conservative electoral success was also based on raising fears of Socialism which were often crude and alarmist, yet Baldwin has often been described as having achieved the 'appeasement of labour'. This involved a mixture of firm resistance to extremism and unconstitutional pressure with the

encouragement of the moderate and parliamentary sides of the Labour movement. Baldwin was not interested in putting the clock back as far as the legal rights of trade unions were concerned, or in punitive measures; trade unionism if practised in its proper sphere was an accepted part of the landscape. Baldwin refused to believe that there was anything to fear as far as the British working class was concerned, provided it was treated fairly and with respect. In early 1924 he ruled out any intrigues to prevent Labour from taking office for the first time, and insisted that the government be given a fair chance. His focus on industrial relations directly addressed the social and economic concerns of the day, casting the labour movement as one side of the solution rather than as all of the problem. He addressed these issues in a spirit of justice and balance, in the wider national interest placing demands and responsibilities upon owners and managers as much as unions and workers. Baldwin's promotion of social harmony and industrial reconciliation played a significant role in soothing tensions in the 1920s, and in encouraging the trade unions to leave political issues to the parliamentary leadership of the Labour Party. Baldwin's relations with the latter were cordial and constructive, and he was careful to accord the new official Opposition all its rights and privileges. Baldwin was noted for his generous treatment of opponents: in the words of a friend and Cabinet colleague, 'he never attacked them when they were down, and always treated them with a remarkable consideration'.[8] On several occasions in the 1920s, Baldwin warned Neville Chamberlain against showing a contemptuous attitude towards the Labour Party in the Commons.

With the Conservative Party electorally successful and with such a reassuring figure as Baldwin as its leader, the middle classes felt safe and secure. Although unemployment peaked in the early 1930s, the National Government presided over economic stability and a slow but increasingly visible recovery. Above all, there was no inflation and no collapse in basic social and economic confidence. At the same time the Conservative Party stood for a developing Empire, and patriotic sentiment was appeased by quiet pride rather than bellicosity or chauvinism. Despite the moderation of his leadership, Baldwin ensured that the Conservative Party left no fertile opening to the Right. There were critics and occasional periods of turmoil and unrest, but the underlying cohesive strength of the party ensured that it did not splinter. It was for these reasons, as much as its alien origins, ideology and methods, that Fascism failed to find a following in Britain between the wars. Baldwin did more than any other individual to confine Sir Oswald Mosley and his British Union of Fascists to the margins of political life.

Only one area of politics consistently aroused Baldwin's interest: threats to the general political stability enshrined in the parliamentary Constitution. All his major battles were fought in this area, from the cynicism and corruption of the Lloyd George Coalition, through the General Strike, the pretensions of the press barons and the future of India, to the abdication crisis. Once he shifted political conflict to this ground he was unbeatable, a fact found to their cost by apparently more able politicians such as Lloyd George and Winston Churchill, who continually underestimated his skill and resistance.

The failures of appeasement and rearmament
Criticism of Baldwin's record focuses upon the area which he left mainly to others: foreign affairs. The approach of his governments in the 1920s, and especially in the 1930s, has been denounced as lacking in foresight, overly cautious and feebly missing opportunities to deter the aggressors. By 1929 relations with the United States had become strained, and friction and mutual misunderstanding with France was a consistent problem from the Ruhr occupation of 1923 to the Rhineland crisis of 1936. The issue of whether the League of Nations could have been made to work is impossible to resolve, and the failure to check the ambitions of the dictators is a complex matter. In 1936 would the British people, with their vivid memories of the horrors of the Western Front and the new fear of massive bombing from the air, have fought to prevent German soldiers parading in the Rhineland, a part of Germany itself? Although German actions were breaches of the Versailles settlement, that treaty had become thoroughly discredited and it was commonly accepted that a new basis of peace and understanding was required. The Anglo-German Naval Agreement of 1935 was intended as a first step towards this, and can be claimed as a partial success: during the Second World War the German surface fleet was never to pose a serious danger. Hitler was adept at finding justifications for his actions, and it should not be forgotten that until March 1939 his claims for the incorporation of German population within the Reich were based on the accepted principle of nationality. The most determined efforts to achieve peace by appeasement took place after Baldwin's retirement, and his approach was more limited and sceptical than that of his successor.

Excess of caution is also the charge against Baldwin in the parallel area of defence: that having disarmed in the 1920s in the hope that others would follow, British rearmament in the 1930s was too late and too slow. It was limited by problems of finance in the wake of the slump, and constrained by political anxieties: not to affront public opinion, especially before the 1935 general election, and not to raise taxation or interfere in private business. Baldwin was judged as principally culpable here: his famous declaration in 1932 that 'the bomber will always get through' had an air of fatalism and defeatism, and did not lead to action. Events such as the East Fulham by-election of 1933 and the 'Peace Ballot' organised by supporters of the League of Nations in late 1934 seemed to inhibit him, and the 1935 manifesto spoke quietly only of doing 'what is necessary to repair the gaps in our defences'. Even so, a programme of rearmament began in 1934 and had grown massively by the time Baldwin retired in 1937. Much of this equipment had to be abandoned when France fell and the Army was evacuated from the Channel beaches in 1940; the state of the country's defences as it faced invasion after Dunkirk was not a fair reflection of the National Government's rearmament efforts, but this was the image which sank into popular mythology. This perception was fostered from two directions: by the polemics of left-wing journalists, such as *Guilty Men*,[9] and by the criticisms of the Conservative anti-appeasers, who were in the ascendancy for more than twenty-five years after Churchill's rise to the Premiership in 1940.

During the wartime years the reputation of the National Government and of its leading figures sank into disrepute. This was not just a matter of its foreign and defence policies, but also of its economic record – above all on unemployment, the popular symbols of which were the dole queues and the Jarrow march. Baldwin's standing was at its lowest from the 1940s to the 1960s, while wartime memories were still fresh and the new methods of Keynesian economic management appeared to guarantee prosperity. Since the late 1960s, economic decline and the return of mass unemployment have combined with revisionist analyses of appeasement to produce a more balanced – but still critical – picture.

Significance
Baldwin did much to bring stability to British politics. On the Right he played a major part in the success of the Conservatives and the failure of Fascism; on the Left he drew the teeth of trade union-based Syndicalism, marginalised revolutionary Communism and fostered the primacy of moderate parliamentary Socialism. A further contribution was the preservation of a popular constitutional monarchy in 1936. The governments of 1924–29 and 1931–37 had constructive records in domestic affairs, with measures such as widows' pensions and Poor Law reform in the 1920s and slum clearance and agricultural marketing schemes in the 1930s. However, their orthodox economic approach did not tackle the structural weaknesses of British industry, and had limited impact on unemployment. His commitment to negotiated devolution in India was never intended to lead to the end of the Empire, but its spirit began the process of peaceful decolonisation which culminated in the post-war independent Commonwealth, with its successful preservation of ties of trade and goodwill. Perhaps Baldwin's greatest legacy was Britain's 'secret weapon' of the Second World War: the bedrock of social unity and the willingness of all classes to work together, and the acceptance that all that could have been done to avoid war had been done, which enabled public morale to withstand the onslaught in the dark and lonely days of 1940–42.

Baldwin was a formative influence on a generation of younger Conservatives who shaped the party's response in the post-war era, and Anthony Eden, R. A. Butler and Harold Macmillian all drew consciously on his example. The degree of public trust and confidence which Baldwin enjoyed has been the envy and inspiration of later politicians. He was a model for Macmillian and Harold Wilson, who deliberately adopted Baldwin's pipe-smoking as more avuncular and reassuring than cigarettes or cigars. The unifying images which Baldwin used were still powerful enough for his shade to be evoked by John Major in the 1990s. Since 1945 Baldwin has become the emblem of a type of paternalist Conservatism, non-confrontational, infused by a sense of social responsibility, principled and generous. This overlaps with the concept of 'one nation' Toryism and similarly is used as a shorthand term, often with an incomplete understanding of the original.

Chronology

1867	born, 3 August
1888	graduates from Cambridge University with third class honours
1892	marriage to Lucy Ridsdale
1906	contests Kidderminster, defeated by 271 votes
1908	elected MP for the Bewdley division of Worcestershire
1917	appointed as Bonar Law's Parliamentary Private Secretary and a Junior Lord of the Treasury. Later appointed Financial Secretary to the Treasury (held jointly to May 1919)
1920	made a Privy Councillor
1921	enters the Cabinet as President of the Board of Trade on 1 April
1922	Carlton Club meeting overthrows the Lloyd George Coalition. Appointed Chancellor of the Exchequer
1923	Cabinet crisis over the American debt settlement. Becomes Prime Minister, after Law's resignation, on 22 May declares for protection in speech to the Conservative Party Conference at Plymouth in October but the tariff policy rejected in the general election in December
1924	government defeated in the Commons, resigns as Prime Minister next day. Conservative Party meeting at the Hotel Cecil confirms Baldwin's leadership; becomes Prime Minister for the second time on 4 November
1925	establishes authority by his speech on Macquisten's Trade Union Bill. Cabinet crisis over the budget for the Navy. Announcement of subsidy for the coal industry. Refusal of application for safeguarding duties from the steel industry
1926	General Strike
1927	Trade Disputes Bill
1928	publicly rules out a general tariff or duties on food from the next manifesto
1929	resigns Premiership in June after defeat in election of 30 May. Endorses the Irwin Declaration on future dominion status for India in November
1930	wins votes of confidence at two party meetings in June and October
1931	attacks the press lords in the Westminster St George's by-election. Agrees to serve under Ramsay MacDonald in a National Government on 24 August
1932	Imperial Conference at Ottawa. Later alarms public with declaration that 'the bomber will always get through'
1933	the Conservative Party's Central Council narrowly approves the India policy
1934	narrow victory on India policy at the annual party conference
1935	crisis over new unemployment payments and Wavertree by-election in

	February; on 7 June exchanges posts with MacDonald and becomes Prime Minister for third term. Election victory in November followed by crisis over the Hoare–Laval plan
1936	Rhineland crisis. Abdication of King Edward VIII
1937	retires from Premiership on 28 May; made a Knight of the Garter, created 1st Earl Baldwin of Bewdley
1947	dies, 14 December

Notes

1 Thomas Jones, *A Diary with Letters 1931–1950* (London, Oxford University Press, 1954), p. xxx.
2 Speech at Queen's Hall, Westminister, 17 March 1931, reported in *The Times*, 18 March 1931.
3 L. S. Amery, *My Political Life: II – War and Peace, 1914–1929* (London, Hutchinson, 1953), p. 505.
4 Bayford diary, 18 March 1925, in John Ramsden (ed.), *Real Old Tory Politics: The Political Diaries of Sir Robert Sanders, Lord Bayford: 1910–1935* (London, The Historians' Press, 1984).
5 Martin Wiener, *English Culture and the Decline of the Industrial Spirit 1850–1980* (Cambridge, Cambridge University Press, 1981), pp. 101–2, 108–9, 120–2.
6 Austen to Ida Chamberlain, 2 July 1931, Austen Chamberlain papers, AC/5/1/545, Birmingham University Library.
7 Amery, *My Political Life: II*, p. 398.
8 Entry on Baldwin, November 1929, in Philip Williamson (ed.), *The Modernisation of Conservative Politics: The Diaries and Letters of William Bridgeman 1904–1935* (London, The Historians' Press, 1988), p. 227.
9 'Cato' (Michael Foot, Peter Howard and Frank Owen), *Guilty Men* (London, Gollancz, 1940).

Further reading

For a general discussion of Conservative politics in the Baldwin era see Stuart Ball, *The Conservative Party and British Politics 1902–1951* (London, Longman, 1995) and, in more detail, John Ramsden, *The Age of Balfour and Baldwin 1902–1940* (London, Longman, 1978). The most accessible full-length biography remains H. Montgomery Hyde, *Baldwin* (London, Hart-Davis and MacGibbon, 1973). The earlier and massive life by Keith Middlemas and John Barnes, *Baldwin* (London, Weidenfeld and Nicolson, 1969), reflected a desire to redress the balance after the post-war criticism of his role in appeasement and rearmament. The best short biography is the lucid sketch by Kenneth Young, *Baldwin* (London, Weidenfeld and Nicolson, 1976); Roy Jenkins, *Baldwin* (London, Collins, 1987) is readable but was based only upon other biographies. The crisis in the middle of Baldwin's leadership is analysed in Stuart Ball, *Baldwin and the Conservative Party: The Crisis of 1929–1931* (New Haven and London, Yale University Press, 1988). There are also four important and perceptive articles: a subtle review of Baldwin's thought by Philip Williamson, 'The doctrinal politics of Stanley Baldwin', in Michael Bentley (ed.), *Public and Private Doctrine: Essays in*

British History Presented to Maurice Cowling (Cambridge, Cambridge University Press, 1993); the lucid and critical essay 'Stanley Baldwin' by John Campbell in J. P. Mackintosh (ed.), *British Prime Ministers in the Twentieth Century, Volume 1: Balfour to Chamberlain* (London, Weidenfeld and Nicolson, 1977); and two studies which focus upon the construction of Baldwin's public image – David Cannadine, 'Politics, propaganda and art: the case of two "Worcestershire lads"', *Midland History*, Vol. IV (1977), and John Ramsden, 'Baldwin and film', in N. Pronay and D. W. Spring (eds), *Politics, Propaganda and Film 1918–1945* (Basingstoke, Macmillan, 1982). Baldwin's character is refracted more immediately through the papers of his confidants Thomas Jones, *A Diary with Letters 1931–1950* (London, Oxford University Press, 1954), and J. C. C. Davidson, edited by Robert Rhodes James as *Memoirs of a Conservative: J. C. C. Davidson's Memoirs and Papers 1910–1937* (London, Weidenfeld and Nicolson, 1969); the most important of his published collections of speeches is Stanley Baldwin, *On England* (London, Philip Allan, 1926).

Neville Chamberlain

Nick Smart

In photographs and video footage, Neville Chamberlain appears as the quintessential British politician of the inter-war era. With wing-collar and tightly rolled umbrella, he is forever remembered as the gullible Premier who personified appeasement and promised 'peace in our time'. Yet within a year, this same Premier was leading his country to war with Germany announcing that 'everything I have believed in during my public life has crashed in ruins'.[1] Toppled from office in May 1940, he died the following November in a strange house, scarcely lamented as the country fought for its life.

Background

There was much that was deeply conventional about Neville Chamberlain. His tastes and habits were those of the typical, upper-middle-class family. No biographer has found, or even cared to look for, a scrap of scandal. A shy man with a strong sense of family, he took his hobbies seriously, was well travelled and, to a point, cultivated. He never seems to have kicked against his upbringing or rebelled against the formidable expectations imposed upon him by his family name. His diary, but above all his letters to his sisters, constitute a vast and rich source from which historians have been able to equate the private self with the public man. (His surviving papers reside at Birmingham University.)

Yet for all its conventional aspects, attempts to fit Chamberlain's life into the categories of early, middle and late fall foul of a distinctly unconventional chronology. Until well into his forties, he devoted his life to what was expected of it: business and municipal good works. His illustrious father, Joseph, had decreed that Austen (Joseph's first son and Neville's half-brother) would pursue a career in politics, whereas Neville should not go to university, must work for his living and might not form associations far removed from the family network. Neville did as he was bid. As a twenty-one-year-old, he was despatched to the Bahamas to manage a 20,000 acre sisal plantation – a hard and expensive exercise in self-reliance. The project failed after seven years, with the loss of some £2 million in today's terms. The memory of his lonely life on the island of Andros, 'where the plants did not grow', stayed with him.

Andros was in no conscious sense a political apprenticeship. Nor were the next twenty years as a businessman in Birmingham. As his father had once remarked, Neville was the abler of the two sons but without interest in politics.[2] It was only in 1911, the year of his marriage, that he was elected as a Liberal Unionist to Birmingham city council. He was nearly fifty when he entered the House of Commons: no Prime Minister of modern times began his career so late in life. Coupled to the paradox that, of all the Chamberlains, he was the least expected to ascend the greasy pole, this would now be remembered as a truly remarkable story. Appeasement, however, was to prove an ineradicable slur upon his reputation.

Apart from the Andros interlude, Chamberlain's life up to 1914 seems exceptionally dull. Apologists praise his civic virtue and accumulated respectability, while the judgement that his was 'an ideally happy marriage' seems reasonable.[3] Yet it has also been recorded that here was a man of 'passionless rigidity' whose 'private emotional world was an arid wasteland devoid of personal satisfaction'.[4] Such divergence of opinion shows how difficult it is to reconcile the portrait of a dry, respectable public servant with that of an emotionally stunted and demonically driven figure (this author leans towards the former position). It needs to be acknowledged, however, that the tragic nature of Chamberlain's Premiership inevitably encourages a search for some fatal flaw in his psyche.

Apprenticeship

Chamberlain may have had a 'father haunted' view of life, but he had an uncluttered and eclectic approach to political questions – beyond the obvious inherited ones of tariff reform and resistance to Irish Home Rule. Taking up his father's cudgels as an improver of 'the Empire's second city', he believed in extending the role of the state, with high-profile local authorities bringing better housing, education and health care to the people. Social policy fired his political imagination: public spirited, enlightened and, if necessary, authoritarian. Problems were there to be solved on a clinical basis, and he despised blimpish opponents of progress.

In short, the body of ideas he echoed most strongly was that of Fabianism – usually associated with Socialism, of course, but at that time not as clearly linked to any political party. When he spoke of transferring, 'the working classes from their hideous and depressing surroundings to ... more wholesome dwellings', he was not delivering a mere sop to working-class voters.[5] An early advocate of town planning, cultural improvement 'on the rates' also interested him. During his spell as Lord Mayor from 1915 to 1916, two pet projects came to fruition: the Birmingham city orchestra and a municipal savings bank.

In December 1916, Lloyd George quite unexpectedly asked Chamberlain to become Director of National Service – one of a batch of government departments established by the new Prime Minister to wage war more efficiently. Hustled to immediate acceptance, it did not take long for Chamberlain to recognise his mistake. For Chamberlain's apologists, the Department of National Service was typical of Lloyd George's ill-conceived ideas – concocted more for its rhetorical impact than as part of any systematic plan. Beneath the grand phrases, administrative chaos reigned. A variety of government departments all felt they had a stake in the deployment of non-military labour and the newly established war Cabinet failed to sort out areas of competence. Chamberlain had neither the experience nor temperament to cope with the Whitehall in-fighting that quickly prevailed. Moreover, the man who had forced the appointment upon him – Lloyd George – never really liked him.[6] No doubt fault lay on all sides but, as can be imagined, his critics make much of this 'failure' and its impact upon his later career. By August 1917, he was back in Birmingham having resigned in humiliating defeat. He may have been resolved never to serve under Lloyd George again, yet he was still impatient to enter parliament at the earliest opportunity.[7]

No Birmingham seat was instantly available and, with large-scale boundary changes taking place, he had to wait until the general election of 1918 for a suitable opportunity. With the help of his wife's vigorous campaign, he was elected for the new inner city constituency of Ladywood. Whatever his thoughts on Lloyd George, he was a clear beneficiary of Lloyd George's leadership of the extended Coalition. Although he took to parliamentary life easily, busying himself in committee work, Chamberlain was in a frustrating predicament. A middle-aged man in a hurry, he wanted office; this was why he had become an MP. But with Lloyd George as Premier and Austen such a major shareholder in the Coalition (first as Chancellor and then as Unionist leader), his path to progress was blocked.

Limelight

Chamberlain took no direct part in the downfall of Lloyd George. He had joined the Carlton Club early in 1922 but, at the time of the fateful meeting of Conservative MPs that October, was *en route* home from a holiday in Canada. Nevertheless, he benefited from the event – accepting Bonar Law's invitation to be Postmaster General in his new government and, in doing so, emotionally outmanoeuvred his half-brother. Austen – the deposed Unionist leader – reacted to Neville's decision as though it was 'the last drop of bitterness in the cup'.[8] It was certainly the moment when Neville at last moved from under Austen's shadow.

After a series of breathtaking promotions, Neville Chamberlain was within a year Chancellor of the Exchequer in Baldwin's first government. Along the way he had been Minister of Health and was sworn into the Privy Council, flourishing while Austen endured his exile in sulky stiffness. During a period of revived Tory government, this was ironic; for while Austen was by temperament a Tory, Neville claimed to care little for party politics, finding the term 'Conservative' especially 'odious'.[9] If Austen had a heightened sense of a social order which needed protecting from Socialism, Neville professed the need for changes in post-war political alignments. By rights, Neville should have been the one to prosper in Coalition while declining afterwards. Yet the political scene following the downfall of Lloyd George's government was like improvised theatre: there were scripts and parts initially, but these tended to get mixed up once performances got underway.

Though few would have predicted it at the time, Lloyd George never again held public office after 1922. Between 1922 and 1923, there was much talk within Tory circles of the need to wean Austen, Lord Birkenhead and other Coalitionist Conservatives away from Lloyd George's embrace and back towards traditional Tory partisanship. Neville Chamberlain strongly supported this, yet oddly – after each failed attempt to reunite these leading Conservatives – he was promoted. To add to the general bewilderment, Baldwin decided (after only five months as Prime Minister and with an adequate majority) to pursue a policy of protection and, to that end, called a general election in November 1923. Whatever prompted Baldwin's decision, it was certainly not Chamberlain's own ideas on fiscal policy; neither was it a ploy to reunite the Tory party.[10] It took the shock general election defeat and the first Labour government to do that.

Chamberlain was not depressed by Labour taking office. His guess that 'they would be too weak to do much harm but not too weak to get discredited' proved astute.[11] He reasoned that a minority Labour government limping on for a year would allow the Conservatives to regroup and put their house in order, while the Liberals would continue on their path to self-destruction. Like Baldwin (though unlike many other Conservatives at that time), Chamberlain was not afraid of Labour. If Baldwin envisaged a kind of house-trained Labourism, schooled in the ways of Westminster, Chamberlain's aim was to take on Labour at its own game, demonstrating a Conservative commitment to social reform that was at least as genuine and more effective. The two were not soul-mates. But the combination of Baldwin's strategic vision and Chamberlain's more abrasive tactics represented what was called from 1924 the 'New Conservatism'. With the 'red scare' election of that year returning the Tories to office with a large majority, Chamberlain expedited the return to the Tory fold of both Churchill and Birkenhead, helping to secure them ministries to which their talents proved unsuited. Believing that the government would stand or fall by its social reforms, Chamberlain thereby set out to be 'a great Minister of Health'.[12]

There seems to be general agreement that, if not quite 'great', Chamberlain was certainly a very good Minister of Health between 1924 and 1929. His energy and drive raised the status of his department and earned him the reputation of a thoroughly competent minister. Churchill's 1925 Budget provided the finance for Chamberlain's legislative assault on the conditions of widows, orphans and old-age pensioners. His mastery of detail during the passage of the Rating and Valuation Bill 'put him in the first rank of parliamentarians', while his Local Government Act reformed the Poor Law and recast the financial relations of central and local government.[13] That he could contemplate, by 1929, a record that included twenty-one separate pieces of legislation, 800,000 houses built and fifty-eight slum clearance schemes in operation was a source of great personal satisfaction. If his achievement fell a little short of being 'massive and unquestioned',[14] and was not quite perhaps 'the link between the Liberal programme of social reform in 1906 and the Labour programme of 1945'[15] – as some historians evidently think – the judgement that he was 'the only minister in Baldwin's government of 1924–29 with a consistent record of achievement on the domestic front' seems more than justified.[16]

As a team player in that 1924–29 government, Chamberlain brought to it a sense of discipline and motivation, while his paternalistic social policies offered to the public a firm controlling hand. Yet his achievements carried costs. His strengths as a minister often made him appear to other politicians as 'more like a machine than a man'.[17] Never the 'clubbable' type, this 'cold fishy creature who puts your back up in five minutes'[18] developed a rasping parliamentary manner which so infuriated the Opposition that, for the rest of his life, he was 'hated by the Labour party with a quite remarkable degree of venom'.[19] In Cabinet, his decisiveness won much respect; but his inability to suffer fools gladly and, as he put it himself, '[in]capacity for looking on and seeing other people mismanaging things' were often interpreted as arrogance.[20]

Chamberlain's apologists excuse his 'too often combative manner' by referring to his 'exceptional sensitivity' and 'unflinching honesty of mind'.[21] Yet Chamberlain's less attractive features during this period are also used to explain his eventual, tragic demise; his 'incapacity for self-criticism' and his 'touchy vanity' have been seen as portents for his 'complete failure in foreign policy and ... posthumous derision'.[22] Even his apologists often describe his qualities at the Ministry of Health in a way that makes his later failures abroad seem predictable, echoing the jibe that he was a man of 'rigid competency' and 'an adequate Lord Mayor of Birmingham in a lean year' – the implication being that in any emergency he was lost[23] and that outside domestic affairs he 'ran into ... tides he could not measure'.[24]

Yet, as a conclusion, this would be unfair. Chamberlain in debate more often bettered Lloyd George and Churchill than they bettered him, and he was a more rounded politician than many allow. His record between 1929 and 1931, when he held no departmental office, shows a very different kind of politician: still rather cold and somewhat unendearing, yet tough, pragmatic, flexible and doggedly determined. He wrote around this time that his pleasure was 'in administration rather than the game of politics'.[25] This was typical but arch. During the 'games' which surrounded both the Conservative leadership crisis and the formation of the National Government, Chamberlain proved a formidable player.

The story of the 1929–31 Conservative leadership crisis is generally told in stark and dramatic terms – usually from Baldwin's point of view and culminating in his famous attack on the press lords in March 1931 (claiming that their 'power without responsibility' was akin to 'the prerogative of the harlot'). The issues of India and tariff reform overlap the personal efforts of Churchill and Beaverbrook to oust Baldwin, whether through the rousing of diehard opinion or the fielding of candidates in by-elections to challenge official Conservatives. Chamberlain himself, who became Party Chairman in June 1930 (earning the hatred of his predecessor, Davidson), is sometimes attributed with 'rather ambiguous motives',[26] maintaining only a formal loyalty while 'biding his time to gain the leadership without a fight'.[27] However, the evidence for this is as thin as Davidson's motives for criticism are transparent.[28]

Chamberlain certainly thought himself fit to succeed 'his friend and leader'. But he also knew that, in the Conservative Party, mixing the wish to succeed with the wish to replace is always a dangerous game. Though 'driven nearly to despair over SB's ways', he kept his head and resisted numerous requests to show his hand more forcefully.[29] As Party Chairman, he had to work closely with the leader, and Austen (who had his own motives for wishing Baldwin out) was sorry his half-brother had undertaken the post, fearing it would jeopardise Neville's own prospects of succession.[30]

Yet the role of adjutant suited him. Unlike Churchill, he had the sense not to acquire a reputation for disloyalty. Thanks to his efforts, the party could at least defend itself from the charge of vacuous sterility while in Opposition. Trimming to the Right, his 'unauthorised programme' of September 1930 (offering drastic economies in unemployment insurance and measures to improve imperial trade) became Shadow Cabinet policy within a month. By Christmas, he was also doing his best to wean dissident Liberals away from their unhappy acceptance of Lloyd George's leadership.

All this added to the party's fire-power at a time when an election seemed a possibility. There were misunderstandings with Baldwin, most famously in March 1931 during 'the supreme crisis in Baldwin's leadership'.[31] But this was at a time when Baldwin's attitude to anyone bearing bad news was to kill the messenger. When Chamberlain resigned the Party Chairmanship in 1931, Baldwin characteristically expressed 'not a word of surprise, regret or satisfaction'.[32]

No less characteristically, Baldwin was on holiday during the financial crisis of August 1931 – a crisis which led to the disintegration of the Labour government. It was left to Chamberlain to cancel his holiday arrangements and carry on inter-party negotiations with MacDonald and Samuel, which on 24 August produced the National Government. It fell to him not just to persuade the weary (yet ultra-sensitive) MacDonald that he should sever links with his party and lead a Coalition Government, but also to sell the idea to Tory colleagues who would normally expect a dissolution of parliament and the return of a Tory ministry.[33]

In the peculiar circumstances of August 1931, resolving the crisis depended on the swift decisions of a few key figures, all operating in a foggy climate. There was no conspiracy to bring down the Labour government. The problem was forming a new administration which could produce a balanced budget, restore financial confidence and maintain social harmony. Chamberlain's role in the crisis was decisive. As the Labour government collapsed amid fears of a financial apocalypse, he reached two quick and crucial decisions: that an immediate general election was too slow and unpredictable a way of resolving the crisis, and that the prospect of a new, minority Conservative administration was fraught with danger. He was in no doubt that, should a Conservative government try to enact the drastic economies judged necessary, the political and social consequences could be disastrous.

Chamberlain therefore played a major part in persuading MacDonald to stay on as Prime Minister and made more acceptable the idea that Baldwin should follow his lieutenant's lead. Whatever the motives of MacDonald, George V or Baldwin himself, it was Chamberlain's discreet salesmanship that 'shaped the situation'.[34] Thanks largely to his influence, what began as an expedient turned into a lasting political edifice. With expert ruthlessness, he persuaded Cabinet colleagues in September that an election was after all necessary, both for the government to clarify its own uncertainties and in order to inflict a decisive defeat upon Labour. He may not have been the National Government's architect – its construction was too complex for any one man – but in its consolidation and electoral triumph Chamberlain was chief strategist.

Emerging from the crisis with reputation enhanced, the 1931 settlement still put a brake on Chamberlain's own progress. Having helped to lengthen the queue to the Premiership, he had to bide his time with as much patience as he could muster. Yet Chamberlain's performance between 1929 and 1931 should dispel any notion that he was a bumbling, over-promoted figure, or that he was rendered outstanding only because he lived 'in a day of the lesser men'.[35] The crisis years of 1929 to 1931 posed the severest test of any politician's mettle.

Chamberlain did not possess great charm; that by 1932 it amused him to 'find a policy for each of my colleagues in turn' shows him in an ever more vain and unattractive light.[36] But it is still important to record that the description of him as an 'earnest and opinionated provincial' was very wide of the mark. No man possessing only 'a narrow sharp-edged efficiency' or 'limited outlook' would have had the wit or physical stamina to survive the events of 1929–31.[37] He had proved he had all the equipment necessary to fill the highest offices of state. His status as crown prince was symbolically confirmed in February 1932 when, as Chancellor of the Exchequer, he launched his Import Duties Bill in the House of Commons. Amid the waving of order papers that greeted the introduction of protection, Austen descended from his backbench seat to shake Neville's hand. Neville might well have whispered, as Napoleon once said to his brother, 'if only our father could see us now'.

Austen did not live to see his half-brother become Prime Minister five years later. Before then, Chamberlain had assumed a wide brief as Chancellor. In part, this stemmed from his holding the purse strings of departmental spending, helped also by his continuing Chairmanship of the Conservative Research Department which allowed him to affect long-term policy planning and party publicity. Yet with MacDonald ailing, and Baldwin's distaste for detail growing with the years, Chamberlain was the man who carried the government on his back. Few Cabinet colleagues dared stand up to him. The force of his personality played its part in this; but the almost certain knowledge that Chamberlain would soon be their leader also served to fortify his position.

Chamberlain is credited with presiding over an economy which, from deepest slump in 1931–32, reached surprising levels of buoyancy. The traditional charge is that the government could have been less devoted to balanced budgets and done more to alleviate the distressed areas – particularly during the period of private sector growth. But economic historians have recently formed a kinder opinion, arguing that Chamberlain was wise to follow orthodox policies.[38] All six of his Budgets were certainly well received at the time and, for a politician sensitive to electoral needs, he could draw immense satisfaction from the government's comfortable re-election in 1935.

Over rearmament, he was much less orthodox. With the Treasury as 'the fourth arm of defence', he did not veto expenditure. The sums allocated from 1934 were considerable by any standards and numerous schemes for raising further revenue were tried. Yet by insisting upon 'value for money', he consciously intervened in defence and foreign policy, irritating the services' ministers. Yet this also represented sound training for a Premier-in-waiting. At a time when foreign policy became central, Chamberlain formed a negative impression of the Foreign Office and devised his own plan of action.

Given the mounting crisis in Europe, and the obvious frailty of the League of Nations, Chamberlain perceived a large gap between Britain's

Continental commitments and national resources. Diplomacy would have to fill that gap by reducing diplomatic liabilities while satisfying, to a respectable extent, the demands of the dictators. The imprint he left upon the policy of appeasement while Prime Minister was one he fully rehearsed – in his mind – while Chancellor.

His accession to the Premiership was so smooth that it could have been stage-managed; Churchill actually seconded the resolution which confirmed Chamberlain as party leader. There had indeed been no slip twixt cup and lip during Chamberlain's 'years of waiting', and he 'exuded confidence' as he assumed the highest office.[39] Yet for all his new-broom style of leadership, his first Cabinet saw few changes in personnel. By and large, he was content to accept the team he had inherited and, mindful of the need to preserve his government's 'national' credentials, did not swamp it with Conservatives. There were no places for Amery and Churchill, for example, even though the Tory Chief-Whip (Margesson) had advised a post for the latter on the grounds that it would keep him 'out of mischief'.[40] It was also interesting that Eden – who he inherited as Foreign Secretary – was so impressed with his new leader's grip of affairs that he felt able to remove his own permanent undersecretary to a more marginal position.[41]

Chamberlain did have some difficulties with ministers. The list of those he sacked or who resigned during his thirty-five months as Premier bolsters the view that he liked to be 'adored and set on a pedestal ... by unquestioning admirers'.[42] Yet there is no clear evidence that he surrounded himself with cronies. In keeping government supporters in line, Margesson did not exceed his powers, nor was there anything unusual or sinister about Chamberlain's reliance upon his civil servant adviser, Sir Horace Wilson. Although he told Lady Astor that he meant to be 'his own Foreign Minister', there is no evidence that this 'drove Eden to resignation' in February 1938.[43]

In spite of efforts in his memoirs to claim the contrary, Eden was no consistent anti-appeaser – nor was Chamberlain as ignorant of foreign affairs as those memoirs implied.[44] Because the resignation 'was not obviously about anything in particular',[45] it created so little damage that even Eden's supporters were 'inclined to think that Chamberlain was right'.[46] Nevertheless, the idea that Eden sought to destroy the government is intriguing, not because it shows Eden 'overestimat[ing] his indispensability,[47] but for the implication that Chamberlain's leadership was not as unquestioned as is generally supposed. That Eden was advised, 'the country is unenthusiastic about the PM',[48] while Thomas Jones thought Chamberlain's team 'not a very loyal one',[49] undermines the traditional view that Chamberlain was so dominant he could pursue his foreign policy with 'complacent obstinacy.'[50]

Whatever the morality of that policy, there was a clear domestic imperative for it to succeed. A general election could not long be delayed; nor for that matter could the question of his succession. Chamberlain's visit to Hitler in September 1938 was a brilliant public relations exercise and, despite Duff

Cooper's resignation, the support the Premier received from the Commons directly after Munich was overwhelming.

The political success of Munich would eventually destroy both Chamberlain's career and reputation. He thought that the agreement he secured would ensure that Germany and Britain never went to war again. He thought that Hitler had been the one who backed down. He believed that the basis of a lasting peace had been established. If the dictators kept their word, any domestic criticism could easily be ignored. But the dictators did not keep their word. Hitler's behaviour after Munich, and the 'moral disturbance' it created, led to mounting criticism to which Chamberlain eventually succumbed.[51]

Public opinion may not quite have 'exploded' after Germany's occupation of Prague in March 1939, but in parliament a block of resistance – comprising 'an excitable mass of socialists, Tory ultras and the inevitable waverers and opportunists' – steadily mounted.[52] Although it lacked the backing of Churchill and Eden after September 1939, it was this unlikely alliance which contributed to the 'crushing moral defeat' in the Norway debate of May 1940.[53] It would be pleasing to record that this was an occasion where parliament recovered its conscience and spoke in Cromwellian tones for the nation. Yet for all the debate's significance, it was an event two days later which determined Chamberlain's resignation.[54] By refusing to serve under Chamberlain, the National Executive of the Labour Party paved the way for Churchill's own Coalition. It was cruel yet fitting that the politician who helped exclude Labour from office in 1931 should be shorn of office himself by the politics of the Labour Party.

Legacy

The 'verdict of history', which Chamberlain anticipated before he died proved so severe that the revisionist backlash has been correspondingly sharp.[55] There is no currency now in arguing that he was weak, ignorant or pursued peace at any price. The 'guilty men' interpretations of the 1940s are now out of fashion, and it has even been suggested that he took a covert lead in plans to replace Hitler with Goring at the beginning of the war.[56] His brand of appeasement has lately been portrayed as plausible and appropriate, one that was unavoidable and even predetermined.[57]

Yet the process of rehabilitation can only go so far, and the notion that there was simply no alternative to his appeasement policy is difficult to accept. Although it may not have been any character defect which led Chamberlain to believe in the Munich settlement, it was still a calamitous misjudgement. It involved his adherence to the view that conciliation could render Hitler's Germany peaceful – long after contrary evidence had surfaced. Had he thought and acted as if Munich bought no more than time, and had he been less anxious to reassure the dictators, then things might have turned out less disastrously. Above all, there remains the criticism that, in his search for *detente*, he sent the wrong signals to the dictators. Hitler can only have reasoned that, if the British and French would not march to save Czechoslovakia, they would not do so to save Poland. It was Chamberlain's fault, as well as misfortune, that the Anglo-French threat to honour the guarantee to Poland was not taken seriously in either Berlin or Moscow.

One can take a dim view of Chamberlain's foreign policy without using the language of tragedy. To say that he followed mistaken policies is not to say that he was unable to make sensible decisions using the information available. He may well have been 'obstinate', but is that so very different from the less pejorative 'determined'? His critics do not help our understanding by arguing that his personality *per se* made him unsuitable for high office; his career undeniably ended in failure, but his personality was no more flawed than that of most other politicians. Chamberlain was a tough, dogged and resourceful politician, no less suited for the posts he occupied than most of his predecessors or successors. Unfortunately for Chamberlain, his mistakes were to prove rather more costly and conspicuous.

Chronology

1869	born, Edgbaston, Birmingham, March
1875	death of mother (Florence Chamberlain)
1890	despatched to Andros as a sisal planter
1897	returns from Andros
1911	marries Annie Cole. Elected to Birmingham City Council
1914	death of father (Joseph Chamberlain). Becomes Alderman
1915	elected Lord Mayor of Birmingham
1916	accepts Lloyd George's invitation to become Director of National Service
1917	resigns as Director of National Service
1918	elected to parliament, Member for Ladywood
1922	joins Carlton Club. Becomes Postmaster General
1923	becomes Paymaster General, then Minister of Health and later Chancellor of the Exchequer
1924	Minister of Health
1925	Rating and Valuation Act
1929	Local Government Act. Becomes Head of Conservative Research Department
1930	becomes Conservative Party Chairman
1931	resigns as Party Chairman, becomes Minister of Health and then Chancellor of the Exchequer
1932	Import Duties Act
1937	becomes Prime Minister
1938	Eden resigns. Munich Agreement
1939	Polish guarantee. Nazi–Soviet non-aggression pact. Declaration of war on Germany
1940	Norway debate. Chamberlain resigns Premiership but remains in War

Cabinet as Lord President and retains party leadership. Resigns all offices in September due to illness. Refuses Garter. Dies in November at Heckfield, Hampshire

Notes

1. J. Charmley, *Chamberlain and the Lost Peace* (London, Hodder and Stoughton, 1989), p. 209.
2. K. Feiling, *The Life of Neville Chamberlain* (London, Macmillan, 1946), p. 34.
3. D. Dilks, *Neville Chamberlain*, Vol. I (Cambridge, Cambridge University Press, 1984), pp. 119–22.
4. L. W. Fuchser, *Neville Chamberlain and Appeasement* (New York, Norton, 1982), pp. xi and 199.
5. H. Montgomery Hyde, *Neville Chamberlain* (London, Weidenfeld and Nicolson, 1976), p. 24.
6. Dilks, *Chamberlain*, p. 195.
7. Feiling, *Chamberlain*, p. 63.
8. I. Macleod, *Neville Chamberlain* (London, Frederick Muller, 1961), p. 87.
9. J. Ramsden, *The Age of Balfour and Baldwin* (London, Longman, 1978), p. 356.
10. R. Self, 'Conservative reunion and the general election of 1923', *Twentieth Century British History*, 3 (1992), 249–73.
11. Dilks, *Chamberlain*, p. 360.
12. Feiling, *Chamberlain*, p. 117.
13. W. W. Hadley, entry in *Dictionary of National Biography 1931–1940* (Oxford, Oxford University Press, 1949).
14. Feiling, *Chamberlain*, p. 127.
15. Macleod, *Chamberlain*, p. 114.
16. B. Lenman, *The Eclipse of Parliament* (London, Edward Arnold, 1991), p. 118.
17. S. Ball (ed.), *Parliament and Politics in the Age of Baldwin and MacDonald: The Headlam Diaries 1923–1935* (London, Historians' Press, 1992), p. 113.
18. S. Ball, *Baldwin and the Conservative Party* (New Haven, Yale University Press, 1988), p. 136.
19. Ramsden, *Balfour and Baldwin*, p. 357.
20. Viscount Templewood (Sir Samuel Hoare), *Nine Troubled Years* (London, Collins, 1954), p. 36.
21. Macleod, *Chamberlain*, p. 203.
22. R. A. C. Parker, *Chamberlain and Appeasement* (London, Macmillan, 1993), p. 11.
23. D. Lloyd George, *War Memoirs* (2nd edn, London, Odhams, 1938), p. 811.
24. W. S. Churchill, *The Second World War: Volume 1* (London, Cassell, 1948), p. 174.
25. Dilks, *Chamberlain*, p. 586.
26. R. Blake, *The Conservative Party from Peel to Thatcher* (London, Fontana, 1985), p. 234.
27. Ramsden, *Balfour and Baldwin*, p. 311.
28. R. Rhodes James (ed.), *Memoirs of a Conservative: J. C. C. Davidson's Memoirs and Papers 1910–1937* (London, Weidenfeld and Nicolson, 1969), pp. 356–8.
29. Montgomery Hyde, *Chamberlain*, p. 54.

30 R. Self (ed), *The Austen Chamberlain Diaries and Letters* (Cambridge, Cambridge University Press, 1995), p. 354.
31 Rhodes James, *Davidson's Memoirs*, p. 356.
32 Macleod, *Chamberlain*, p. 143.
33 Ball, *Baldwin*, p. 176.
34 P. Williamson, *National Crisis and National Government: British Politics, the Economy and Empire 1926–1932* (Cambridge, Cambridge University Press, 1992), p. 337.
35 C. L. Mowat, *Britain Between the Wars* (London, Methuen, 1955), p. 414.
36 Macleod, *Chamberlain*, p. 164.
37 Churchill, *Second World War*, pp. 173–4.
38 A. Thorpe, *Britain in the 1930s* (Oxford, Blackwell, 1992), p. 78.
39 Ramsden, *Balfour and Baldwin*, p. 357.
40 Secret memo, Margesson to Chamberlain, March 1937; Birmingham University Library, NC 8/24/1.
41 D. Carlton, *Anthony Eden* (London, Allen and Unwin, 1986), p. 99.
42 J. Colville, *The Fringes of Power: Downing Street Diaries 1939–1955* (London, Hodder and Stoughton, 1985), p. 79.
43 H. Macmillan, *The Past Masters* (London, Macmillan, 1975), p. 138.
44 Lord Avon, *Facing the Dictators* (London, Cassell, 1962), p. 455.
45 M. Cowling, *The Impact of Hitler* (Cambridge, Cambridge University Press, 1975), p. 267.
46 N. Smart (ed.) *The Diaries and Letters of Robert Bernays* (Lewiston, Edwin Mellen, 1996), p. 342.
47 Carlton, *Eden*, p. 132.
48 J. Harvey (ed), *The Diplomatic Papers of Oliver Harvey 1937–1940* (London, Collins, 1970), pp. 88–9.
49 T. Jones, *A Diary with Letters 1931–1950* (Oxford, Oxford University Press, 1954), p. 350.
50 Parker, *Chamberlain and Appeasement*, p. 94.
51 M. Cowling, *The Impact of Labour* (Cambridge, Cambridge University Press, 1976), pp. 201 and 280.
52 R. Holland, *The Pursuit of Greatness: Britain and the World Role 1900–1970* (London, Fontana, 1991), p. 157.
53 P. Addison, *The Road to 1945* (London, Sphere Books, 1977), pp. 97–8.
54 R. Rhodes James (ed.), *'Chips': The Diaries of Chips Channon* (Harmondsworth, Penguin, 1984), p. 303.
55 J. Charmley, *Churchill: The End of Glory* (London, Sceptre, 1995), p. 235.
56 See S. Newton, *Profits of Peace: The Political Economy of Anglo-German Appeasement* (Oxford, Clarendon, 1996).
57 See P. Kennedy, 'Appeasement', in G. Martel (ed.), *The Origins of the Second World War Reconsidered* (Boston, Allen and Unwin, 1986), p. 155.

Further reading

Dilks' first (and still only) volume on Chamberlain, *Neville Chamberlain* (Cambridge, Cambridge University Press, 1984), is the best all-round guide, although it is widely considered somewhat dull. Ramsden's *Age of Balfour and Baldwin* (London, Longman, 1978) is orthodox in its interpretations but still offers a useful treatment of Chamberlain's career. Parker's *Chamberlain and Appeasement* (London, Macmillan, 1993) provides a 'post-revisionist', and often hard-hitting, assessment of Chamberlain's foreign policy. Cowling's *Impact of Hitler* (Cambridge, Cambridge University Press, 1975), though not always as readable as some students might wish, still assembles much useful information while offering a number of challenging conclusions.

Winston Churchill

Owen Hartley

Background

The most important elements in Churchill's background were his aristocratic connections, his relative poverty within a sometimes scandalous family, the influence of his father, Lord Randolph, his enthusiasm, energy and determination to make a name, and the provisional character of his political philosophy.

Blenheim Palace was built, partly at public expense, to commemorate the victories of the 1st Duke of Marlborough against the European ambitions of Louis XIV. It was here that Churchill was born in 1874. He was potentially a future Duke of Marlborough himself, and only the birth of a son to his father's elder brother prevented a translation of Churchill's energies to the tending of estates and a seat in the House of Lords. Churchill was to write biographies of both his father and the first Duke and chose to be buried close to his birthplace. He was at all times a conscious member of a distinguished tradition with all the duties, public and private, which that position required.

Yet the Churchill family was rather poor, only able to sustain itself with the influx of American monied wives (Churchill's own mother was the daughter of an American millionaire), such was the level of financial incompetence in the family. The young Churchill was sufficiently favoured with resources and contacts to be able to go to Harrow and Sandhurst and obtain a commission in a good cavalry regiment, but he had little money to squander and as a younger son was, in any event, expected to make his own fortune. The later Churchillian ruthlessness with regard to money and financial security rested upon a sharp early recognition that these things were not to be taken for granted.

Within the historic family, Winston was one of the few, including his own children, with anything that might pass for a sense of moral awareness. His father, in particular, was notoriously loose living and wayward. Lord Randolph, while expressing disappointment in his son's activities, was dedicated to a flashy and poorly judged political life; he died early, it is believed, of the syphilis that the young Winston may have thought he had inherited. Churchill felt compelled to seek fame in order to come to terms with his father's view of him and to fulfil in politics what his father had only partly attained: high and long office.

Churchill's brief army career saw a considerable amount of fighting on the Indian North West frontier and in the Sudan. By 1899, however, he had decided that life in a costly polo-playing regiment (Churchill scored three goals for his regiment when they won the inter-regimental polo cup in 1898) was less interesting than a career in journalism and politics. His experiences as a war correspondent in South Africa and with the South African Horse regiment were again of a lively and distinguished kind. There was little doubt to most of his contemporaries that Churchill was personally brave, pushy for recognition and altogether a man on the verge of an interesting career in politics.

Quite what his politics were, especially party politics, was something of a mystery, possibly even to himself. Following in Lord Randolph's footsteps, he was a Conservative Unionist when elected in 1900, but already had doubts about the party that, in his view, had treated his father so shabbily and which seemed less interested in reform than he felt appropriate to the times. It was possible to be a Unionist on Ireland, an ardent supporter of the Empire and be a Liberal too. On most points in the contemporary political debate, Churchill was with the Liberals. To move over to them in 1904 on the free-trade issue when the Conservatives flirted with protection was easy. Reform and renewal at home while preserving British interests abroad was a good basis for a young politician eager for office. Churchill had already become convinced that politics were more about national issues than party concerns and ideas, an approach more common in the Victorian period than the twentieth century. This was to be both a long-term weakness and his strength for Coalition Government.

Apprenticeship

Churchill's apprenticeship was characterised by weak political skills, energy in ministerial office, doubts about his judgement of people and issues, and his continuing estimation of his own ability to serve in high office.

One continuing theme in Churchill's long apprenticeship as a politician is that he was never very good at his trade. Out of office he had little grasp and, while he was a very good minister, he managed to annoy colleagues and lose friends. A symptom of this was that he never had a secure constituency base. He had to move from Oldham, where he had been elected in 1900, to

Manchester North West in 1906 and thence, on losing the by-election then necessary for ministers on attaining Cabinet rank, to Dundee in 1908. He lost Dundee in 1922 and failed in his next two attempts to re-enter parliament in 1923 and 1924 before being found a safe seat by Baldwin in the latter year. There is no evidence that he then became any more than a perfunctory constituency member.

A further point about Churchill as a politician was that, though he professed to love parliament and Cabinet government dependent on parliament, he was, in fact, both a very poor parliamentarian and Cabinet colleague. He disliked the business of the House and the existence of many Members who were held together by party and personal loyalties and rewards rather than by the force of argument and oratory. He enjoyed making speeches but parliament was no longer a body that responded to the impulses of speeches, however good. Churchill relished office above all else. Being a minister was to have, use and be close to power; it meant making decisions, explaining them in speeches and being involved in the whole firmament of high politics. This latter activity Churchill enjoyed to the dismay of his colleagues; he interfered with their work while never being personally loyal to their conclusions. Only as Chancellor of the Exchequer did Churchill have an institutional base for the kind of involvement with other departments that he so enjoyed.

The circumstances of Churchill's early political apprenticeship, between 1904 and 1915, made him aloof from parliamentary party politics: he obtained office early, was part of a large Commons majority and, after 1908, worked in a Cabinet that enabled him to develop habits of independent action. The experiences of 1904–15 were such that Churchill never became a modern party politician. Neither did participation in a large Coalition between 1917 and 1922, or the holding of office as an ex-Liberal in a Conservative administration between 1924 and 1929, promote his understanding of party politics. Changing parties twice, from Conservative to Liberal in 1904 and then back again twenty years later, did little to dispel the earlier uncertainties about him as a party politician.

As a minister, Churchill was very successful and proved himself to be the practical and sure holder of office that Premiers prefer. At the Colonial Office, 1905–08, Churchill was concerned with South African issues and arrangements for the newly annexed East Africa. At the Board of Trade, 1908–10, he was responsible for Labour Exchanges, the introduction of Wages Boards for the 'sweated labour trades' and unemployment insurance. As Home Secretary, 1910–11, Churchill encouraged prison reform and attempted a reform of the legislation relating to shopping hours; he was more famous, however, for his presence at the death of three anarchists in the 'Seige of Sidney Street' and for his military intervention in the coal miners' strike at Tonypandy and other industrial disputes. When appointed First Lord of the Admiralty in 1911, Churchill moved to that concern for war and high politics that he instinctively preferred and the measures he implemented focused on preparations for war. But it was during the war that Churchill finally failed. The defence of Antwerp in 1914 and the Dardanelles expedition of March 1915, a campaign that Churchill had enthusiastically supported against the doubts of his best professional and political advisers, were regarded as ultimate proof of his unfitness to govern both among Liberal colleagues and many Conservatives. He was transferred to the Duchy of Lancaster but, keenly aware of his demotion, Churchill volunteered to serve in France, where a good war could restore both reputation and career.

The first apprenticeship, 1904–15, was over: Churchill was recognised as a man of talent and energy but he had few party political friends – the Conservatives regarded him as a traitor, the Liberal reformers saw him as one of them but they were necessarily close to a Labour Party who saw Churchill as decidedly unsympathetic after his use of the military in industrial disputes. Moreover, after the Dardanelles fiasco, his judgement, even in areas where he thought of himself as having a special insight, was suspect. Nevertheless, a persistent man could always engineer a return; there was no doubt that he had been a good minister and he had the personal regard in that respect of two men who were to become Prime Ministers: Lloyd George and Baldwin.

Having served in the trenches, Churchill was able to take advantage of a battalion reorganisation to resume his parliamentary activities. In 1917 Lloyd George found him an office at Munitions where his energies were concentrated on the production of shells, gas and tanks. Promoted to War and Air in 1919, Churchill oversaw a successful demobilisation programme, though he backed the wrong horse with his support for the anti-Bolshevik forces in Russia. Moving to the Colonial Office in 1921, Churchill helped to bring about much of the post-war settlement in the Middle East, including Jewish immigration to Palestine; he was also a leading protagonist in the resolution of the Irish problem. By the time of the fall of the Coalition in October 1922, Churchill had done enough to be regarded as a serious politician once again. At this point the context in which Churchill had operated fell apart.

At the 1922 election the Liberals were driven into third place and it was plain to many that the future of party politics was going to be Conservative versus Labour. Liberal politicians with constructive ambitions would have to make a choice, and for Churchill such a choice could only mean a return to the party he had left in 1904. A parallel problem for Churchill was that he lost his parliamentary seat in 1922. At a crucial moment in his rehabilitation as a serious politician, he was left on the margins.

He was able to return through the generosity of Baldwin, who found him a safe seat at Epping and made him Chancellor of the Exchequer in the new Conservative government of 1924. Though best known for his time at the Treasury for his decision to return to the Gold Standard in 1925 or his rough handling of the unions during the General Strike of 1926, most significant to contemporaries were his policies on interstate debt, and tax and rating reforms. At the point of the Conservative defeat in the election of 1929,

Churchill could be seen as a major figure in the party. He had amply demonstrated that, while not popular or completely immune from occasional bouts of rashness, he was a good and competent minister.

At this point Churchill made a major political error. In a bid for political leadership against Baldwin he resigned from the Conservative Business Committee (a forerunner of the Shadow Cabinet) in 1931. This was an act of personal disloyalty to Baldwin and clearly contemptuous of the party, which was willing to follow Baldwin's lead. It is customary to regard Churchill's views on India as being reactionary and biased by his previous military service. In fact, they read much better in the light of the later history of British India, and deserve reassessment. The timing of Churchill's protest was also unfortunate coming only a few months before the financial crisis of 1931 which swept the Conservatives back into power as part of the National Government. A period of silence would have seen Churchill in office again.

Churchill's reputation among Conservatives plummeted. He continued to give vent to his views on the India legislation of the new government, so confirming his place on the backbenches. His other theme in the 1930s was the problem of appeasing Italy and Germany. Quite what he wanted to do was much less clear at the time than the vehement, anti-appeaser role Churchill's own history later suggested. In any event, it had no resonance with the rest of his party, though it sometimes played well with Labour. Churchill's romantic support for Edward VIII in the abdication crisis of 1936 merely confirmed to observers that his judgement was now fatally impaired. Of the major domestic issues, such as unemployment, he had little to say. In a political wilderness on policies, Churchill compounded his distance from party matters by basking in the adulation of a group of friends and cronies, including Brendon Brackan and Bob Boothby, who had little reputation. Serious political dissidents from the government, such as Eden after 1937, avoided too close a contact with Churchill.

Churchill was occupied in these years with journalism and serious historical writing. For him to be so engaged was to some observers a real relief: Churchill had abilities and literary flair but he was not a plausible politician of the first rank. His weakness had been exposed and he did nothing to recover favour. He was the senior Privy Counsellor in the party and thus was the man to second Neville Chamberlain to become the new party leader in 1937; he could have cultivated the role of the somewhat dissident elder statesman (like Heath after 1975). But Churchill believed, against all the evidence, that he had a future role in which he might serve his country. Throughout the 1930s, he never wavered in his belief that, while not a saviour in the political realm as some Continental leaders regarded themselves, there was one last task for him to accomplish.

As it happened, the distance of Churchill from politics in the 1930s was precisely what made him such a valuable prospect in returning to power. He was not associated with the failings of the Conservatives after 1931. Though he had a past, Labour could give him the benefit of the doubt that he would be a leader whom they could follow. Churchill was an elder statesman who had warned of dangers that were above and beyond the concerns of party politics. If only he could get some policy right while the government got it wrong – and the Opposition would accept that analysis – then there was a hope. At last he would have shown that his reputation for poor judgement was unfair. Churchill clung to that hope.

Limelight

Churchill's wartime triumph rested upon his leadership of coalition politics, his grasp of the grand strategy and direction of war, his enthusiasm, energy, courage and conviction, and the contemporary verdict that this was his 'finest hour'.

Churchill's road to the top started with his rejection of the Munich Pact which Chamberlain had negotiated with Hitler in September 1938. Despite the loss of the Sudetenland to Germany, the pact was universally popular and Churchill's hostile speech in the House of Commons was unwelcome. However, when it became clear that Hitler would not be bound by treaty obligations as he occupied Prague against the Munich settlement terms in March 1939, Churchill wisely avoided the temptation to point out in triumph that his warnings about Germany had been thoroughly justified. Such a restrained approach helped to make Churchill acceptable to Chamberlain, who appointed him First Lord of the Admiralty once more. Churchill was a symbol of British willingness to fight. No one else had a plausible claim to that role; everyone, including Labour, was tainted with some element of having flinched from the prospect of war.

At the Admiralty, Churchill was dynamic but not particularly successful. Indeed the issue on which Chamberlain was to fall, the government's handling of the Norwegian campaign, was largely Churchill's responsibility. His defence of his own and the government's conduct won support from the Conservatives even as it became clear that the direction of the war had to be in hands other than Chamberlain's. Everyone but Lord Halifax thought that the latter would be the ideal leader of a new Coalition Government. Halifax preferred Churchill and since no one else had suitable credentials, Churchill became Prime Minister despite his known or suspected weaknesses.

Leading a Coalition Government suited Churchill. He was quite willing to leave domestic issues to the Labour ministers and even delegated to them the organisation of government itself. His loyalty was repaid by the efforts Labour made to make the Coalition work. This allowed Churchill to devote his energies to matters of wartime strategy and direction. When, in 1942, the war was not going well, especially against Japan, Churchill was able to win a confidence vote in the Commons by 464 to 1. However infuriating, eccentric and out of touch with domestic matters he may have been,

Churchill was simply not replaceable.

Churchill's wartime strategy comprised the rallying of the British public to continue the war, the acquisition of allies and the pursuit of a peace settlement that kept Britain as a major player in international affairs but avoided the outcome of 1919 with the USA outside the framework for peace. The first of these objectives was achieved in 1940 when Churchill fine-tuned his political rhetoric to boost morale after the Dunkirk evacuation and prepare for the Battle of Britain. The second was achieved by the rather improbable alliance with the USSR when it was invaded by Germany in 1941, and the more eagerly sought alliance with the USA after Pearl Harbor. Though Churchill may have exaggerated in his war history the speed with which he recognised the shape of the post-war world, he still had a better grasp than anyone else of the emerging power balances. He was particularly anxious to contain the advantages to be gained from the war by Stalin, as evidenced by the attempt in 1944 to apportion interests between Britain and the USSR in the Balkans. The cost of the rebalancing was that Britain's international position was inevitably tied to that of the USA and that Britain's imperial position was irretrievably weakened, much against Churchill's instincts.

All these elements of the strategic picture are controversial. It was and still is questioned whether fighting Hitler was worth any sacrifice, especially since Bolshevik Russia was to be identified as the next enemy. But in 1940 no one thought that Hitler would either give or respect an honourable peace settlement. The alliance that emerged, and the round of conferences that ensured a common direction, owed much to Churchill's capacity for seeing and negotiating an overview and for mastering the arts of diplomatic brokerage. In retrospect, Churchill played his hand carefully, distrusting Stalin and losing little to Roosevelt. That the USA, as the only democratic superpower, would emerge as the major world force at the end of the war was perhaps inevitable. If the war was worth fighting then US dominance was to be a consequence. The main task, therefore, was to ensure that the US was committed to broadly British perspectives on world affairs. Churchill essentially invented 'the special relationship' to ensure that outcome.

Throughout the war Churchill exhibited enthusiasm and energy as well as courage and conviction. His habit of firing off memoranda to his colleagues and the Chiefs of Staff with the annotation 'Action this Day' was hardly endearing, yet those who could stand the bombardment loved being part of a system where things did happen and where decisions were made. Churchill routinely worked ninety hour weeks, slept at odd times, rushed around the world seeing people, constantly received briefs on new problems and still spent time explaining as much as he could to the House of Commons. It was a phenomenal performance, totally neglectful of his own health and infirmities, but always done with the whole-hearted conviction that there was no way of doing the task other than the way he did it.

Churchill's style as Premier can be seen as the last gasp of the old Britain.

He rather self-consciously behaved as a Victorian grandee with the aristocratic symbol of cigar in hand. His concern for the high politics of interstate relations and Empire distinguished him from a political agenda in which domestic issues of employment, education, housing and planning were the currency of debate between Labour and the reforming Tories who now dominated his own party. He had never excelled at the new party politics, preferring a people-based approach; but neither was he close to any of the new personalities in politics, always gravitating towards old friends, even to the exclusion of those who claimed, like Eden and Macmillan, to be heirs to his political insight. He appealed to an England rather than a Britain, and an England that was supremely self-confident about its own value and place in the world. He could thus offer no real threat to the new men of party politics who had, they believed, grasped the reality of Britain's position in the world and what would make it great again. Churchill was not likely to speak against this new Britain – he was still a Tory reformer – but he was not relevant to it. This might seem to be an astute political position to ensure his political survival, but the bulk of it came from his heart rather than his head.

Drawing up the balance sheet on Churchill's wartime Premiership has so far hinged on the answers to a small number of questions. Was it worth continuing the war in 1940? Was the neglect of domestic policy the foundation of an ultimately debilitating domestic consensus? Was too much conceded to the USA in the strategic settlement after the war (the Empire, a world role, the necessity for the anti-Communist crusade)? Future historians may raise other questions but the answers given so far by Churchill's supporters suggest that 'there was no alternative', while detractors claim that 'these were the mistakes to be expected of this kind of man'. The two standpoints are much closer in analysis than the proponents might wish. In part this is because no one has yet sensibly integrated the wartime Churchill with the post-war Churchill in continuities of interest and style.

Churchill, like his party, did not expect to be defeated in the 1945 election. He had wanted to continue the Coalition at least until the war with Japan was concluded; but the Labour Party, in contrast to the views of some of its leaders, was eager for office. Churchill, at something of a loose end after the hectic life he had led for over five years, took poorly to the task of Leader of the Opposition. He made the necessary ritual speeches on Labour's domestic policies, but many were policies he had himself supported in his earlier career. More significant was his role as statesman. He was able to combine very substantial support for the emerging Labour foreign policy, opposing the USSR with public speeches that gave new directions to policy that could be accepted or disregarded by the new leaders of Britain and the USA at will. They very often found Churchill's points helpful. The 'Iron Curtain' speech at Fulton, Missouri, was one that gave a shape to the growing opposition by the USA to Soviet expansion in Europe. Similarly, his speeches on a united or common European policy promoted Franco-German reconciliation, gave British blessing to the restoration of a new Germany and promised British co-operation in European affairs. This satisfied both US and British policy which was rarely explained with quite the same eloquence or passion. The statesman also had his war memoirs to write, partly motivated by his wish to sustain his role as the prophet once ignored with the obvious implication that his current warnings deserved consideration.

The conventional view is that Churchill continued in politics long past his best and should have retired gracefully in 1945. These sentiments were certainly shared by colleagues in his post-war government of 1951 to 1955 (though Churchill believed, perhaps rightly, that they, and especially Eden, were not up to the task either). This conventional view places too much emphasis on the need for domestic activity from Churchill and neglects the point that both he and his party were unwilling to contemplate a return to real 'Conservatism' after 1945. Domestic consensus was what Churchill and most of the Conservative leadership sought. The concern for international affairs was a most sensible priority: war in Europe and elsewhere was not impossible with new uncertainties over the futures of Germany and Japan, the US commitment to world affairs and the behaviour of Communist China and Russia. Churchill's capacity to see these issues clearly has been neglected because the framework of interpretation that he used was the old-fashioned balance of power thesis which, it is held, overestimated how the British contribution to that balance could be decisive. On both matters, Churchill's post-war performance may well be the beneficiary of revisionist interpretations, with today's Labour Party discerning the advantages of consensus, and post-Cold War analyses of Britain's role exploring the problems of operating within an environment of uncertainty.

Legacy

Churchill left office in 1955, retired to the backbenches and made irregular appearances in the House of Commons until he gave up his seat in 1964. He did not enjoy the infirmities of old age or the lack of excitement on being relieved of office and seems to have welcomed death in 1965. His state funeral was a magnificent affair. Everyone, including old enemies, paid tribute to a man who was larger than life and embodied virtues and values no longer present in a greyer world.

The first legacy Churchill left was to historians. They have had to ponder how to deal with a long and complex career, without the traditional props of domestic party hagiography and including major elements of international and imperial affairs for which few historians are equipped. There is no doubt that almost everyone who works on Churchill develops some kind of affection for the man. He wrote well and at length. Though Churchill could speak harshly of opponents, he was personally a man devoid of sustained malice. Of the politicians of his own period, only Ramsay MacDonald had an equivalent sweetness of temper. It is hard for historians not to warm to him.

Even so, the historical tradition has until recently, like this chapter, identified 1940–45 as the peak of Churchill's career, with a preceding apprenticeship and a subsequent anti-climax. Addison's brave effort on *Churchill on the Home Front*[1] invites a reconsideration of Churchill's formidable domestic record: for a man not close to becoming Prime Minister, his record of achievement, 1904–31, is unparalleled. It has been suggested here that a similar reconsideration of 1945–55 could be made around the theme of reconciliation in domestic and international affairs. Much of this reflects contemporary concerns; the verdict of history is revised in every generation as each new generation of political leaders seeks to use those parts of the past that help present purposes – much as Churchill himself did in his historical writings.

For post-1945 politics, the Churchill legacy has been a grammar of improving myths and stories. Churchill's long experience in political isolation, followed by a return to power and recognition of his rightness, has comforted other exiles from Tony Benn to Enoch Powell. The 'Dunkirk spirit' can be found in any crisis from the collapse of sterling to the Falklands War. The concern for Europe or US involvement in world affairs can still be cited as a prophecy relevant to our times. Even Addison's work on the Home Front has a small message for any anti-welfare Conservative government to heed. One major strength of the Churchill story is that it is not purely party or even nationally political; it belongs to anyone as a common currency, as much a part of Anglo-American history as British domestic concerns.

Yet the actual legacy of Churchill is now very slight: in the domestic sphere, new reforms and new problems shape our understanding of what is needed; in foreign affairs being firm with dictators is all very well as a slogan but, as Churchill himself demonstrated during the 1930s, such toughness is not always easy to achieve; furthermore, almost nothing survives of the world Churchill helped to shape now that the Cold War is over. It would appear that Churchill has already joined the great figures of history sporting such names as Marlborough and the Elder and Younger Pitt. This would have pleased Churchill enormously for he always thought of politics and history in this way – what you do is less important than the style in which you are remembered for having done it. The myth is ultimately more important than the Churchill who lived.

Chronology

1874	born at Blenheim Palace, Oxfordshire, November
1886	Lord Randolph Churchill briefly becomes Chancellor of the Exchequer
1888	enters Harrow School
1893	enters Royal Military College, Sandhurst
1895	death of Lord Randolph Churchill. Commissioned and joins 4th Hussars

1896	posted to India
1898	takes part in Battle of Omdurman
1899	war correspondent in South Africa; captured by Boers and escapes
1900	elected Unionist MP for Oldham
1904	joins Liberal Party
1905	appointed Parliamentary Under-Secretary for the Colonies
1906	elected Liberal MP for Manchester North West
1908	appointed President of the Board of Trade. Loses by-election in Manchester and becomes MP for Dundee. Marries Clementine Hozier
1910	appointed Home Secretary. South Wales miners' strike
1911	Seige of Sidney Street. Appointed First Lord of the Admiralty
1915	Dardanelles campaign. Appointed Chancellor of the Duchy of Lancaster in new Coalition Government. Resigns and goes to France
1916	commands 6th Battalion, Royal Scots Fusiliers. Returns to London in May
1917	appointed Minister for Munitions
1919	appointed Secretary of State for War and Air
1921	appointed Secretary of State for the Colonies (retaining Air but losing War)
1922	loses Dundee in general election
1923	fails to be elected as a Liberal in West Leicester in general election
1924	fails to be elected as an Independent Anti-Socialist in Abbey Division, Westminster, in by-election. Elected MP for Epping as a Constitutionalist with full Conservative support. Appointed Chancellor of the Exchequer
1925	returns Britain to the Gold Standard
1926	appointed editor of the *British Gazette* during General Strike
1931	resigns from Shadow Cabinet over India
1936	supports Edward VIII during abdication crisis
1939	appointed First Lord of the Admiralty
1940	appointed Prime Minister and Minister of Defence
1941	British–Soviet agreement. Signs Atlantic Charter with Roosevelt. Declares war on Japan after Pearl Harbor. Addresses US Congress
1942	fall of Singapore. Cairo and Moscow visits. Victory at El Alamein
1943	round of conferences: Casablanca, Washington, Algiers, Quebec, Tehran
1944	D-Day landings. Second Quebec Conference. Meeting with Stalin in Moscow
1945	Yalta Conference. VE Day. Heads Caretaker Government pending general election. Potsdam Conference. Elected National Conservative MP for Woodford. Labour wins general election
1946	Iron Curtain speech at Fulton, Missouri
1948	attends The Hague United Europe Conference
1951	wins general election and becomes Prime Minister again
1953	receives Nobel Prize for Literature
1955	resigns as Prime Minister
1964	leaves House of Commons
1965	dies in London, January. Buried after state funeral at Bladon near Blenheim, Oxfordshire

Note

1   Paul Addison, *Churchill on the Home Front 1900–1955* (London, Cape, 1992).

Further Reading

The eight volumes of the Official Biography, Vols I and II by Randolph Churchill and the others by Martin Gilbert (London, Heinemann, 1966–88), with the companion volumes of documents for Vols I to V, provide an indispensible start for the serious explorer. The one-volume work by Martin Gilbert, *Churchill – A Life* (London, Heinemann, 1991), is a selection of the official biography with a sharper focus. Henry Pelling, *Winston Churchill* (London, Macmillan, 1974), has stood the test of time as an affectionate and critical appraisal. A very much shorter recent book by Keith Robbins, *Churchill* (London, Longman, 1992), is ideal for those wishing to grasp the salient points quickly.

Two volumes of collected essays give a full picture of the range of Churchill's interests. Charles Eade (ed.), *Churchill by his Contemporaries* (London, Hutchinson, 1953), is unashamedly partisan and sees Churchill in the light of 1940. For a more academic compilation see Robert Blake and W. Roger Louis (eds), *Churchill* (Oxford, Oxford University Press, 1993).

On particular aspects of Churchill, there are many volumes deserving mention but only four will be listed here. Robert Rhodes James, *Churchill – A Study in Failure 1900–1939* (London, Weidenfeld and Nicolson, 1970) states the conventional position on the early Churchill. This view is partly refuted in Paul Addison, *Churchill on the Home Front 1900–1955* (London, Cape, 1992), which re-evaluates Churchill's domestic achievements. John Charmley, *Churchill: The End of Glory* (London, Hodder and Stoughton, 1993) reconsiders the wartime myths, and Ronald Lewin's, *Churchill as Warlord* (London, Batsford, 1973) remains one of the most sensitive accounts of Churchillian strategic thinking.

Churchill was a prolific author, not least about himself, and his own account of his role against appeasement can be found in *The Gathering Storm*, Vol. 1 of *The Second World War* (London, Cassell, 1954).

Appendix 1
Governments and major office holders, 1866–1945

Party	Date formed	Prime Minister	Chancellor of Exchequer	Home Secretary	Foreign Secretary
Conservative	Jun. 1866	E. of Derby (14th)	B. Disraeili	S. H. Walpole	Ld Stanley
Conservative	Feb. 1868	B. Disraeli	G. Ward Hunt	S. H. Walpole	Ld Stanley
Liberal	Dec. 1868	W. E. Gladstone	R. Lowe W. E. Gladstone (Aug. 1873)	H. A. Bruce R. Lowe (Aug. 1873)	E. of Clarendon Ld Granville (Jun. 1870)
Conservative	Feb. 1874	B. Disraeli	Sir S. Northcote	R. A. Cross	E. of Derby (15th) Ld Salisbury (Apr. 1878)
Liberal	Apr. 1880	W. E. Gladstone	W. E. Gladstone H. C. E. Childers (Dec. 1882)	Sir W. Harcourt	Ld Granville
Conservative	Jun. 1885	Ld Salisbury	Sir M. Hicks Beach	Sir R. A. Cross	Ld Salisbury
Liberal	Feb. 1886	W. E. Gladstone	Sir W. Harcourt	H. C. E. Childers	Ld Rosebery
Conservative	Jul. 1886	Ld Salisbury	Ld R. Churchill G. J. Goschen (Jan. 1887)	H. Matthews	E. of Iddesleigh Ld Salisbury (Jan. 1887)
Liberal	Aug. 1892	W. E. Gladstone	Sir W. Harcourt	H. H. Asquith	Ld Rosebery
Liberal	Mar. 1894	Ld Rosebery	Sir W. Harcourt	H. H. Asquith	E. of Kimberley
Conservative	Jun. 1895	Ld Salisbury	Sir M. Hicks Beach C. T. Ritchie (Oct. 1900)	Sir M. W. Ridley	Ld Salisbury Ld Lansdowne (Oct. 1900)
Conservative	Jul. 1902	A. J. Balfour	C. T. Richie A. Chamberlain (Sep. 1903)	A. Akers Douglas	Ld Lansdowne
Liberal	Dec. 1905	Sir H. Campbell-Bannerman	H. H. Asquith	H. J. Gladstone	Sir E. Grey
Liberal	Apr. 1908	H. H. Asquith	D. Lloyd George	H. J. Gladstone W. S. Churchill (Feb. 1910) R. McKenna (Oct. 1911)	Sir E. Grey
Coalition	May 1915	H. H. Asquith	R. McKenna	Sir J. Simon Sir H. Samuel (Jan. 1916)	Sir E. Grey
Coalition	Dec. 1916	D. Lloyd George	A. Bonar Law	Sir G. Cave	A. J. Balfour

Party	Date formed	Prime Minister	Chancellor of Exchequer	Home Secretary	Foreign Secretary
Coalition	Jan. 1919	D. Lloyd George	A. Chamberlain Sir R. Horne (Apr. 1921)	E. Shortt	A. J. Balfour Ld Curzon (Oct. 1919)
Conservative	Oct. 1922	A. Bonar Law	S. Baldwin	W. C. Bridgeman	Ld Curzon
Conservative	May 1923	S. Baldwin	S. Baldwin N. Chamberlain (Aug. 1923)	W. C. Bridgeman	Ld Curzon
Labour	Jan. 1924	J. R. MacDonald	P. Snowden	A. Henderson	J. R. MacDonald
Conservative	Nov. 1924	S. Baldwin	W. S. Churchill	Sir W. Joynson-Hicks	A. Chamberlain
Labour	Jun. 1929	J. R. MacDonald	P. Snowden	J. R. Clynes	A. Henderson
National	Aug. 1931	J. R. MacDonald	P. Snowden	Sir H. Samuel	Ld Reading
National	Nov. 1931	J. R. MacDonald	N. Chamberlain	Sir H. Samuel	Sir J. Simon
National	Jun. 1935	S. Baldwin	N. Chamberlain	Sir J. Simon	Sir S. Hoare A. Eden (Dec. 1935)
National	May 1937	N. Chamberlain	Sir J. Simon	Sir S. Hoare	A. Eden Ld Halifax (Feb. 1938)
National	Sep. 1939	N. Chamberlain	Sir J. Simon	Sir J. Anderson	Ld Halifax
National	May 1940	W. S. Churchill	Sir K. Wood	Sir J. Anderson H. Morrison (Oct. 1940)	Ld Halifax A. Eden (Dec. 1940)
Conservative	May 1945	W. S. Churchill	Sir J. Anderson	Sir D. Somervell	A. Eden

Appendix 2
Leaders of principal political parties, 1867–1945

The Conservative Party

The title 'Leader of the Conservative Party' did not officially exist until it was conferred upon Bonar Law in October 1922. Before this there was a separate leader in each of the two Houses of Parliament. The recognised leader was either the Prime Minister, when the party was in office, or the most recent ex-Prime Minister or, failing that, the most long-serving or most prestigious of the two leaders, when the party was in Opposition.

Leaders of the party (or of the Commons)

14th Earl of Derby	1867
Benjamin Disraeli	Feb. 1868
(created Lord Beaconsfield 1876)	
Sir Stafford Northcote*	May 1881
3rd Marquess of Salisbury	June 1885
Arthur Balfour	July 1902
Andrew Bonar Law*	Nov. 1911
Austen Chamberlain*	Mar. 1921
Andrew Bonar Law	Oct. 1922
Stanley Baldwin	May. 1923
Neville Chamberlain	May 1937
Winston Churchill	Oct. 1940

*Leaders in the Commons only

Leaders of the party in the House of Lords, 1867–1922

14th Earl of Derby	1867
Earl of Malmesbury	Feb. 1868
Lord Cairns	Feb. 1869
Duke of Richmond	Feb. 1870
Earl of Beaconsfield	Aug. 1876

3rd Marquess of Salisbury	May. 1881
8th Duke of Devonshire	July 1902
5th Marquess of Lansdowne	Oct. 1903
1st Earl Curzon	Dec. 1916

The Liberal Party

Since the House of Lords was essentially a Conservative Chamber it was not an appropriate base for successful Liberal leadership which, with two brief exceptions, came from the Lower House. After Asquith's defeat at the 1918 general election, Sir Donald Maclean was elected leader of the parliamentary party but relinquished that post when Asquith was returned at a by-election in March 1920

Leaders of the Liberal Party

William Ewart Gladstone	Dec. 1867
Lord Hartington	Feb. 1875
William Ewart Gladstone	Apr. 1880
5th Earl of Rosebery	Mar. 1894
Sir William Harcourt	Oct. 1896
Sir Henry Campbell-Bannerman	Feb. 1899
Herbert Henry Asquith (created Lord Oxford and Asquith 1925)	Apr. 1908
David Lloyd George	Oct. 1926
Sir Herbert Samuel	Nov. 1931
Sir Archibald Sinclair	Nov. 1935
Clement Davies	Aug. 1945

The Labour Party

The leader of the Labour Party was designated 'Chairman' between 1906 and 1922 and, until 1970, 'Chairman and Leader'.

Leaders of the Labour Party

James Keir Hardie	1906
Arthur Henderson	1908
George Barnes	1910
James Ramsay MacDonald	1911
Arthur Henderson	1914

William Adamson	1917
John Robert Clynes	1921
James Ramsay MacDonald	1922
Arthur Henderson*	1931
George Lansbury	1932
Clement Attlee	1935

*Henderson lost his seat in the October 1931 general election. He retained the title 'Leader' for the next twelve months, with Lansbury elected as 'Chairman' of the party by his parliamentary colleagues.

Appendix 3
Government revenue and income tax, 1867–1945

	Net national income (£m)	Central govt income (£m)	Central govt income as % of net national income	Standard rate of income tax
1867	840	68	8.1	4d
1868	836	68	8.1	5d
1869	867	71	8.2	6d
1870	936	74	7.9	5d
1871	1,015	68	6.7	4d
1872	1,072	73	6.8	6d
1873	1,149	75	6.5	4d
1874	1,126	76	6.7	3d
1875	1,113	74	6.7	2d
1876	1,099	76	6.9	2d
1877	1,089	77	7.1	3d
1878	1,059	78	7.3	3d
1879	1,032	81	7.9	5d
1880	1,076	73	6.8	5d
1881	1,117	82	7.3	6d
1882	1,160	84	7.2	5d
1883	1,153	87	7.6	6.5d
1884	1,124	86	7.7	5d
1885	1,115	88	7.9	6d
1886	1,136	90	7.9	8d
1887	1,185	91	7.7	8d
1888	1,259	90	7.1	7d
1889	1,350	90	6.7	6d
1890	1,385	95	6.8	6d
1891	1,373	97	7.0	6d
1892	1,335	99	7.4	6d
1893	1,339	98	7.3	6d

Appendix 3 211

	Net national income (£m)	Central govt income (£m)	Central govt income as % of net national income	Standard rate of income tax
1894	1,418	98	6.9	7*d*
1895	1,447	102	7.0	8*d*
1896	1,484	109	7.4	8*d*
1897	1,538	112	7.3	8*d*
1898	1,618	116	7.2	8*d*
1899	1,700	118	6.9	8*d*
1900	1,750	130	7.4	8*d*
1901	1,727	140	8.1	1*s*
1902	1,740	153	8.8	1/2*d*
1903	1,717	161	9.4	1/3*d*
1904	1,704	151	8.9	11*d*
1905	1,776	153	8.6	1*s*
1906	1,874	154	8.2	1*s*
1907	1,966	155	7.9	1*s*
1908	1,875	157	8.3	1*s*
1909	1,907	152	7.9	1*s*
1910	1,984	132	6.6	1/2*d*
1911	2,076	204	9.8	1/2*d*
1912	2,181	185	8.5	1/2*d*
1913	2,265	189	8.3	1/2*d*
1914	2,209	198	9.0	1/2*d*
1915	2,591	227	8.7	1/8*d*
1916	3,064	337	11.0	3*s*
1917	3,631	573	15.8	5*s*
1918	4,372	707	16.2	5*s*
1919	5,461	889	16.3	6*s*
1920	5,664	1,340	23.7	6*s*
1921	4,460	1,426	32.0	6*s*
1922	3,856	1,125	29.2	6*s*
1923	3,844	914	23.8	5*s*
1924	3,919	837	21.4	4/6*d*
1925	3,980	799	20.1	4/6*d*
1926	3,914	812	20.7	4*s*
1927	4,145	806	19.4	4*s*
1928	4,154	843	20.3	4*s*
1929	4,178	836	20.0	4*s*
1930	3,957	815	20.6	4*s*

	Net national income (£m)	Central govt income (£m)	Central govt income as % of net national income	Standard rate of income tax
1931	3,666	858	23.4	4/6d
1932	3,568	851	23.9	5s
1933	3,728	827	22.2	5s
1934	3,881	809	20.9	4/6d
1935	4,109	805	19.6	4/6d
1936	4,388	845	19.3	4/9d
1937	4,616	897	19.4	4/9d
1938	4,671	949	20.3	5s
1939	5,037	1,006	20.0	5/6d
1940	5,980	1,132	18.9	7s
1941	6,941	1,495	21.5	8/6d
1942	7,664	2,175	28.4	10s
1943	8,171	2,922	35.8	10s
1944	8,366	3,149	37.6	10s
1945	8,340	3,355	40.2	10s

Appendix 4
General election results, 1867–1945

	Total votes	MPs elected	Candidates	Unopposed returns	% share of total vote
1868 Nov.					
Conservative	903,318	271	436	91	38.4
Liberal	1,428,776	387	600	121	61.5
Other	1,157	0	3	0	0.1
Elec. 2,484,713	2,333,251	658	1,039	212	100.0
Turnout 68.5%					
1874 Jan.					
Conservative	1,091,622	350	507	125	43.9
Liberal	1,281,330	242	489	52	52.7
Home Rule	90,234	60	80	10	3.3
Other	2,936	0	4	0	0.1
Elec. 2,751,547	2,466,122	652	1,080	187	100.0
Turnout 66.4%					
1880 March					
Conservative	1,426,351	237	521	58	42.0
Liberal	1,836,223	352	499	41	55.4
Home Rule	95,535	63	81	10	2.6
Other	1,107	0	2	0	0.0
Elec. 3,040,050	3,359,216	652	1,103	109	100.0
Turnout 72.2%					
1885 Nov.					
Conservative	2,020,927	249	602	10	43.5
Liberal	2,199,998	319	572	14	47.4
Irish Nat.	310,608	86	94	19	6.9
Other	106,702	16	70	0	2.2
Elec. 5,708,030	4,638,235	670	1,338	43	100.0
Turnout 81.2%					
1886 June					
Con. & Lib. Unionist	1,520,886	393 (77 LU)	563	118	51.4
Liberal	1,353,581	192	449	40	45.0
Irish Nat.	97,905	85	100	66	3.5
Other	1,791	0	3	0	0.1
Elec. 5,708,030	2,974,163	670	1,115	224	100.0
Turnout 74.2%					

	Total votes	MPs elected	Candidates	Unopposed returns	% share of total vote
1892 July					
Con. & Lib. Unionist	2,159,150	313 (45 LU)	606	40	47.0
Liberal	2,088,019	272	532	13	45.1
Irish Nat.	311,509	81	134	9	7.0
Other	39,641	4	31	1	0.9
Elec. 6,160,541	4,598,319	670	1,303	63	100.0
Turnout 77.4%					
1895 July					
Con. & Lib Unionist	1,894,772	411 (71 LU)	588	132	49.1
Liberal	1,765,266	177	447	11	45.7
ILP	44,325	0	28	0	1.0
Irish Nat.	152,959	82	105	46	4.0
Other	8,960	0	12	0	0.2
Elec. 6,330,519	3,866,282	670	1,180	189	100.0
Turnout 78.4%					
1900 Sep.					
Conservative	1,797,444	402	579	163	51.1
Liberal	1,568,141	184	406	22	44.6
LRC	63,304	2	15	0	1.8
Irish Nat.	90,076	82	100	58	2.5
Others	544	0	2	0	0.0
Elec. 6,730,935	3,519,509	670	1,102	243	100.0
Turnout 74.6%					
1906 Jan.					
Conservative	2,451,454	157	574	13	43.6
Liberal	2,757,883	400	539	27	49.0
LRC	329,748	30	51	0	5.9
Irish Nat.	35,031	83	87	87	0.6
Other	52,387	0	22	0	0.9
Elec. 7,694,741	6,667,404	670	1,315	75	100.0
Turnout 82.6%					
1910 Jan.					
Conservative	3,127,887	273	600	19	46.9
Liberal	2,880,581	275	516	1	43.2
Labour	505,657	40	78	0	7.6
Irish Nat.	124,586	82	104	55	1.9
Other	28,693	0	17	0	0.4
Elec. 7,694,741	6,667,404	670	1,315	75	100.0
Turnout 86.6%					
1910 Dec.					
Conservative	2,420,566	272	550	72	46.3
Liberal	2,295,888	272	467	35	43.9
Labour	371,772	42	56	3	7.1
Irish Nat.	131,375	84	106	53	2.5
Other	8,768	0	11	0	0.2
Elec. 7,709,981	5,228,369	670	1,190	163	100.0
Turnout 81.1%					

Appendix 4

	Total votes	MPs elected	Candidates	Unopposed returns	% share of total vote
1918 Dec.					
Coalition Unionist	3,504,198	335	374	42	32.6
Coalition Liberal	1,455,640	133	158	27	13.5
Coalition Labour	161,521	10	18	0	1.5
Coalition	5,121,359	478	550	69	47.6
Conservative	370,375	23	37	0	3.4
Irish Unionist	292,722	25	38	0	2.7
Liberal	1,298,808	28	253	0	12.1
Labour	2,385,472	63	388	12	22.2
Irish Nat.	238,477	7	60	1	2.2
Sinn Fein	486,867	73	102	25	4.5
Other	572,503	10	197	0	5.3
Elec. 21,392,322 Turnout 58.9%	10,766,583	707	1,625	107	100.0
1922 Nov.					
Conservative	5,500,382	345	483	42	38.2
National Liberal	1,673,240	62	162	5	11.6
Liberal	2,516,287	54	328	5	17.5
Labour	4,241,383	142	411	4	29.5
Other	462,340	12	59	1	3.2
Elec. 21,127,663 Turnout 71.3%	14,393,632	615	1,443	57	100.0
1923 Dec.					
Conservative	5,538,824	258	540	35	38.1
Liberal	4,311,147	159	453	11	29.6
Labour	4,438,508	191	422	3	30.5
Other	260,042	7	31	1	1.8
Elec. 21,281,232 Turnout 70.8%	14,548,521	615	1,446	50	100.0
1924 Oct.					
Conservative	8,039,598	419	552	16	48.3
Liberal	2,928,747	40	340	6	17.6
Labour	5,489,077	151	512	9	33.0
Communist	55,346	1	8	0	0.3
Other	126,511	4	16	1	0.8
Elec. 21,731,320 Turnout 76.6%	16,639,279	615	1,428	32	100.0
1929 May					
Conservative	8,656,473	260	590	4	38.2
Liberal	5,308,510	59	513	0	23.4
Labour	8,389,512	288	571	0	37.1
Communist	50,614	0	25	0	0.3
Other	243,266	8	31	3	1.0
Elec. 28,850,870 Turnout 76.1%	22,648,375	615	1,730	7	100.0

	Total votes	MPs elected	Candidates	Unopposed returns	% share of total vote
1931 Oct.					
Conservative	11,978,745	473	523	56	55.2
National Labour	341,370	13	20	0	1.6
Liberal National	809,302	35	41	0	3.7
Liberal	1,403,102	33	112	5	6.5
Nat. Govt	14,532,519	554	696	61	67.0
Ind. Liberal	106,106	4	7	0	0.5
Labour	6,649,630	52	515	6	30.6
Communist	74,824	0	26	0	0.3
New Party	36,377	0	24	0	0.2
Other	256,917	5	24	0	1.2
Elec. 29,960,071 Turnout 76.3%	21,656,373	615	1,292	67	100.0
1935 Nov.					
Conservative	11,810,158	432	585	26	53.7
Liberal	1,422,116	21	161	0	6.4
Labour	8,325,491	154	552	13	37.9
ILP	139,577	4	17	0	0.7
Communist	27,117	1	2	0	0.1
Other	272,595	4	31	1	1.2
Elec. 31,379,050 Turnout 71.2%	21,997,054	615	1,348	40	100.0
1945 July					
Conservative	9,988,306	213	624	1	39.8
Liberal	2,248,226	12	306	0	9.0
Labour	11,995,152	393	604	2	47.8
Communist	102,780	2	21	0	0.4
Common Wealth	110,634	1	23	0	0.4
Others	640,880	19	104	0	2.0
Elec. 33,240,391 Turnout 72.7%	25,085,978	640	1,682	3	100.0

Appendix 5
Biographical summaries, 1867–1945

Anderson, Sir (1919) John, 1st Viscount Waverley (1952) (1882–1958): Chairman of Board of Inland Revenue, 1918–22. Permanent Under-Secretary to the Home Office, 1922–32. Governor of Bengal, 1932–37. MP (Nat.) for Scottish Universities, 1938–50. Entered Cabinet as Lord Privy Seal, 1938–39. Home Secretary and Minister of Home Security, 1939–40. Lord President of the Council, 1940–43. Chancellor of the Exchequer, 1943–45. See J. Wheeler-Bennett, *John Anderson, Viscount Waverley* (London, Macmillan, 1962).

Birkenhead, 1st Earl of (1922), Sir (1915) Frederick Edwin Smith, 1st Lord Birkenhead (1919), 1st Viscount (1921) (1872–1930): MP (Con.) for Walton, Liverpool, 1906–18 and for West Derby, Liverpool, 1918. Entered Cabinet as Attorney-General, 1915–18. Lord Chancellor, 1919–22. Secretary for India, 1924–28. Appeared for the Crown in the trial of Roger Casement, 1916. See John Campbell, *F. E. Smith, 1st Earl of Birkenhead*, (London, Jonathan Cape, 1983).

Bright, John (1811–89): MP (Rad.) for Durham, 1843–47, (Lib.) Manchester, 1847–57, Birmingham, 1857–85 and for Birmingham Central, 1885–89. Entered Cabinet as President of the Board of Trade, 1868–70. Chancellor of Duchy of Lancaster, 1873–74 and 1880–82. Resigned in protest at bombardment of Alexandria, 1882. Opposed Irish Home Rule. See G. M. Trevelyan, *The Life of John Bright* (London, Constable, 1913) and Keith Robbins, *John Bright* (London, Routledge and Kegan Paul, 1979).

Campbell-Bannerman, Sir Henry (1836–1908): MP (Lib.) for Stirling Burghs, 1868–1908. Financial Secretary to War Office, 1871–74 and 1880–82. Financial Secretary to Admiralty, 1882–84. Chief Secretary for Ireland, 1884–85. Entered Cabinet as Secretary for War, 1886 and 1892–95. Leader of Liberal Party in the Commons, 1899–1908. Prime Minister, Dec. 1905–April 1908. Resigned due to ill health. Condemned system of warfare pursued during Boer War as 'methods of barbarism'. Principal achievement lay in reuniting the Liberal Party and leading them to a landslide victory in the 1906 general election. See J. Wilson, *C-B: A Life of Sir Henry Campbell-Bannerman* (New York, St. Martin's Press, 1973).

Carson, Sir Edward (1854–1935): MP (Unionist) for Dublin University, 1892–1918 and for Belfast, 1918–21. Solicitor-General, 1900–05. Entered Cabinet as Attorney-General, 1915–16. 1st Lord of Admiralty, 1916–17. Lord of Appeal, 1921–29. As leader of the Ulster Unionists he founded the Ulster

Volunteer Force in 1913. See A. T. Q. Stewart, *Edward Carson* (London, Gill and Macmillan, 1981).

Chamberlain, Sir (1925) Joseph Austen (1863–1937): MP (Con.) for Worcestershire East, 1892–1914 and for Birmingham West, 1914–37. Liberal Unionist Whip, 1892. Civil Lord of Admiralty, 1895–1900. Financial Secretary to Treasury, 1900–02. Postmaster General, 1902–03. Entered Cabinet as Chancellor of Exchequer, 1903–05. Secretary for India, 1915–17. Resigned, 1917. Minister without Portfolio, 1918–19. Chancellor of Exchequer, 1919–21. Lord Privy Seal and Leader of Conservative Party in Commons, 1921–22. Foreign Secretary 1924–29. 1st Lord of Admiralty, 1931. Awarded the Nobel peace prize, along with Charles Dawes, for negotiating the Locarno Pact. Only Conservative leader this century not to become Prime Minister. Birkenhead said of him: 'Austen always played the game and always lost it'. See Sir Charles Petrie, *The Life and Letters of the Rt. Hon. Sir Austen Chamberlain*, two vols (London, Cassell, 1939, 1940); David Dutton, *Austen Chamberlain: Gentlemen in Politics* (Bolton, Ross Anderson, 1985) and D. R. Thorpe, *The Uncrowned Prime Ministers: Austen Chamberlain, Curzon and R. A. Butler*, (London, Darkhorse Publishing, 1980).

Childers, Hugh Culling Eardley (1827–96): MP (Lib.) for Pontefract, 1860–85 and for Edinburgh South, 1886–92. Civil Lord of Admiralty, 1864–66. Financial Secretary to Treasury, 1865–66. Entered Cabinet as 1st Lord of Admiralty, 1868–71. Chancellor of Duchy of Lancaster, 1872–73. Secretary for War, 1880–82. Chancellor of Exchequer, 1882–05. Home Secretary, 1886.

Churchill, Lord Randolph Henry Spencer (1849–95): MP (Con.) for Woodstock, 1874–85 and for Paddington South, 1885–95. Leader of 'Fourth Party' in Commons, 1880–85. Entered Cabinet as Secretary for India, 1885–86. Chancellor of Exchequer and Leader of Commons, 1886. Resigned over estimates. See W. S. Churchill, *Lord Randolph Churchill*, two vols (London, Macmillan, 1906); R. Rhodes James, *Lord Randolph Churchill*, (London, Weidenfeld and Nicolson, 1959) and R. F. Foster, *Lord Randolph Churchill: A Political Life* (Oxford, Oxford University Press, 1981).

Cross, Richard Assheton, Viscount (1886) (1823–1914): MP (Con.) for Preston, 1857–62 and for South West Lancashire 1868–86. Entered Cabinet as Home Secretary 1874–80. Secretary for India, 1886–92. Lord Privy Seal, 1895–1900.

Curzon, George Nathaniel, Lord Curzon (1898), 1st Earl (1911), 1st Marquess Curzon of Kedleston (1921) (1859–1925): MP (Con.) for Southport, 1886–98. Under-Secretary India Office, 1891–92. Under-Secretary Foreign Office, 1895–98. Viceroy of India, 1899–1905. Entered Cabinet as Lord Privy Seal, 1915–16. President of Air Board, 1916. Lord President of the Council, 1916–19. Leader of Lords, 1916–24. Foreign Secretary 1919–24. Lord President of the Council, 1924–25. Leader of Conservative Party in the Lords, 1916–25. See Leonard Mosley, *Curzon: The End of an Epoch* (London, Longman, 1960) and Kenneth Rose, *Curzon: A Most Superior Person* (London, Weidenfeld and Nicolson, 1969).

Derby, 15th Earl of (1869), Edward Henry Stanley (1826–93): MP (Con.) for Lynn Regis, 1848–69. Under-Secretary at Foreign Office, 1852. Entered Cabinet as Colonial Secretary 1858. President of Board of Control, 1858. Secretary for India, 1858–59. Foreign Secretary 1866–68 and 1874–78. Resigned over Eastern Question, 1878. Left Conservative Party, 1879 and joined Liberals. Colonial Secretary 1882–85. Leader of Liberal Unionists in Lords, 1886–91. Declined throne of Greece, 1863.

Devonshire, Spencer Compton Cavendish, Marquess of Hartington (1858) and 8th Duke of (1891) (1833–1908): MP (Lib.), 1857–91. Civil Lord of the Admiralty, 1863. Under-Secretary for War, 1863. Entered Cabinet as Secretary for War, 1866. Postmaster General, 1868–71. Chief Secretary for Ireland, 1871–74. During Gladstone's semi-retirement he acted as party leader but chose to serve under Gladstone following the Liberals' election victory in 1880. Secretary for India, 1880–82. Secretary for War, 1882–85. Voted against government on first Home Rule Bill, 1886, and became a leading Liberal Unionist. Lord President of the Council, 1895–1903. Resigned over tariff reform. See Bernard Holland, *Life of the Duke of Devonshire*, 2 vols, (London, Longman, 1911); Patrick Jackson, *The Last of the Whigs: A Political Biography of Lord Hartington* (London, Fairleigh Dickinson University Press, 1994).

Goschen, George Joachim, 1st Viscount Goschen (1900), (1831–1907): MP (Lib.) for City of London, 1863–80, Ripon, 1880–85, Edinburgh South, 1885–87, and (Con.) St George's, Hanover Square, 1887–1900. Vice-President of the Board of Trade and Paymaster General, 1865–66. Entered Cabinet as Chancellor of Duchy of Lancaster, 1866. President of Poor Law Board, 1868–71. 1st Lord of Admiralty, 1871–74. Voted against first Irish Home Rule Bill and became a Liberal Unionist, 1886. Chancellor of Exchequer, 1887–92. 1st Lord of Admiralty, 1895–1900. See T. J. Spinner, *G. J. Goschen* (Cambridge, Cambridge University Press, 1973).

Granville, 2nd Earl (1846), Granville George Levenson-Gower (1815–91): MP (Whig) for Morpeth, 1837–40 and Lichfield, 1841–46. Vice-President of Board of Trade and Paymaster General, 1848–51. Entered Cabinet as Foreign Secretary 1851–52. Lord President of the Council, 1852–54. Chancellor of Duchy of Lancaster, 1854–55. Lord President of the Council, 1855–58 and 1859–66. Colonial Secretary 1868–70. Foreign Secretary 1870–74 and 1880–85. Colonial Secretary 1886. Liberal leader in Lords, 1855–91.

Grey, Sir Edward, 1st Viscount Grey of Fallodon (1916) (1862–1933): MP (Lib.) for Berwick on Tweed, 1885 1916. Under Secretary, Foreign Office, 1892–95. Entered Cabinet as Foreign Secretary 1905–16. Leader of the Liberal Party in the Lords, 1923–24. See Keith Robbins, *Edward Grey* (London, Cassell, 1971).

Halifax, 3rd Viscount (1934), Edward Frederick Lindley Wood, 1st Lord Irwin (1925), 1st Earl of (1944), (1881–1959): MP (Con.) for Ripon, 1910–25. Under-Secretary Colonial Office, 1921–22. Entered Cabinet as President of the Board of Education, 1922–24. Minister of Agriculture, 1924–25. Viceroy of

India, 1926–31. President of the Board of Education, 1932–35. Secretary for War, 1935. Lord Privy Seal, 1935–37. Leader of Lords, 1935–38. Lord President of the Council, 1937–38. Foreign Secretary 1938–40. Leader of Lords, 1940. British Ambassador to USA, 1941–46. See A. Roberts, *The Holy Fox: A Biography of Lord Halifax* (London, Weidenfeld and Nicolson, 1991).

Harcourt, Sir (1873) William Vernon (1827–1904): MP (Lib.) for Oxford City, 1868–70, for Derby, 1880–95 and for Monmouth West, 1895–1904. Solicitor-General, 1873–74. Entered Cabinet as Home Secretary 1880–85. Chancellor of Exchequer, 1886 and 1892–95. Leader of Commons, 1894–95. Leader of Liberal Party, 1896–98. See A. G. Gardiner, *The Life of Sir William Harcourt*, 2 vols, (London, Constable, 1923).

Hardie, James Keir (1856–1915): MP (Ind. Lab.) for West Ham, 1892–95 and (Lab.) for Merthyr Tydfil, 1900–15. Chairman of ILP, 1893–1900 and 1913–15. Chairman of the Labour Party, 1906–08. Established Scottish Labour Party, 1888. See K. O. Morgan, *Keir Hardie – Radical and Socialist* (London, Weidenfeld and Nicolson, 1975) and I. S. McLean, *Keir Hardie* (London, Allen Lane, 1975).

Henderson, Arthur (1863–1935): MP (Lab.) for Barnard Castle, 1903–18, Widnes, 1919–22, Newcastle East, 1923, Burnley, 1924–31 and for Clay Cross, 1933–35. Secretary of Labour Party, 1911–34. Treasurer of Labour Party, 1930–35. Chairman of Labour Party, 1908–10 and 1914–17. Chief Whip, 1914. Entered Cabinet as President of the Board of Education, 1915–16. Paymaster General, 1916. Minister without Portfolio, 1916–17. Resigned from Cabinet over 'doormat incident' 1917. Chief Labour Party Whip, 1920–24 and 1925–27. Home Secretary 1924. Foreign Secretary 1929–31. Leader of Labour Opposition, 1931–32. One of main architects of the 1918 Labour Party Constitution. See F. M. Leventhal, *Arthur Henderson* (Manchester, Manchester University Press, 1989)

Hicks Beach, Sir Michael Edward, 9th Baronet (1854), 1st Viscount St Aldwyn (1906), 1st Earl (1915), (1837–1916): MP (Con.) for East Gloucestershire, 1864–85 and for Bristol West, 1885–1906. Secretary of Poor Law Board, 1868. Under-Secretary in Home Office, 1868. Chief Secretary for Ireland, 1874–78. Entered Cabinet, 1876. Colonial Secretary 1878–80. Chancellor of Exchequer and Leader of Commons, 1885–86. Leader of Opposition in Commons, 1886. Chief Secretary for Ireland, 1886–87. Resigned, 1887, but remained in Cabinet without portfolio. President of Board of Trade, 1888–92. Chancellor of Exchequer, 1895–1902. Resigned, 1902.

Hoare, Sir Samuel John Gurney, 2nd Baronet (1915), 1st Viscount Templewood (1944) (1880–1959): MP (Con.) for Chelsea, 1910–44. Entered Cabinet as Secretary for Air, 1922–24 and 1924–29. Secretary for India, 1931–35. Foreign Secretary 1935. Resigned over Hoare–Laval Pact, 1935. 1st Lord of Admiralty, 1936–37. Home Secretary 1937–39. Lord Privy Seal, 1939–40. Secretary for Air, 1940. British Ambassador to Spain, 1940–44. See J. A. Cross, *Sir Samuel Hoare*, (London, Jonathan Cape, 1977).

Horne, Sir Robert Stevenson, 1st Viscount Horne of Slamannan (1937) (1871–1940): MP (Con.) for Hillhead, Glasgow, 1918–37. Entered Cabinet as

Minister of Labour, 1919–20. President of Board of Trade, 1920–21. Chancellor of Exchequer, 1921–22.

Lansbury, George (1859–1940): MP (Lab.) for Poplar, Bow and Bromley, 1910–12 and 1922–40. Entered Cabinet as First Commissioner of Works, 1929–31. Chairman and Leader of Labour Party, 1932–35. Founded *Daily Herald*. See R. Postgate, *The Life of George Lansbury* (London, Longman, 1951).

Lansdowne, Henry Petty-Fitzmaurice, 5th Marquess of (1866) (1845–1927): Junior Lord of Treasury (Lib.), 1869–72. Under-Secretary for War, 1872–74. Under-Secretary India Office, 1880. Resigned and opposed Liberal government in Lords over Irish policy, 1880. Governor-General of Canada, 1883–88. Viceroy of India, 1888–94. Entered Cabinet as Secretary for War (Con.), 1895–1900. Foreign Secretary 1900–05. Leader of Conservative Party in Lords, 1903–16. Minister without Portfolio, 1915–16. Left Conservative Party, 1917. See Lord Newton, *Lansdowne* (London, Macmillan, 1929) and Dennis Barker, *Prominent Edwardians*, (London, Allen and Unwin, 1969).

Law, Andrew Bonar (1858–1923): MP (Con.) for Blackfriars, for Glasgow, 1900–06, for Dulwich, 1906–10, for Bootle, 1911–18 and for Glasgow Central, 1918–23. Parliamentary Secretary to Board of Trade, 1902–05. Leader of Conservative Party in Commons, 1911–21. Entered Cabinet as Colonial Secretary 1915–16. Chancellor of Exchequer, 1916–18. Lord Privy Seal and Leader of Commons, 1919–21. Resigned 1921. Prime Minister and leader of Conservative Party, October 1922–May1923. Played a crucial role in the overthrow of Lloyd George at the Carlton Club in October 1922. See R. Blake, *The Unknown Prime Minister, The Life and Times of Andrew Bonar Law 1858–1923* (London, Eyre and Spottiswoode, 1955).

Lowe, Robert, 1st Viscount Sherbrooke (1880) (1811–92): MP (Lib.) for Kidderminster, 1852–59, Calne, 1859–68 and for London University, 1868–80. Joint Secretary of Board of Control, 1853–55. Vice President of Board of Trade and Paymaster-General, 1855–58. Vice-President of Privy Council Committee on Education, 1859–64. Leader of Adullamites against Gladstone's Reform Bill, 1866. Chancellor of Exchequer, 1868–73. Home Secretary 1873–74. See James Winter, *Robert Lowe* (Toronto, University of Toronto Press, 1976).

McKenna, Reginald (1863–1943): MP (Lib.) for North Monmouthshire, 1895–1918. Financial Secretary to Treasury, 1905–07. Entered Cabinet as President of Board of Education, 1907–08. 1st Lord of Admiralty, 1908–11. Home Secretary 1911–15. Chancellor of Exchequer, 1915–16. Chairman of Midland Bank, 1919–43. See Stephen McKenna, *Reginald McKenna* (London, Eyre and Spottiswoode, 1948).

Milner, 1st Viscount (1902), Sir (1895) Alfred Milner, 1st Lord (1901) (1854–1925): Chairman of Board of Inland Revenue, 1892–97. High Commissioner for South Africa, 1897–1905. Entered Cabinet as Minister without Portfolio 1916–18. Secretary for War, 1918–19. Colonial Secretary 1919–21. See J. Marlowe, *Milner: Apostle of Empire* (London, Hamish Hamilton, 1976), and T. O'Brien, *Milner* (London, Constable, 1979).

Mosley, Sir Oswald Ernald (1896–1980): MP (Con.) for Harrow, 1918–22, (Ind.)

1922–24 and (Lab.) for Smethwick, 1926–31. Chancellor of Duchy of Lancaster, 1929–30. Resigned when Cabinet rejected his memorandum for regenerating the economy. Founded New Party in 1931 which unsuccessfully contested twenty-one seats in 1931 general election. Formed British Union of Fascists in 1932. Interned 1940–43. Founded the Union Movement, a right-wing organisation in 1948. See Robert Skidelsky, *Oswald Mosley* (London, Macmillan, 1975).

Northcote, Sir Stafford Henry, 8th Baronet (1851), 1st Earl of Iddesleigh (1885) (1818–87): MP (Con.) for Dudley, 1855–57, Stamford, 1858–66 and for North Devon, 1866–85. Financial Secretary to Treasury, 1859. Entered Cabinet as President of the Board of Trade, 1866–67. Chancellor of Exchequer, 1874–80. Leader of the Commons, 1877–80. Upon death of Disraeli became joint leader of the Conservative Party with Salisbury until 1885. 1st Lord of Treasury, 1885–86. Foreign Secretary 1886–87.

Reading, 1st Marquis of (1926), Sir Rufus Daniel Isaacs, 1st Lord (1914), 1st Viscount (1916), 1st Earl of (1917) (1860–1935): MP (Lib.) for Reading, 1904–13. Solicitor-General, 1910. Attorney-General, 1910–13. Entered Cabinet, 1912. Lord Chief Justice, 1913–21. British Ambassador to USA, 1918–19. Viceroy of India, 1921–26. Foreign Secretary 1931. Leader of Lords, 1931. Leader of Liberal Party in Lords, 1930–35.

Redmond, John Edward (1856–1918): MP (Irish Nat.) for New Ross, North Wexford, 1885–91 and for Waterford, 1891–1918. Leader of reunited Nationlist Party from 1900. Worked for Home Rule by constitutional means until the Easter Rising of 1916 placed the political initiative in the hands of Sinn Fein.

Ritchie, Charles Thomson, 1st Lord Ritchie of Dundee (1905) (1838–1906): MP (Con.) for Tower Hamlets, 1874–85, St George's in the East, 1885–92 and for Croydon, 1895–1903. Financial Secretary to Admiralty, 1885–86. President of Local Government Board, 1886–92. President of Board of Trade, 1895–1900. Home Secretary 1900–02. Chancellor of Exchequer, 1902–03. Resigned, 1903, over the defence of free trade.

Rosebery, 5th Earl of (1868), Archibald Philip Primrose, 1st Earl of Midlothian (1911) (1847–1929) Under-Secretary to Home Office, 1881–83. 1st Commissioner of Works, 1885. Entered Cabinet as Lord Privy Seal, 1885. Foreign Secretary 1886 and 1892–94. Prime Minister and Lord President of the Council, 1894–95. Chairman of the London County Council, 1889, 1890 and 1892. Resigned Liberal Party leadership in 1896. A successful racehorse owner, he won the Derby three times, twice while Premier. See Robert Rhodes James, *Rosebery* (London, Weidenfeld and Nicolson, 1963).

Samuel, 1st Viscount (1937). Sir (1920) Herbert Louis (1870–1963): MP (Lib.), 1902–18 and 1929–37. Under-Secretary to Treasury, 1905–08. Under-Secretary to Home Office, 1908–09. Entered Cabinet as Chancellor of Duchy of Lancaster, 1909–10. Postmaster General, 1910–14. President of Local Government Board, 1914–15. Postmaster General, 1915. Chancellor of Duchy of Lancaster, 1915–16. Home Secretary 1916 and 1931–32. High Commissioner for Palestine, 1920–25. Chairman of Samuel Commission,

1925–26. Leader of main group of Liberal MPs, 1931–35. Leader of Liberals in Lords, 1944–55.

Simon, Sir (1910) John Allsebrook. 1st Viscount Simon (1940) (1873–1954): MP (Lib.) for Walthamstow, 1906–18, Spen Valley, 1922–31 and (Lib. Nat.) Spen Valley, 1931–40. Solicitor-General, 1910–13. Entered Cabinet as Attorney-General, 1913–15. Home Secretary 1915–16. Foreign Secretary 1931–35. Leader of Liberal National Party, 1931–40. Home Secretary and Deputy Leader of Commons, 1935–37. Chancellor of Exchequer, 1937–40. Lord Chancellor, 1940–45.

Snowden, 1st Viscount, Philip Snowden (1864–1937): MP (Lab.) for Blackburn, 1906–18 and for Colne Valley, 1922–31. Chancellor of Exchequer, 1924 and 1929–31. Lord Privy Seal, 1931–32. Chairman of the Independent Labour Party, 1903–06 and 1917–20. Followed MacDonald into the National Government in 1931 but resigned in 1932 over the adoption of Imperial Preference. See Keith Laybourn, *Philip Snowden* (Aldershot, Gower Publications, 1988).

Thomas, James Henry (1874–1949): MP (Lab.) for Derby, 1910–36. Entered Cabinet as Colonial Secretary 1924. Lord Privy Seal with responsibility for unemployment, 1929–31. Dominions Secretary 1930–35. Colonial Secretary 1935–36. General Secretary of National Union of Railwaymen (NUR), 1918–31. Expelled from Labour Party and NUR for joining MacDonald in National Government of 1931. See Gregory Blaxland, *J. H. Thomas. A Life for Unity*, (London, Muller, 1964).

Webb, Sidney James, 1st Baron Passfield (1929), (1859–1947): MP (Lab.) for Seaham, 1922–29. Entered Cabinet as President of Board of Trade, 1924. Dominions Secretary 1929–30. Colonial Secretary 1930–31. Founder member of Fabian Society, 1884. With his wife Beatrice, founded London School of Economics and the *New Statesman*.

Wood, Sir Kingsley (1881–1943): MP (Con.) for West Woolwich, 1918–43. Parliamentary Private Secretary to Minister of Health, 1919–22. Parliamentary Secretary to Minister of Health, 1924–29. Parliamentary Secretary to Board of Education, 1931. Postmaster General, 1931–35. Entered Cabinet, 1933. Minister of Health, 1935–38. Secretary for Air, 1938–40. Lord Privy Seal, 1940. Chancellor of Exchequer, 1940–43.

Index

Acts of Parliament
  Artisan's Dwelling Act (1875) 4
  Ballot Act (1872) 33
  Congested Districts Act (1890) 100
  Corn Production Act (1917) 10
  Crimes Act (1887) 100
  Criminal Law Amendment Act (1871) 33
  Defence of the Realm Act (1914) 10
  Education Act (1870) 7, 33, 82
  Education Act (1891) 69
  Education Act (1902) 102, 129
  Education Act (1918) 11
  Education Act (1944) 11
  Emergency Powers Act (1940) 11
  Equal Franchise Act (1928) 6
  Factory Act (1874) 4
  Housing Act (1919) 5, 136
  Housing of the Working Classes Act (1890) 5
  India Act (1935) 168
  Irish Church Act (1869) 36–7
  Irish Land Act (1870) 36–7
  Irish Land Act (1881) 37, 51
  Judicature Act (1873) 7
  Licensing Act (1872) 34
  Local Government Act (1888) 5, 69
  Mining Industry Act (1926) 6
  National Insurance Act (1911) 132
  Parliament Act (1911) 104, 116–17
  Public Health Act (1875) 4
  Reform Act (1867) 4, 18–19, 24, 66
  Reform Act (1884) 36, 53, 85
  Royal Titles Act (1876) 22
  Special Areas Act (1934) 7
  Technical Instruction Act (1889) 5
  Trade Boards Act (1909) 8
  Trade Union Act (1871) 33
  Unemployment Insurance Act (1920) 136
  University Test Act (1871) 33
Armenian massacres (1894–97) 70
Asquith, Herbert
  Chancellor of the Exchequer (1905–08) 115
  constitutional crisis (1909–11) 116–17
  early life and education 113
  elected MP (1886) 114
  first Labour Government (1924) 120, 122
  First World War leadership 123
  Home Rule Bill (1912) 117
  Home Secretary (1892–95) 114
  legal career 113–14
  Maurice debate (1918) 119
  Prime Minister 115–19, 122
  women's movement 117–18
Attlee, Clement 14

Baldwin, Stanley
  abdication crisis 168
  adopts protection (1923) 165, 182
  'appeasement of labour' 172–3
  appointed Prime Minister (1923) 165
  business experience 162

Index   225

Chancellor of the Exchequer
    (1922–23) 164
Conservative leadership crisis
    (1929–31) 167–8, 184
contribution to Conservatism 171–2
elected MP (1908) 163
family background and education
    161–2
Financial Secretary (1917–21) 163
foreign affairs and rearmament
    174–5
General Strike 166
Leader of Opposition (1924) 165;
    (1929–31) 167–8
loathing of Lloyd George 164
President of Board of Trade
    (1921–22) 163
Prime Minister of National
    Government (1935–37) 168
second administration (1924–29)
    166–7
serves under MacDonald in National
    Government (1931–35) 168, 185
Balfour, Arthur J.
    Balfour Declaration (1917) 105
    Boer war 101
    Committee Imperial Defence 102
    Constitutional Crisis (1909–11) 104,
        109
    defence policy 107–8
    early government posts 99
    Education Act (1902) 102
    First Lord of Admiralty (1915) 105
    Foreign Secretary (1916–19) 105–6
    Hotel 'Cecil' 100–1, 107
    influence of Lord Salisbury 98
    Irish Chief Secretary (1887–91)
        99–100
    Leader of the House (1891–1902)
        100–1
    Leader of the Opposition (1906–11)
        103–4, 109
    length of Cabinet service 108
    Lord President (1919–22) 106
    member of the 'Fourth Party' 99
    member of the 'Souls' 98
    party reorganisation (1910–11) 109
    Prime Minister (1902–05) 101–3

Battle of Isandhlwana (1879) 22
Battle of Ulundi (1879) 22
Beveridge Report (1942) 11
Boer war 72, 90
Butt, Isaac 48, 49

Cardwell, Edward 34
Carlton Club meeting (Oct. 1922) 137,
    164
Cecil, Lord Robert 73
Chamberlain, Austen 181, 182, 186
Chamberlain, Joseph
    Birmingham Liberal Association 82
    Colonial Secretary (1895–1903) 72,
        89–90, 102
    education and early work experience
        80
    elected MP (1876) 84
    family background 80
    Home Rule 85–6
    imperialism 87, 88
    influence of Birmingham 81
    Liberal Unionist Association 88
    marriage 81, 87
    Mayor of Birmingham 83–4
    National Education League 33, 82
    National Liberal Federation
    political outlook 92–3
    President of Board of Trade
        (1880–85) 84–5
    reformist approach 81
    social reform 88
    tariff reform 5, 91
    unauthorised programme 85
    unitarian beliefs 80–1
Chamberlain, Neville
    appeasement 187–9
    appointed Prime Minister (1937)
        187
    business experience 180
    Chancellor of the Exchequer
        (1931–37) 186
    Conservative Party Chairman
        (1930–31) 184
    Director of National Service
        (1916–17) 181
    elected MP (1918) 181
    first Labour Government 182

formation of National Government 185
Import Duties Act (1932) 186
influence of father 180
influence within National Government (1931–37) 186
leadership crisis (1929–31) 184
Minister of Health (1924–29) 183
Munich (1938) 187–8
municipal interests 180–1
Norway debate (1940) 188
Postmaster General (1922–23) 181–2
Churchill, Lord Randolph 67–8, 85, 86, 87, 99, 100, 194
Churchill, Sir Winston S.
anti-appeaser 197–8
army career 194
becomes Prime Minister (1940) 198
Chancellor of Exchequer (1924–29) 196
family background and education 193
First Lord of Admiralty (1939) 198
general election (1945) 200
influence of father 194
Iron Curtain speech 200
joins Liberal Party (1904) 194
ministerial abilities (1905–15) 195–6
Munich (1938) 198
office under Lloyd George (1917–22) 196
party politician 195
rejoins Conservative Party (1924) 196
resigns from Conservative Business Committee 197
wartime strategy 199
Civil Service reforms (1870) 33
Coalition Government (1918–22) 5
Communist Party 150
Conservatism
contribution of Baldwin 171–2
contribution of Disraeli 20–1, 24, 27
contribution of Salisbury 75–6
Conservative Government (1874–80) 4, 21–3; (1885–86) 67; (1886–92) 68–9; (1895–1902) 69–72; (1902–05) 101–3; (1922–23) 164–5; (1924–29) 6, 166–7
Conservative National Union 4, 67–8
Curzon, Lord George 71, 164

Davitt, Michael 51
Dilke, Sir Charles 38, 82–3, 84
Disraeli, Benjamin
ambition 17
attacks Peel over Corn Laws 17, 18
Chancellor of the Exchequer (1852, 1858–59, 1867) 16, 18
Congress of Berlin (1878) 23, 35
differences with Gladstone over foreign and imperial issues 25
distrusted by Conservative traditionalists 19
early political style 16–17
Eastern Question 22–3
elected MP (1837) 16
fiscal policies 27
franchise reform (1866–67) 18–19, 24
imperialism 21–2, 24
jewish background 16
novel writing 16
opportunism 26–7
Peelite policies 24
reaction to Gladstone over Bulgarian Horrors 23
relations with Queen Victoria 28
reshaping of Conservatism 20–1, 24
second administration (1874–80) 21–2
Second Afghan War 22
social reform 21, 25
Suez Canal shares 22
Tory Democracy 18
Young England 17
Zulu War (1879) 22

Fashoda (1898) 71
First World War (1914–18) 10–11

General Elections (1874) 20, 34, 39; (1880) 23, 40; (1885) 37, 53; (1886) 67; (1892) 69; (1895) 69;

(1900) 72, 90, 129, 145; (1906) 91, 146, 103–4; (1910 – Jan) 104, 116, 132; (1910 – Dec) 104, 116–17; (1918) 119, 136, 148–9; (1922) 137, 149, 165, 196; (1923) 150, 182; (1924) 165; (1929) 138, 152, 167; (1931) 14, 153; (1935) 14; (1945) 1, 200
General Strike (1926) 166
Gladstone, William E.
  attack on Beaconsfieldism 35
  becomes Prime Minister (1868) 32
  Chancellor of the Exchequer (1852–55, 1859–65) 32
  character 31
  death of General Gordon 36
  differences with Disraeli 42
  Eastern Question 34–5
  élitism 40
  estrangement from radicals 41
  first administration (1868–74) 33–4, 38–9
  Irish policy 36–8, 41
  Liberalism 39
  Midlothian campaign (1879) 35–6, 39
  occupation of Egypt (1882) 36
  populist 39
  relations with Queen Victoria 40
  second administration (1880–85) 36
  veneration for Peel 32
Gordon, General Charles 36
Goschen, George 68
Grey, Sir Edward 118, 123

Harney, George 74
Hartington, Lord Spencer 35
Henderson, Arthur 148, 149

Irish Home Rule Bill (1886) 38, 53–5, 67
Irish Home Rule Bill (1893) 38
Irish National League 52
Irish University Bill (1873) 36–7

Keynes, John Maynard 9
Kilmainham Treaty (1882) 37, 51

Labour Government (1924) 120, 122, 150–1, 182; (1929–31) 152–3; (1945–51) 3, 12
Lansdowne, Lord Henry 73, 75, 104
Law, Andrew Bonar 136, 164
Liberal Government (1868–74) 20, 33–4, 38–9; (1880–85) 36; (1892–95) 69; (1905–15) 115–18
Liberal Unionists 54, 67, 69, 75, 86, 87, 99
Lloyd George, David
  Boer war 129
  Budget (1909) 131–2
  Carlton Club meeting (1922) 137
  Chanak crisis 137
  Chancellor of the Exchequer (1908–15) 131–3
  contribution to foreign policy (1908–14) 133
  early influences 128
  Education Bill (1902) 129
  elected MP (1890) 128
  family background and education 127
  'Geddes Axe' 137
  Genoa Conference (1922) 137
  honours scandal 137
  Irish agreement (1921) 137
  leader of Liberal Party (1926) 138
  legal career 127–8
  Marconi scandal (1912) 132
  Minister of Munitions (1915–16) 134, 139
  National Insurance Act (1911) 132, 139
  peacetime Prime Minister (1918–22) 136–7
  President of Board of Trade (1905–08) 130–1
  Secretary of State for War (1916) 134–5
  Stevenson, Frances 132
  wartime Prime Minister 135

MacDonald, James Ramsay
  becomes Prime Minister (1924) 150
  elected leader of PLP (1910) 148
  elected MP 146

first government 150–1
formation of National Government 153, 155, 168
joins ILP (1894) 145
leader of opposition (1924–29) 151–2
loses seat (1918) 148
marriage 145
political writings 146–7
re–elected leader of PLP (1922) 149
relations with Liberalism 145
resigns leadership of PLP (1914) 148
retires as Prime Minister (1935) 154
second government (1929–31) 152–3
Secretary of LRC 145
social origins 144–5
Major, John 108
Mediterranean Agreements (1887) 71

National Education League 33, 82
National Education Union 33
National Government (1931–39) 6–7
New Liberalism 7–10
Northcote, Sir Stafford 66, 99

O'Shea, Captain William 52, 56

Parnell, Charles Stewart
death 58
elected leader of Irish parliamentary party (1890) 50
elected MP (1875) 48
fall 56–8
family background and education 47
Gladstone's conversion to Home Rule 53
Grattan's parliament 47, 59
Home Rule Bill (1886) 53–5
imprisonment (1881) 51
Irish National League 52, 61
Kilmainham Treaty 51
Land Act (1881) 51, 61
Liberal alliance (1886–89) 55
Meath speech (1891) 59
'New Departure' 49, 50
'obstructionism' 48–9
'Plan of Campaign' 55

President of Home Rule Confederation of Great Britain (1877) 49
President of Irish National Land League (1879) 48, 50
relationship with Katherine O'Shea 52, 55, 56
republicanism 59
Special Commission (1888–89) 55–6
'To the People of Ireland' manifesto (1890) 56
tour of North America (1880) 50, 59
Phoenix Park murders (1882) 37

Salisbury, Lord Robert
appointed Foreign Secretary (1878) 66
appointed Prime Minister (1885) 67
appointments 70
attitude to parliamentary reform 65–6, 75
becomes Lord Cranborne (1865) 65
character and beliefs 65, 76
childhood and education 64
class war 75–6
death 72
domestic reform (1886–92) 69, (1895–1902) 69–70
elected MP (1853) 64
family pedigree 64
foreign policy (1886–92) 68; (1895–1902) 70–2
foreign secretary and Prime Minister (1885) 67
general conduct of foreign affairs 73
journalism 65
leader of Conservative Party in Lords (1881–85) 66
leader of opposition and use of House of Lords (1892–95) 69
marriage 64, 65
party organisation 74–5
political thought 75
redistribution (1885) 75
relations with Joseph Chamberlain 72, 74–5
relations with Lord Randolph Churchill 67–8, 75

resigns from Derby administration (1867) 66
social policy 73–4, 75
Tory backbencher (1846–66) 65–6
views on Disraeli 19, 65, 66
views on Joseph Chamberlain's radical programme 85
Second World War (1939–45) 11

Snowden, Philip 151
Social Democratic Federation 1
Social Democratic Party (est. 1981) 2

Tariff Reform (1903–06) 91, 103
Tory Democracy 18, 67, 87, 100
Treaty of Berlin (1878) 23
Treaty of San Stefano (1878) 23